The Privilege
of Aging

"The aging of Baby Boomers worldwide is a hard trend. Fun fact: we will not get chronologically younger! *The Privilege of Aging* provides a powerful guide for embracing our mortality and living a happier and fulfilling life as we age."

DANIEL BURRUS, NEW YORK TIMES BESTSELLING
AUTHOR OF *FLASH FORESIGHT*

"What do you get when you cross an old soul with a life review? Pure alchemy. Kamla Kapur's brave memoir about aging immerses us in the land of old souls—a generation of seekers living beyond aging as denigration, denial, or romance but rather as a privilege to be embraced. A great addition to the growing conscious aging library."

CAROL ORSBORN, AUTHOR OF
THE SPIRITUALITY OF AGE AND *SPIRITUAL AGING*

"A wise and wonderful roadmap for awakening to and harvesting the divine gifts of this life as we ripen."

KEN DRUCK, PH.D., AUTHOR OF
HOW WE GO ON AND *COURAGEOUS AGING*

The Privilege of Aging

Savoring the Fullness of Life

Kamla K. Kapur

Park Street Press
Rochester, Vermont

Park Street Press
One Park Street
Rochester, Vermont 05767
www.ParkStPress.com

Park Street Press is a division of Inner Traditions International

Cataloging-in-Publication Data for this title is available from the Library of Congress

ISBN 979-8-88850-052-1 (print)
ISBN 979-8-88850-053-8 (ebook)

Printed and bound in the United States by Lake Book Manufacturing, LLC

10 9 8 7 6 5 4 3 2 1

Text design and layout by Priscilla Harris Baker
This book was typeset in Garamond Premier Pro with Amster, Autumn Embrace,
Avenir, Fleurons, Legacy Sans, Parisian, and Snell Roundhand used as display
typefaces

To send correspondence to the author of this book, mail a first-class letter to the
author c/o Inner Traditions • Bear & Company, One Park Street, Rochester, VT
05767, and we will forward the communication, or contact the author directly at
KamlaKKapur.com.

Scan the QR code and save 25% at InnerTraditions.com.
Browse over 2,000 titles on spirituality, the occult, ancient
mysteries, new science, holistic health, and natural medicine.

For Payson, my partner
in aging

Old age superbly rising!
O welcome, ineffable grace of dying days!

WALT WHITMAN, "SONG OF MYSELF"

Getting old is like climbing a mountain.
You get a little out of breath, but the view is
much better.

INGRID BERGMAN

Where I am, I don't know, I'll never know,
in the silence you don't know, you must go
on, I can't go on, I'll go on.

SAMUEL BECKETT, *THE UNNAMABLE*

Contents

The Many Privileges of Aging

Grow old along with me!
The best is yet to be,
The last of life, for which the first was made:
Our times are in His hand
Who saith, "A whole I planned,
Youth shows but half; trust God: see all, nor
be afraid!

ROBERT BROWNING, "RABBI BEN EZRA"

The title of this book, at the suggestion of my husband, Payson, was adopted after the book was accepted for publication by Inner Traditions under a different title: *Aging with Ardor: An Odyssey.* Though *The Privilege of Aging* is a better title, I realized the privileges mentioned in this book are scattered throughout the narrative, not consolidated in one place. Nor was the book structured with this focus in mind, though the improvements age brings are among the underlying themes. This preface makes amends by narrating my many privileges of aging. I wrote this book during my seventy-first year and write this preface at age seventy-five. In this interim I have discovered a hoard of treasures available to, and waiting for, the aging if we keep ourselves open to receiving them and do the focused work that old age demands.

To some extent the perspective of old age as privilege is a natural evolution. We enter a different dimension and experience of life with the passage of time. Our views mature, keeping pace with our circumstances. Many studies have shown that people in their dusking years are happier than ever; that nothing is taken away, only given. We know and accept who we are, grow wiser, give gratitude for our lives as they have unfolded, become content with our lot in life. As my ninety-year-old friend Jillian Hensley says, "My whole life has been a privilege!"

This preface is a testament to how far I have come from seventy-one to seventy-five. My life has improved in many ways. So much dross, so many compulsions, nagging desires, dissatisfactions, and discontents have fallen away. And after a lifetime of struggle, I derive a lot of pleasure from my being, my existence, as I move closer to the event horizon.

❧

> Then, welcome each rebuff
> That turns earth's smoothness rough,
> Each sting that bids nor sit nor stand but go!
> Be our joys three-parts pain!
> Strive, and hold cheap the strain;
> Learn, nor account the pang; dare, never grudge the throe!
> ROBERT BROWNING, "RABBI BEN EZRA"

The downsides of aging, together with the gifts bestowed, must be incorporated into the vision of privilege to make it whole. For many, sometimes even me (as demonstrated in this book), "aging sucks." It is true that our deterioration has begun, death is closer than ever, and energy and stamina have diminished. We are more prone to physical and mental ailments and our ambit has decreased. Relationships become unsustainable, fall away, and our social life shrinks. Unlearning the ways we functioned in our youth, changing our mindset to fit our current circumstances has become arduous and sometimes impossible. We are prone to feeling more isolated in a culture in which youth is worshipped and extolled.

So how can we, in addition to Robert Browning's advice in the above stanza to embrace the rough parts, stings, pain, illness, and incapacity, reconcile the two versions of aging, the hopeful and the fearful?

We have heard and know from science, our spiritual guides, and from personal experience that focus determines our reality. We find what we seek. The *New Oxford American Dictionary* definition of the verb "to focus" is revealing: "to adapt to a prevailing level of light and become able to see clearly." The operative word here is "adapt" so we can see clearly. What are the tools that help us adapt—some given in this story—and transform our old age into a thing of wonder and immense gratitude for the amazing gift of life?

I was first made aware that focusing is the decisive factor in creating our reality some forty years ago by a ten-year-old boy. I was living in an apartment complex in Santa Fe, and one day my cat, Chua, did not return from roaming. I was frantic and went looking for him in the entire complex and in the outlying arroyos. I met the boy, who was out looking for his dog, and asked him if he had seen a yellow tabby. He said he hadn't. I was agitated and asked him again, perhaps a trifle angrily, was he sure he hadn't seen the cat? He replied, "If I had been looking for a cat, I would have seen a cat. I was out looking for a dog!"

Chua did return at dusk, but the lesson remained: we find what we seek. The boy may have seen a cat but not registered it because his focus excluded everything but his dog. Similarly, the journey from life sucks to life-as-privilege is a focus, a perspective. The privileges of aging have to be focused on, looked for, discovered, emphasized. And not just once but again and again, for that is the way we humans seem to learn, through repetition. We have to keep reminding ourselves of what we seek. If we don't, all we are left with are ailments, disintegration, illness, loss, regret, and unhappiness.

All these "negative" things are also part of the human experience; pain distracts and we become unfocused. We cannot deny it, and we mustn't. This story doesn't. I have written the spectrum of my aging story. We need to see our circumstances in every stage of our life, every day, hour, in an accurate and honest light, embrace and adapt to our situations in order to see clearly even in dimming light.

❧

I saw Eternity the other night,
Like a great ring of pure and endless light,
All calm, as it was bright;
And round beneath it, Time in hours, days, years,
Driv'n by the spheres
Like a vast shadow mov'd; in which the world
And all her train were hurl'd.

HENRY VAUGHAN, "THE WORLD"

The privileges of aging are so numerous that I must take detours to unfurl them all. Meandering, in life and in writing, is the prerogative of age. I am so entranced with my experiences of aging that I want to tell all. Being oneself in life and in writing is one of the most delicious offerings of age. As is time, that mysterious force that no one can explain or comprehend in any but its practical, empirical applications. In the *Granth Sahib*, the sacred scripture of Sikhism, Guru Gobind Singh, tenth guru of the Sikhs, refers to time as God. Though time passes and passes away, it stays. Time is eternal.

Although there is less time as we age and move toward the end of time as we know it in its linear unfolding, there is also an expansiveness, a deep, wide, soulful adagio before the finale. Less and more of time at once; such are the paradoxes of life.

I became aware of the too-much aspect of time in the transition between working and retiring. I don't mean to make working and retirement an either/or issue or perpetuate the stereotype of old folks as one extreme or the other: hugely productive or useless. The truth, as happens so often, is somewhere between the two. I had a long phase of lostness—eons, it seems—after retirement from my teaching position. I didn't know what to do with myself, with no job I wanted to go to, no volunteer work I wanted to do, no greater social engagement I desired. I would wake up depressed, feeling useless and irrelevant, and unable to find my footing in my days. How long it takes us to become aware of and seek remedies for a problem! So strong are the chains of habit. So powerful the aversion to change. Perhaps it is simply the cycle of things, the slow pace of evolution that we have to accept, not spoil with regret. We cannot, it seems, learn from our follies till the point of despair, which sometimes takes a long time to arrive. Marcel Proust's description of the horse of his fictional hero Golo applies aptly to psychological evolution. "The horse continued at the same jerky trot, and nothing could arrest his slow progress." I am that slow old mare.

Then gradually I began to create and discover pursuits that had been ripening all my life. I now have a new discipline and rhythm to my days that has birthed a new me, still learning to see more clearly in the prevailing light, still stumbling, but adapting, finding gems on the way to adorn the last of life, for which the first was made.

❧

Certainly Mr. Shelley is right in his notions about old age: unless powerfully counteracted by all sorts of opposite agencies, it is a miserable corrupter and blighter to the genial charities of the human heart.

THOMAS QUINCY, *CONFESSIONS OF AN OPIUM EATER*

There is something mysterious about an idea that floats into our brains as a gift from the universe when we are ready and ripe to receive it.

Mornings were a problem in the transition period between teaching and retirement. One day after doing my morning necessities, the wood floor with our favorite Persian rug beckoned my eye. I "grabbed a piece of the floor," as I like to tell it, and began doing some yoga. I had always done yoga sporadically, often with lack of awareness that resulted in injuries, but now it became a study and discipline. I do it attentively, minding my body, my marvelous old mare. Yoga not only dispels my morning blues but gives me energy for the rest of the day. I have developed a sequence of poses: standing, sitting, on my back, on my belly, on my side. It didn't happen in a day, but day by day. I do it almost every day now, sometimes for an hour, at a languid pace, breathing through the poses, paying attention to the parts of my body that are stiff and aching, wrestling with my old self that wants me to hurry through it and get to what I previously considered more important tasks, such as writing. On sluggish mornings I do "geriatric yoga," at a pace even slower than usual, content with even ten minutes of it.

It has made all the difference. At seventy-five I go for walks. I ford the powerful and genial Hirab that flows in front of our Himalayan home in India, Behta Pani, translated as "flowing waters." I swim in the stream on hot days, sometimes against a gentle current, clambering on boulders, climbing from pool to pool on all fours. I make sure to do free weights two or even three times a week to keep my upper body strong. Yoga was the first gift that unraveled other activities and perspectives that I enjoy, activities that keep me young, engaged, and healthy in body, mind, and soul.

My practice is, however, a very flexible discipline. The word "discipline" feels like a straitjacket, too regimented, too anti-life. It brings to mind the image of a horse, an ass, camels I have seen in the deserts of Arabia, snorting and bucking, howling and braying at burdens. I like a healthy spontaneity within the structure of a day. I like balance between sameness and change, between discipline and the lack of it. On very sluggish days I abandon it altogether. This is a huge freedom.

Rather than following an external definition, each of us has to define discipline for ourselves. In order to define it for myself I have to take a detour, play a little, and tell you a story that I heard when I was a child.

An ass had a demanding master who loaded him down with sacks of salt every day to take to another town. Along the way they had to cross a stream. One day as they were crossing the ass slipped on a boulder and fell into the water. When he stood back up he found his burden was much lighter, because the water had dissolved some of the salt. From then on the ass made a practice of either falling down in the stream or wading deep into it. He splashed about in the water and had a jolly old time. But one day the master caught on, and to teach the ass a lesson, he filled his sacks with cotton wool. When the ass waded into the stream to lighten his load, his burden increased tenfold.

The lesson for me is that I am that ass, and as long as I can get away with it, I wade into the stream; I discard the burdens of discipline altogether. But there are days, many days, when my daemon fills my sacks with cotton, when *not* doing yoga, weights, or walks is a greater burden than doing them. Then I return, naturally, spontaneously, without any effort or coercion on my part, to my discipline and carry my burden.

I am getting better as I age in fighting entropy, staying active. I am stronger at seventy-five than I was at seventy. I enumerate my accomplishments with utter humility, knowing anything can happen at any point. I may forget all my blessings when I become a suffering human being. Then I hope I will remember some of the techniques I have so diligently collected over the years and be grateful for my countless blessings.

❧

There is more to life than simply increasing its speed.

MAHATMA GANDHI

Side by side with activity, as I age I have become better at wasting time, not hurrying, going slowly, doing nothing, resting as frequently as I need.

These practices, I believe, are the very essence of spirituality. Certainly they have changed my life for the better in all sorts of wonderful ways.

Doing too much and hurrying have been the bane of my life. When I was young I pinched minutes and hours, squeezed time, did not allow myself to settle into the moment, breathe in it, be. I packed my days with activities and did not let myself relax, be it sitting on the pot, brushing my hair, or taking a bath. I was measuring out my life with coffee spoons, as T. S. Eliot penned in his memorable saga on aging, "The Love Song of J. Alfred Prufrock."

Hurrying is a result of our subconscious awareness that time is limited. I cannot claim I have conquered the urge to hurry. Hurry happens despite us. Right now, for example, I'm hurrying to write these words, wanting to meet a deadline—self-imposed so I can free myself to have some quality time with my husband and my family in the city. I have spent many an impatient hour and sleepless night at its slow progress. We are also packing up our India life for six months and returning to the United States for six months, so I'm juggling the consequent emotions at uprooting. As usual, new tasks pop up that need to be handled. I want to do more than I can and end up tying myself into knots, confused and unhappy. My left brain wants me to write my experience as lists and get it over with. The hurry is interfering with how I write best—slowly, deliberately, without imposing my will on the material.

In the past I often stayed in this tortured hamstrung state for weeks and months, but my techniques to go to nature for solution and solace have shortened my bouts of confusion. Not long ago I went for a swim in the Hirab on a dark, overcast day. The stream carving its path down the mountains at its own pace was a reminder to give up imposing my will on what is happening, but rather to flow with it and not let hurry destroy the joy of my life and writing. It served as a prompt to trust that there is always enough time for it all to turn out well. I am learning, again, to trust my process, to allow this essay to take as much time as it needs to complete itself, to stop forcing my will upon my writing and my life. The following morning the chapter fell into place, and freed of struggle, I moved on to the tasks of preparing and packing.

Aging is teaching me to trust instead of fear. Trusting relieves all my anxieties. I trust life's ways and I trust myself more than ever before. I perceive myself as a whole fragment of God. Like fractals, we humans are self-similar. I trust where I've been, what I was, am, and will be; I trust I will be given the strength to endure the trials of aging that lie ahead.

Trust fructifies all one's efforts and desires. There is something magical about trusting and committing to oneself. And what is this self that we need to trust? It is the higher self within ourselves, the multiverse in a grain of sand, to paraphrase poet William Blake. It is the reflection of the whole in the particle, the self that knows, creates, sees with its vision the vaster pattern in which we are the designs. It is the greater self that we share with the self of the universe, the self of trees and everything that is.

❧

For fast-acting relief, try slowing down.
LILY TOMLIN

One of the greatest gifts of aging is slowing down the pace. It allows us to experience and taste life fully with awareness, attention, senses, and mind awake. For this we need time, and we have it, hallelujah. Going slowly is also imperative to avoid injuries and accidents. I know many who have injured themselves in hurried or inattentive moments, in some cases with repercussions for years.

I know the joys of slowing down, foremost among them doing just one thing at a time and doing it with attention. Though I am aware my time is limited, I know that whatever I complete will be enough. Whatever I leave undone is also fine. I live from the inside out instead of by the tick tock of the clock. There is a tempo to our bodies. We are musical notes in the harmony of life and sense when we are out of tune. Going with our tempos makes our days easier. When daily tasks—brushing my teeth, combing my hair, early morning yoga—feel huge, I make them easier by taking my time over them, not overstepping or hastening my natural, inherent rhythm. Going slowly through life changes our experiences of life. We have more time for all those splendid things that improve the quality of life: cooking, eating right, observing, lingering with beauty wherever it exists (and it exists everywhere, inside and out); reflecting, noticing the subjective and objective, marveling and taking joy in simple things, wondering at the miracles of our workings—our bodies and minds, as well as the awesome universe that includes us. We can take time for loving ourselves and those in our lives, however flawed, while also paying homage to necessity with full attention and engagement.

I am reminded of an aged priest I saw in a little temple built into a rock on an island in an Indian river. Using ash from his cooking fire he was slowly and deliberately scrubbing his utensils and a brass prayer bell; his meditative air made each step of this activity seem part of his discipline, as if all his tasks, his life itself, were a prayer.

When he stood up, his purposeful steps were a dance. Perhaps he had learned from his spiritual path that life does not have to be a scurrying, constant tug-of-war between seeming contraries: the mundane and the spiritual, doing and not doing. The river may have taught him to flow with the course of his life and emotions, even likely doubt and isolation, drifting from prayer to play and from work to watching the river go by.

❧❦

Take it easy.

POPULAR AMERICAN GOODBYE

Doing the difficult, pushing boulders uphill, contorting myself to get things done was easier for me back when I had an excess of stamina to get away with abusing myself. I wasn't very kind to myself in my youth. Taking the easy route, being very kind to myself is another precious gift of aging.

Now I push only when it is necessary to keep from becoming too sedentary. When fatigued I pull my reins gently in easy directions I need to go to preserve myself for further aging, should I be fortunate enough to get there.

In many ways this decrease in stamina has been good for my writing, too. It has forced me to simplify, pare down to the essential instead of the titillatingly different. I ruthlessly eliminate the difficult and flow around the boulders in my path, just as the Hirab flows around and erodes the lichen- and moss-covered boulders in its path. This approach has been helpful in other areas, too. I do not keep to rigid "must-do's" but am very supple when it comes to agendas about my day or my writing. If an appointment is fragmenting my day, I cancel. If my brain rebels at the thought of opening the computer, I indulge it. Aging has made my life a lot easier because after a long, hard struggle and years of effort to meet goals and schedules, I have allowed myself to let it be easier.

Ease. The word glides, slides, expresses itself without too much effort. Doing and thinking the easy includes not giving myself a hard time with self-negating thoughts. I am infinitely kind to myself. I do not indulge regrets. I accept the many facets of who I am and how my life has turned out. Poet Robert Browning in "Rabbi Ben Ezra" phrased it well: "What I aspired to be and was not, comforts me."

I am also being easy around money. We spent our life socking away, preparing for the future. Well, the future is here. The real function of money is peace of mind and comfort. I don't get all knotted up about spending. I take care of money, let it go, give it away. My husband, Payson, and I have been both fortunate and frugal; we've saved and taken responsibility for our financial well-being. Even at our age—How much longer do we have? He is seventy-eight—we never spend more than we have, don't have any grand plans, and use serviceable, well-functioning vehicles that we keep for tens of years. It is a good habit to prepare for old, old age (in my way of thinking we are now in middle-old age). Who knows what sudden health issues might pop up needing expensive cures or full-time support? As my sister Mishi said to me at one point, knowing I was childless, "Money will be your children."

But God herself has loosened my money sphincter. My material mother is the model for my conception of this deity. I am spending thoughtfully on what I need, with small splurges on colorful Indian cotton shifts and tops and a regular tailor to help me play with my mother's silk suits, adapting them for my uses. It gave me joy for my seventy-fifth birthday to give gifts to our household staff: clothing, rain boots and jackets, blankets. Birthdays are for giving.

In addition to the privilege of spending freely, there is some loosening of my claws around the extrinsic rewards of my creative labors. Doing the work, having something to do that engages me, is more than enough. This is freeing and contributes hugely to my peace, my most precious treasure.

Another thing that has made my life easy is that I no longer try to change people or the world, though I retain raging rights. What a relief for the mythological Sisyphus to finally let go! How much pushing the boulder uphill we did fruitlessly in our youth! I let go dysfunctional relationships that resist attempts at conciliation and move openheartedly toward those who respond.

Doing nothing is better than being busy doing nothing.

LAO TZU

Doing nothing has been, and continues to be, one of the most difficult endeavors of my life, perhaps because I am still trying to define and clarify the concept for myself; till we are dead it is impossible to do nothing. Even the phrase "doing nothing" has the word "doing" in it.

Doing is highly addictive. Like all addictions, energy is a happy addiction until it isn't. We love energy so much that when it diminishes, as it must in the varying rhythms of our lives and especially in the process of aging, we expend what remains of life in bemoaning its loss, worrying, *Why can't I do this or that? What happened to the me that I was? Am I dying?*

Doing nothing is an ongoing practice that takes a lifetime to master. Doing nothing is an imperative, an absolute must as we age. I know. I suffer a great deal because I don't know how to do it. Stamina has diminished but the old gears are grinding still, driving me crazy. I have suffered and felt lost over transitions in my day when one activity is done and another not begun. I have driven myself quite crazy, not wanting to do anything but not comfortable with not doing.

Since we can't do away with doing till we are dead, we have to learn to do nothing, make it a conscious practice. Doing nothing is an active choice, an art to be courted and cultivated. I am learning to do much more of nothing than I have ever done before and developed some healthy techniques to deal with my transition periods.

First, I have to be guiltlessly okay with being in bed. The bed has always been my favorite piece of furniture. It is my go-to place to self-soothe. I write in it, nap in it, meditate and do nothing in it. Instead of a flying carpet I have a flying bed. It takes me everywhere. I have had many dreams about my bed, me in it, flying through space, the edges of my bedcover flapping, the sheets transformed to sails.

Transitions between activities, I now know are way stations, inns, places to rest. I lie in bed, eyes closed, and simply, consciously breathe. I combine the breathing with the name of my Beloved, the being who lives in me and in whom I live.

You are never doing nothing if you make breathing deliberate and conscious. Breathing with awareness is an active process. The knowledge that doing nothing is imperative for our flagging energies, that it is highly productive, dispels guilt and also gives me rest when I desperately need to pull back from all activity. Or I just sit in a chair and remind myself that this is a transition and I must stop. I reassure myself that even a few breaths of nothingness will reveal the next move, then I rest some more or do some tiny thing that needs doing, such as brush my hair or eat a snack. Another technique that helps enormously is that I think of my brain as a very large white room—I call it "the White Room"—with open windows and doors without curtains or blinds, and empty of all objects, ideas, thoughts, and people. Even I am not in it. The whole room breathes and I along with it. I can return to this holy space whenever I need.

The trick, again, is to remember that transitions demand rest, even if it is just backing off and taking a few breaths. Remembering there is a solution works magic. I have to be disciplined about attending what I think of as the school for oldies. I memorize my lessons, take care of my tools, hone my techniques, make lists, study. It is important to me to be a good student. Life is an exam and I want to do everything to pass. That being said, a few failures are allowed in the interest of utmost self-kindness.

Meditation is the ultimate in doing nothing. Until recently I practiced meditation off and on, more off than on, but now my school instructions are to do it regularly. I must not waste my mornings doom scrolling on my phone. The phone is also a source of lessons about health and exercise, but it is not something to do first thing in the morning. A little of it while sitting on the pot and leisurely relaxing my bowels is okay. The first thing after morning ablutions—I can take my time over them—I go for my *zafu* cushion, my meditation seat. Meditation is the surest portal to the bliss of nothing.

This is a paradigm shift and has huge spiritual and practical implications. I want to go on and on about meditation, but my brain tires and I think I can just suggest YouTube. There are so many valuable lessons to find there: instructions, benefits, and much more. Brevity is a privilege of old age. Shortcuts are now a valid path.

❧

Is freedom anything other than the right to live as we wish?

EPICTETUS

To ramble while the brain is still ticking is also a privilege of age. Many of my aging gifts have to do with newfound freedoms, trivial and sublime, that I didn't allow myself when I was young. Though freedom from convention, traditions, expectations, and all that bound my spirit has always been the thrust of my life and search, I allow myself to be bound with cords of love and need.

To understand freedom—and I speak only of personal freedom—we have to understand what keeps us from being free. Most of our tyrants are within us. We are captives of our shadows, what the old world called vices and sins. Pride keeps us from the most valuable experiences of love; anger, envy, greed, lust, unchecked despair, and depression are their own hells. Guru Nanak, the founder of Sikhism, says,

> Antar chor guhai ghar mandar in saakat doot naa
>   jaataa hai.
> *"Inner demons are plundering the temple of your home,*
> *O Doubter, acknowledge these ghouls*
> *That pull you this way and that."*

Inner demons are insidious, invisible thoughts and unconscious behaviors that misguide us into suffering. They attack us a thousand times a day. All our downturns and depressions are accompanied by subliminal, self-belittling, self-doubting thoughts, desires, fear, guilt, shame, or regret. *I want more than I have. Why did my life turn out this way? Why am I so terrible? I'm not good enough*, and so on.

No, I haven't tamed my demons and beasts. They are a sly bunch and just when I think they are gone, they surface, take me hostage, and shackle me to suffering. But I have become very aware of them and catch them almost as soon as they surface. The first indication that they are present is unhappiness. Digging to the root of it reveals them. Just acknowledging their presence is a huge accomplishment. I rout them with the tools mentioned in this book. I know how to duck negative thoughts, refuse to go where they are attempting to drag me. I have become better at revolting against them and wresting my freedom from their masticating jaws.

This frees up energy for more fun, rest, reading, and engaging in the business of living. Unshackling, however, is an ongoing daily process.

❧

I cock my hat as I please, indoors or out.
WALT WHITMAN, "SONG OF MYSELF"

There is also more freedom from the vanities of my youth. Comfort takes precedence over appearance. How I feel is more important than how I look in mirrors. For example, in my youth I was anxious about body hair and waxed my legs, arms, and face. I had many dreams in which I was arrested by police for hairy legs. My inner crone doesn't care and is even proud of her gray eyebrows, a cluster of white bristles beneath her lower lip, and some at the corner of her lips. Oh, I care enough to remove them occasionally; I am still here, I am still able to, but there is no compulsion and their presence is no longer an embarrassment. I deliberately let a few persistent gray bristles live in anticipation of a time to come in a hospital or a home, when there will be no energy to pluck them, let alone nourish myself. Finally my corpse will display them in all their glory, appearing even longer compared to the shrinking tissue around them.

But oh, I do wish to die at home in my warm and cozy bed! That would be the ultimate privilege—slip into a dream and never return. Easy, natural, like the falling of a leaf. It entertains me every now and then to wonder how and where and when it will be. I cannot know it, nor can I prepare for every eventuality my fearful mind conjures. You can try to play chess with life but you will lose.

I am freed from thinking of my body as something on display. I am giving away all form-fitting clothes that confine and squeeze my skin, like the newest iteration of corsets: blue jeans and shorts so tight they give me wedgies, and wide, high waistbands that constrict my digestion. I have even given up wearing underwear. My skin is thinner and will brook no chafing.

I still like to dress up sometimes, adorn my body with jewelry or one of my mother's shawls, something different from the clothes I habitually wear, but only when it is something I am doing joyously. I remember my mother, even in her nineties, wearing silk suits and a fancy shawl just to sit in a chair in her garden. A little bit of dressing up for outings (which makes me avoid them) is manageable because earrings alone often do the trick. My inner crone, who is gaining dominance, has no qualms about being a schlump, even outdoors. I love the old hag!

⤕⤔

> Man ray, kyoon chootai bin piar.
> *"Oh my mind, how can you be free without love?"*
>
> GURU NANAK

I can claim I have grown in my capacity to love. This has been a life goal, albeit a subconscious one. I am happier in my marriage, having come to terms with our inevitable differences. We have far fewer fights than the ones you will witness in this book. I love the people in my life who remain after superfluous relationships have been winnowed. Only the power-packed germ remains.

The best way to get love is to give it. I am learning to not project my problems onto others, take responsibility for my own happiness, self-examine, see where I go wrong, take and give space, let hurt go sooner rather than later, and not get sucked into other people's dramas or suffering.

Most of all, I am trying to love myself unconditionally.

⤕⤔

> *I know I am deathless,*
> *I know this orbit of mine cannot be swept by a carpenter's compass.*
>
> WALT WHITMAN, "SONG OF MYSELF"

Though we all fear death, living in its light generates a cascade of gifts. It is like a molting into greater and greater freedom, greater and greater degrees of immateriality. I live by Guru Nanak's words: "*Marnai ki chinta naheen, jeevan kee nahin aas,*" or, to have no anxiety of death and no hope of life.

My earlier desire for more and more life, community, family, renown, and creativity took me to some rotten places. I have now been given, after almost a four-year absence, the opportunity to spend an entire season in my favorite place in the universe, our Himalayan home, and though I hope to return here again next year, I am aware of the tentativeness of all plans. I take nothing for granted and am grateful for what I have experienced instead of wanting more and more of it. I surrender my life to the Force that gives and takes away. I huddle in silence in the center of "no hope." It is a good, calm, salubrious place in which I count my blessings. I move my finger on the keyboard and am grateful I can move my finger; I see and feel the rays of the sun hitting my face and give thanks. My blessings are infinite. I move through my day aware of seemingly infinite abundance. It is not gratitude for life as opposed to death, although it is definitely that as well. I hope (there it is again; there is no getting rid of hope entirely) to surrender to death however, whenever it comes, to surrender to God again and again and again, for the mind tends to forget its own demise and then it must birth its death all over again. In surrendering I will be carried like a child in its mother's embrace through darkness into the light described by all who have returned to tell.

As I near the finish line (I have, I pray, more time than I fear) where everything I have and am will be sloughed off like an outgrown carapace, I trust that the unknown, larger, newer me will fly away to an unknown adventure, shackles shed, the greatest benefaction of all.

1

The Adventure
That I Am

I don't want to wait for old age and death. At seventy-one I shall prepare for the encounter and meet them head-on in the pages of this book. A snippet from a dream a week ago, seemingly forgotten, surfaces in my consciousness as I write here: a *sadhu*, a guru wearing a red turban so bright it stood out brilliantly against the dark grayness of the scene, is walking up a jagged incline at dusk. Sometimes he is a guru, no one I can name, sometimes a guru conflated with my father. He beckons me and I follow. The scene shifts and a series of nightmarish misadventures follows. I am going on a long journey up the Himalayas, but I have forgotten to prepare for it. I have no money nor any of the gear needed: food, water, tents, poles, supplies, or medication. I don't know who I am because the person I have been would have prepared. In real life I begin preparing for our annual trip to India months before the trip. It is a six-month stay, so the preparations are elaborate considering I am addicted to my comforts and must have them about me at all times, wherever I am.

Things turn out well at the end of the dream. I find a branch of my bank on the wayside, and shops where I buy gear and food. But the warning remains: Prepare!

I will have to ask myself some essential questions as I age: Who am I when I am no longer the person I was? What can I be? What sort of old person do I want to be and how do I get there? How should I live, from day to day, from hour to hour? How should I think to attain psychological health? What shall I do with the remaining time? What is my purpose now that the world and life as it is lived by younger folk is falling away from me?

Every stage of our lives demands a new set of eyes that are not looking at the present through the filters of past habits and definitions. I need to cleanse and upgrade the lenses of my mind to look at the constantly shifting circumstances of my body-mind. The lens is the lens of perspective, of the mind, the wizard that can make us wither or bloom. John Milton in *Paradise Lost* wrote, "The mind is its own place and in itself can make a heaven of hell, a hell of heaven."

I replace the idea that I am decaying with, *I am being born to a new way of being and living.* I am youthful still. And beautiful, not only in my own eyes but in the eyes of my faithful partner, Payson, his wonderful eyes that pierce through gray hair and wrinkles to the soul. He loves and cares for the hunchback woman, Gomti, in our village in the Himalayas. He hugs and kisses her, gives her money, clothing, and shoes. She is more than ten years younger than I but arched over from carrying firewood and sacks of flour up the steep dirt path to her home. She looks like a human table: vertical from feet to waist, horizontal at the waist, twisting her neck to look up at us when she talks. The light-filled smile in her weathered, toothless face is contagious. We don't speak each other's languages; she speaks only Pahari, yet communication happens. The few words I understand are *badiyaa* (great, as in she's feeling great) and *kya karna* (what to do? whenever we commiserate with her about an illness or loss). And always with a smile.

Some mysterious power within my body is transforming my face and body, and I must soften and surrender with trust. Some days I am full of hope that even though in one dimension of time I am closer to my exit, all is, and will be, forever well; that even dying will be the greatest adventure of them all. When we die we fade into the invisible from which we separated and emerged, with which we now merge again. We pass to a place beyond sight, dwelling place of love, compassion, commitment, loyalty, responsibility, values, God, and all those abstract, amorphous thoughts and feelings so palpably pervasive and more real than matter. And then we return again, eternally. Our destiny is the destiny of water, changing form, from vapor to matter, in an endless cycle, remaining constant and indestructible, like air.

Now more than ever, when demons—pessimistic thoughts, despair, failure, regret, self-pity, ailments—attack my increasingly fragile body and mind and inflict damage to my heart, I will make myself strong, physically and mentally, through exercise, meditation, and courage. I need to become a hero and warrior again on the hazardous battle-field that my life, with its chronic health challenges and encroaching hopelessness, has become. These demons must be fought and subdued. Often during the day my happiness is hijacked by their harsh and grating voices in my mind: *I've gained weight. I'm not successful enough. I've failed. Where is the recognition I deserve? I'm getting old and feeble.* These thoughts drag me by my hair all day long, sometimes for weeks or months. Many a day I fall off my horse entirely and am bruised, sometimes for a reason and sometimes for no other reason than that I fell off when I least expected or wanted to. Some days when the journey becomes perilous I become an antihero, a vulnerable and scared wimp. A type of rigor mortis sets in and I can't get going; entropy is visible now not only in mirrors but closer, in the murmurs of my heart. Then the word and concept "adventure" vanishes, leaving only an amorphous, directionless suffering.

Aging is unknown territory with no map. I will think of it as a new type of adventure. My companions and allies will be guides, gurus, and ghosts. I need all manner of fellowship, visible and invisible, on this solo journey.

I know one thing, taught to me by my guides, my allies in the sky: as the veil of the material world thins in my journey to invisibility, the mythic view of our lives as journeys is the only view worth living by, the only one that makes utter sense.

The mind precedes sight and light. Thoughts, airy and invisible, chart the course of our minds, our lives, our destinies. In the plasma of consciousness, how we see something is how it becomes. As soon as I see aging as an adventure, it calls to me, enlists my passion, and gives me the necessary energy to prepare for it with commitment, determination, and consciousness, all of which I need as I navigate the tumultuous terrain of my attenuating life.

Even when I do not budge from my home, I am brought to other places in the constantly shifting kaleidoscope of my body-mind and environment. Earth moves me with her moving, my weather changing with her twirling. Inner, outer, these boundaries, too, are breaking down. Achieving my goal to make inward and outward seamless depends less on my own efforts than grace. Seamless! A feminine word. A whole cloth patched with stitches that are part of its beauty, the pieces invisibly lapped together at their margins in continuous and indivisible wholeness.

I don't have to go anywhere on this journey but stay in the comfort of my own home, inside my skin and my mind, commit to inner explorations in the always unknown territory that is me. Without this inner voyage, outer world adventures fail to satisfy. I do not fear I am withdrawing from the world, missing out on life, for all life is here within my skin. An American woman asked a yogi living in a cave near Rishikesh, "Don't you miss the world?" His happy reply, "Madam, I *am* the world."

What else has it been all along but adventure? My internal journey, hand in hand with the events of my life, is the journey of the lotus, my namesake. My recurring, cyclical journey is from suffering and darkness where my rhizome sucks sustenance, up through murky waters to light and back again. My long, brief journey on this planet goes all the way back to the first protozoa that unfurled into this spreading, variegated, world tree. In this particular incarnation it began with the union of my mother and father, ova and sperm commingling into a singularity, a tiny jelly-like blood seed in the spongy red soil of my mother's womb. Where did I begin? In India, in a small town, Hoshiarpur, Panjab, "land of five waters," land of my foremothers and fathers, transported across continents to a small coastal town in Southern California on the shores of the Pacific.

Adventure. The word and idea excites. Excitement is diminishing with age, though not absent. I had a rare spurt of it just the other day, sitting outside on the terrace of a restaurant here in Del Mar, looking out at the Pacific, the sky aflame with clouds of gold, red, black, white, all morphing even as we watched, mingling and parting on the background of blue and gray. I felt happy, my fading tastebuds blooming with the varied tastes of grilled vegetables, salmon, chicken, salad, bread, and butter. I had an unholy appetite. I tore through the bread, gnawed the chicken bones to suck the marrow, dug out the liver and heart from the breast of the bird. I still get ravenously hungry at times, and how good it feels now that eating has become fuel rather than pleasure, and hungers are shrinking. Hunger is God's gift to the living, and I must continue to stoke it every now and then. Oh, I have many hungers still! Ambition, little delights, a shelf here, something organized there, a beautiful piece of Polish pottery to buy, a small table here or there to add to convenience and beauty, a piece of clothing, a hat, shoes, earrings, a touch of lipstick. I cherish my material self. It keeps me plugged in and alive. I am like my mother who took care of her house, embellished it and her garden, wore good clothing not only in her garden but on errands and appointments into her late eighties.

Sitting on the terrace that day, eating the bounty of earth, I was in the very prow of life, on the very tip of yet another adventure. *What will it be? How will things unfold between now and the inevitable end?*

Will I die in the United States or in India? Will I die first or will Payson? Will I bloom again, or is this blooming my last? And when I fall into an unmoving heap of decay, merge with the mud from which I am formed, will there be another transformation, continuance, the cycle I see manifest all around me, or the end of my cells and spirit?

Somewhere in the questions a worm of worry began to infect my excitement. The thought of parting from Payson, sitting across the table from me, both of us chowing down, made all the losses that have shadowed my aging—mother, father, a husband, friends, pets—bloom. Our after-dinner walk on the shore was tinged with darkness at my edges and in my heart, dispelled somewhat by the beauty of the red and orange smudge at the horizon past the mercurial midnight-blue sea undulating in the dusk, still glowing with last light, and the soothing sibilance of its ebb and flow. I knew, as we entered our home, that it would be a Valium night.

This alternating of light and dark, yin and yang, is increasing in frequency as I age. My inner climate is much like Southern California weather that Groucho Marx described as "chilly today, hot tamale." Perhaps it is nature's way of introducing me gradually to the idea of surcease. *Adventure*, the word, is related to "advent," the arrival of something important. What could be more important than the arrival of—let me say it—death? It is what old age whispers loud and clear, though we rarely hear it. Yet hear it we must, if only to deny it. Death always posits life. It is losing life—with all its beauty and all its sorrow—that we fear when we fear death.

Death is the basis of our fear of getting older, through and beyond the loss of loved ones, youth, beauty, ambition, and energy. And it isn't that we don't have beauty, youth, ambition, energy, and passion when we are older, but they fade and sometimes mute. That part of my life was a different dimension. Shapes change, patterns shift, matter morphs. Can I change with the changing? Can I learn not to resist change and death, even when my heart is breaking?

Anything is possible as I move through my moments. I tripped and fell twice this year, and just sitting on a chair threw out my back. Despite daily yoga I am limping from *peroneal tendonitis* that makes it difficult for me to get about, not made easier by the heavy boots I wear inside the house to protect my foot. Payson had to be rushed to the hospital last month because of chest pain. He needs surgery soon to intercept his prostate cancer. A breath separates each of us from death. That is why I must be present at every turn to everything, particularly in how I interact with my husband with infinite kindness, knowing there are no forevers here. Our union is brief, getting briefer. I try to stay present as I move around the house and outdoors, cook, eat, bathe, and above all, I guard vigilantly against despairing, self-negating thoughts. I want to stop being a captive of my own default mental processes. I resolve to practice the teaching of Guru Nanak: Conquer your mind and conquer the world. I will endeavor to dispel, though I will often fail, thoughts that disempower me and hurt my soul, become a sleuth of my processes, a samurai decapitating errant thoughts that poison this holy time of my life. How rich my life becomes when I pay attention and attend to the minutiae of it, observe myself, and cultivate happiness and peace.

Happiness is not a state but an attitude, a perspective. Happiness requires reformatting and restructuring old habits of thought and body and developing new ones. We are creatures of habit. We must learn to break the ones that keep us in our old, tight skins and craft new ones that are habitable, congenial, easier. Ah, easy! We have to begin with openness to new ways of being, of seeing, of making nano inner gestures toward light. It is a daily, hourly practice. I expect my demons to return, clasp me in their bony arms, dunk me in dark waters. The work of extrication never stops.

I need to travel further into what Nanak calls the pilgrimage to Self. Few embark on it though most of us have heard its call. Unhappiness, depression, discontent—the moaning of our souls—are reminders of something more important than our repetitive lives. The call is the call of the inner frontier. It demands nothing less than total commitment, dedication, and devotion. "Know thyself" is a dictum of all our allies. We know so little about the stranger we meet in the mirror, the stranger so near we live in his or her skin, think his or her thoughts, live his or her life.

This much is certain and clear: I want a successful old age. My quest is to find the always elusive still point, the eye of the storm, the peace that bypasses the brain and all thoughts, conflict, and striving. It is where the heart, content and hopeful, is at rest. I want to fashion who I want to become, live as I want to live, with ease, in my dusking years. I want easy, the very flower of my desiring. The still point and the flow. I am nowhere near my goal. As Rainer Maria Rilke wrote in *Letter to a Friend*, "I tell you that I have a long way to go before I am where one begins."

Perhaps there is no goal, only the going. I have to return to school to learn and master crucial life lessons; practice, practice, practice techniques and skills without which I know I can drown in my own despair, and without which, as I have already experienced and continue to experience, old age can suck.

I will remember, too, that no adventure worth having is ever easy; remind myself that the path *must* wind down through darkness to rise to light, even while knowing that I will forget. But the responsibility for picking myself up after failures, losses, fears, and adversity, after allowing myself the requisite suffering, some of which seeks to be described in these pages, rests with me. After many falls and broken limbs, both literal and figurative, I must remember the tools of the spiritual trade, regroup my cognitive and spiritual army, and get back on my horse. The view is better when I am in the saddle. I can see further.

The first of my rules is kindness, to myself most of all. Everything is allowed. Falling off the horse is allowed. Failing and forgetting is allowed. Everything presented to me in the passage of my day will be faced and endured. I have to accept, with love and compassion, every part of myself, demons, shadows, and all. I am a shifty thing, a cloud, flowing from shape to shifting shape, from faith to doubt, from happiness to despair and back again. I am a coagulum of contraries: god, human, animal. I must let myself be in my entirety.

My aging story is the story of the difficult, sometimes impossible challenge and rewards of striving for grace, falling, and continuing over and over again. As Samuel Beckett wrote in *Worstward Ho*, "Try again. Fail again. Fail better." It is the story of my adventures, external and internal. It is about India, America, and my story mixed in with the stories of places and people I love and who love me. It is also the story of my journey to the event horizon, the black hole from which nothing returns, or returns only in dreams, and where words, images, and stories cease.

I ask the universe to let me have my adventure of aging before I grow too old to enjoy it. Let me experience all the opportunities and gifts that aging brings. I discover more invaluable ones every day. Of course, no gift in this dual world comes without a curse, and I am cursed as well. I'm also blessed beyond imagining and gratitude.

What can be more enriching than experiencing this life I have been given, soon to be over, in a new, more aware way, living my life with greater intensity in the light of death?

Going where I am going, staying where I am, preferring the given, will be my greatest challenge.

Will you help me, Spirit, when I fail?

2

My Old Age Project

As our relevance in the external world decreases, we need to invent and create our own relevance, especially and above all to ourselves: aged, but engaged with whatever and wherever our bliss lies.

I have no children or grandchildren on whom to focus my attention and affection; no employment to go to; no pets, only Bhalli, my part-time dog for the six months we spend in India each year; no country, no home, though we have beautiful residences on two continents; no clan or tribe to which I belong. I am a writer in exile wherever I am. The page is where I live and breathe.

I am compelled to explore, find, reveal, chronicle my aging story; to weave and reweave my life with its tangled ganglion of time, memory, and events swirling like unanchored tumbleweed in the field of my mind where there is neither time, distance, nor distinction among the many tenses I use to keep my story straight. I'm driven to look at the present together with the many layers of my past before turning in the direction from which there is no return, where time, mind, and the senses retract to the singularity from which they unfurl.

Now as the body moves toward disintegration, I want to lay myself bare, pinned on the table of these pages. I hope to dissect beneath the skin and muscle of my physical appearance to the psychic organs ticking, revealing raw tissue of my body-mind-soul, not always without fear, question, or shame. Ambition and exhibitionism combine in my desire to share myself as an aging human specimen with others. Like the spider weaving instinctually, making transparent and fleeting webs of shimmering beauty, I weave the pages of this book.

I do not know if there's time to tell the infinitely unraveling fractal tale of my life. Limited by my physical existence, my question remains unanswered: How long do I have to finish it? But William Blake, one of my many guides, shows me the way in his book *The Marriage of Heaven and Hell*: "He who desires, and acts not, breeds pestilence." The encouraging chorus of my guides and angels, whom I keep around me for the light they cast upon my darkling paths, come to my aid, too: *Go for it, girl! What else are you going to do with what remains of your time? You wear it as a garment ten times your size. The more time contracts, the denser it becomes; with less energy to do things, it hangs heavy in your hands. Doing defines time as objects define space. Shake off paralysis, tell your story; take fistfuls of the endless fleece of your life, embrace labor with the atrophying limbs of your mind, spin like Penelope, wife of Ulysses, spun her tapestries for meaningful engagement while waiting for her long-lost groom. Do it without fear, for it all unravels at the end. Body boundaries collapse as the true merging marriage for which you have been ripening all your life arrives.*

I must proceed without delay. Nothing excites or gets me out of bed except this labor of words calling to me from sleep and dreams. This weaving my own shroud helps me to remake my life as I want to live it now, even in my disintegration—consciously, easily, vitally, still quick and pulsing, though I have begun to taste a host of new, age-related vulnerabilities and anxieties. I will not speak about them too much, just enough to let you know you are not alone when you suffer your own story your own way.

Let me write on aging before I am too old to write, remember, or care. Let the labor continue with commitment till the book is somewhat complete, which is my hope, or till it is snatched away from me—part of the fear and anxiety that steals my sleep. Let me accept, even when I cannot, that Morta, the Roman goddess of death, may snip my thread before my tapestry is done. Let it remain, survive, die, and resurrect in some future archaeologist's dig as a valuable fragment. The shard, the time-eaten loose-weave cloth, the bead from a necklace from Mohenjo-Daro*—are they not complete in themselves, even without the names of the artists to go along with the artifacts? Name, bonded to the body, which is everything on this shore, counts for nothing in geologic deep time where I am headed.

I begin my project with a prayer. I believe there is Something out there and in here that listens to our pleas, even though I often doubt it. But the purpose of doubt is to strengthen our faith, so I try not to resist it, even though it feels like hell. Whether this Something is a fantasy or reality doesn't concern me. I have tasted, palpably, the sweet fruit of the experiences that cannot be described or visualized, only felt. *Help me, please,* I pray, as I toss on the stormy seas of senescence, doubt, and fear. *Take the helm of my ship, replot my course, swell my sails with hope even though I know my end. Take me gently through the many storms that await, to the other, safer shore.*

I am encouraged by a 2020 article by John McPhee that I read in *The New Yorker*, titled "Tabula Rasa: Volume 1." He talks about Thornton Wilder and Mark Twain's "old-man project." As a young man McPhee questioned the older Wilder's project, twelve years before his death, of reading and cataloguing Lope de Vega's four hundred and thirty-one surviving plays (he wrote eighteen hundred full-length plays). To the young McPhee's "Why would anyone want to do that?" Wilder replied furiously, "Young man, do not ever question the purpose of scholarship." At age eighty-eight McPhee finally understands the answer to his question. "I am eighty-eight years old at this writing," McPhee wrote,

---

*This archaeological site of a former well-developed city on the banks of the Indus River, now in Pakistan, dates from 2500 BCE.

"and I know that those four hundred and thirty-one plays were serving to extend Thornton Wilder's life. Reading and cataloguing them was something to do, and do, and do. It beat dying. It was a project meant not to end."

This is my old-woman project. I can go on and on recording and so reliving my today, yesterday, and tomorrow of this infinitely unravelling tale. As McPhee noted, "Old-people projects keep old people old. You're no longer old when you are dead."

Can I learn not to get ambitious about it? Not get wounded by rejections?

3

What Does It Mean to Be Present?

*P*ayson—companion, husband, friend, family in this stretch of my life—said yesterday, "I have accepted I am a nobody. Now I just want to be present." There was a glow on his face I hadn't seen in a while through all his years of striving to succeed as an artist, and it both pleased me enormously and filled me with regret that I wasn't where he was, at the place I both desire and fear: life without ambition. Is it possible? I will make it so if need be. I know only that I do not want to die a bitter, regretful person.

Being present. What does it mean? For P, as he always says and demonstrates, it is the Zen proverb: "chop wood, carry water." He shies from no task, taking care of our finances (even though it is getting harder for him at seventy-five), the maintenance of our home, planting and watering and pruning the garden. Before she died, he changed his mother's diapers, He is always engaged with whatever it is he is doing, whether painting, writing, making music, reading, doing the dishes, or sweeping the floor.

What does being present mean to me? Can I learn, or will I persist in my own increasing resistance to doing things—dishes, cooking, finances, laundry, taxes? It is time to embrace the quotidian, to be present in my house and life.

Payson is not always present to his body, nor I to mine. We push to get everything done, forget our age, do too much, and tire ourselves out. I am learning to take steps to remedy my tiredness no matter where I am, to pull back, take a few conscious breaths, acknowledge and respect my tiredness unquestioningly, and retreat to rest. But I have not mastered the art of resting. When tired, P becomes a grumpy, unavailable, non-present troll. His screws go loose in times of shared stress when I most want loving, caring togetherness. I will tell you the story, later, of when I first encountered his troll, a short time after our meeting while on an RV trip through Northern California, where we had a near-fatal accident. It was on this trip, too, that he asked me to marry him as we sat under giant Cedars of Lebanon trees in the backyard of the courthouse in the town of Independence. When I said yes I didn't realize I had said yes to the troll, too. I have fought his troll tooth and nail. It has been a long, often painful, instructive journey to learn to recognize, name, accept, and hopefully—for this is the intention now—to embrace and love his troll who pushes my buttons and elicits my own closed-hearted, hard harridan, blinded by pride and anger, ready to run out the door. At this age, what else remains but love?

Can I be more present to myself, to Payson, to my life as it is moment to moment—demon fears, monster regrets, and the mute pleas of my body, my old mare, to slow down, stop, and be kind to myself? Can I become aware of the multitude of ways in which I still push, pull, twist, and contort myself? Can I learn to wear my dreams lightly? Will I be content, as P seems, to be a nobody, yet a hero in my own eyes? A hero who ultimately accepts the imperatives of her destiny and surrenders to the fate over which she has no recourse?

4

Small Cosmic Dramas

*M*oving through many membranes of my many lives, I have arrived here: Del Mar, California. It is home, not destination. But it may be a good place to pause, take stock, and prepare.

I delude myself that pauses are possible. Spaceship Earth, as Buckminster Fuller called her, is twirling on her axis at a thousand miles an hour at the equator, spinning giddily through our solar system, taking our molecules along with it. There is never cessation. And that is why God made night. To give us the illusion of stillness, so easily disrupted by dreams.

The river of my life, having made its journey from its beginnings (When and where was it? No birthday can tell), bounding through the gorges of youth, carving its own path down high mountain ridges these many decades, has arrived at sea level. There are no heights remaining to climb to or descend. All is leveled; easy, almost, so easy. The river I am turns to dreaming, letting go parts of itself that have been held tightly together by banks and bounds, takes its own time in the sun like Alph, the Sacred River, "meandering with a mazy motion," as Samuel Taylor Coleridge wrote in *Kubla Khan*. Soon the wide arms of the ocean will reach for me, our mouths will suck each into the other, and I will lose myself and my too-long held identity.

In a dream about my Holy Marriage with my Beloved, at once a man and God, I am in a large compound. The One I have loved all my life, the One from whom I was separated at birth, the One who has a face that is both real and a mask for love has finally chosen me. I am dressed in a red chiffon sari like an Indian bride, adorned in gold and jewels. Soon I am naked under the sheets with my Beloved. It is our first night and we just sleep together, as Payson and I often do, on our angled sides, spooning, his front nestled contour-to-contour into my back, embracing and cozy in the comfort and trust of presence. The sexual under- and overtones have been transmuted to a whole-body experience, a glow that radiates outward from my heart to the edges of my cells that expand to include and become the Other.

May I, as my holy guides before me who lived their lives and deaths creatively, go to old age and death with some trepidation, yes, but with vision, hope, love, and joy. This is my prayer and my endeavor. It will take a lot of work and vigilance, I know, but I am ready for it.

There's so much talk about immortality projects, science, medicine, and technology finding the cure to aging and dying. I expect, with some luck and help from the universe, to get old and die.

Walking into town holding hands with Payson the other day, feeling tired, depressed, old, my stomach distended with trapped, ballooning gas like a dirigible, my right knee creaking, a heavy-duty brace on my left wrist from severe *tenosynovitis* (Ah, I have a name for it! Treatment is near at hand!), I said to him, "I hope to die before I grow old."

"I hope to grow old before I die," he laughed.

His words ripped a veil in my mind and I saw for an instant another way of thinking and being. A future, always so closed and unknown, unrolled before me and I was excited at the prospect of my many transformations yet to come. How will my little old lady be? Where will she be? What will then be her inner terrain and weather? What will be her dreams? Will some of the techniques I am developing now to prepare for aging come to my aid even then, or will I have to develop new ones in my ongoing re-creation of myself? I was reminded of Robert Browning's line in "Rabbi Ben Ezra": "The best is yet to be, the last of life for which the first was made." Is it possible, I wondered, that in some essential way life is getting better? The question was enough to set my soul singing.

Let me count the ways. I did not know going slowly creates time. Time now to putter from thing to thing, to ramble through life allowing each activity, desire, and chore to unfold naturally, organically, without pushing and hurrying; to take hours to wake up, laze sleepily in bed, chew the cud of dreams, be quiet, or schmooze with Payson. It's also refreshing to take time out for a good BM. How hurried and constipated I was in my youth, and how grateful I am now to sit in the wide space of no time, relaxing my bowels, lax, loose, releasing anxieties and rigidities of a lifetime habit of ungodly haste. How good it feels, this return to basics, the healthy indulgences of the body as it pleasures itself through elimination.

Time now to watch the inner-outer drama of the skies. Sunrises and sunsets have become the main events of our lives. The first thing I see on waking every morning is our deck facing west, built on the roof of our three-story house, jutting out like the deck of a ship; and beyond it the whole fat sky, its scumbled predawn colors, soft washes of pinks, blues, and violets on the horizon of the waters of the Pacific, vast and unbounded. There is nothing between us and Japan, more than six thousand miles away, except small islands.

The deck has been the venue and launchpad for many an event and journey. When Payson and I first met, we would lie out on warm evenings on our sheepskin rug, cuddling under the stars, being a part of the show in the sky. This is where the wedding party, five including friends and relatives, gathered in fall of 1998, ate meals, drank wine, sang songs, strung marigolds and roses to make garlands for each of the attendees, and played the harmonium, lyre, drums, and saxophones. Payson and I both had had previous marriages in hasty civil ceremonies.

I was never into wedding rituals, expensive and overrated, but this one, coming five years after my previous husband Donald's suicide, I wanted to make special in simple ways. I bathed in fresh cream and red rose petals and my friends wove fragrant plumeria into my hair. I felt youthful even at fifty. The young-old bride. How long ago it seems, and how near, as if it were yesterday.

This was as close as I got to a traditional marriage ceremony. I had never wanted a garish Indian wedding. Mishi, my older sister, had just gotten engaged the old-fashioned way: arranged by relatives. She had always wanted to get married, dress up and wear jewelry the way Mom did. I didn't want to be an arranged person who had to fall into a submissive role. Marriage was not on my radar in my youth, and because I was next in line for an arranged marriage, I had to flee far away: to America. I was accepted at Kent State but Dad had just retired as a brigadier in the army. We had lived in style, but cash flow was always limited. He didn't own a house and he had two daughters and a son to marry off—always a big expense in India. I asked if I could take the dowry money he had set aside for my marriage to get an education in America. My liberal, supportive father agreed. My destiny was decided. More likely, my destiny made me flee. I was going to fulfill myself in many ways and resolved never to be a wife to any man I did not choose. I would be free! I did not know then that there can be no freedom without love; that boundaries set us free.

From this same deck we often see sprays and spouts of whales as they migrate south to Baja to spawn in warm waters and bays, then back north with their calves, their exhalations and flukes a message and signature of the planet's well-being. How rare these sightings are now! And dolphins, how infrequent, almost non-existent their appearance. But let me not go into the clutches of ecological despair; I want to stay with beauty that man's greed and testosterone will never destroy. Let me keep hope alive that I, together with our Earth and the multiverse with its infinite spaces in which we are embedded, am part of an infinite cycle of time. The Earth and I, old women now, are part of the recurrence, this time beyond mind.

We witnessed the blood red blue moon from our deck. Bundled in blankets on lounge chairs, front row seats to the greatest night show on Earth, we experienced the total lunar eclipse in the synergy of sun, Earth, and moon. In my youth I was deluded by my senses. I forgot that Earth is turning within many turnings, counterclockwise on her own axis, spinning once every twenty-four hours in relation to the sun at an estimated 67,100 miles an hour. It is dizzying. That is why we have been given the illusion of stability.

What I was expecting to happen and what occurred during the eclipse were two different things. I thought the shadow of Earth would start from the top of the moon, like a cap, then creep downward to engulf the pearlescent globe. Instead, the shadow crept up from south-west of the moon, growing like the dark receptacle of an acorn seed up the silver planet till it covered the whole lunar globe. The shadow wasn't dark as I had expected but amber colored from the sun's reflection on the moon. There it hung in the night sky, the whole round, mottled marble turned amber by the sun's reflection, brighter and larger than ever before. Then we on the earth whirled north, the sun south below the horizon. The moon grew gradually pregnant with light, casting its pink reflective glow on the rippling water, the liquid skin of our earth. When the eclipse began to move into penumbra, light having arrived, the moon's colors became liquid and flowing, streaks and washes of pinks against baby blues and violets, translucent before swirling and sinking below the horizon into invisibility.

We stayed till our bodies turned cold, and our eyes, not wanting to miss even a second of it, grew weary. Then, with almost a sense of relief, our old bones descended to our warm kitchen to make some tea and to wonder at the cosmic wheeling in which all parts, including us, are so choreographed in the celestial dance that the marvelous minds of mathematicians and astronomers can predict it.

My expectation of what would happen during the eclipse and what actually happened were two different things, which was a lesson about future fears: What if Payson dies before me? I will have to experience the same anguish I felt when Donald committed suicide. I will be abandoned, alone, without children. Who will take care of me? What if I get dementia, as my grandmother did?

Nanak's words *"Mat man janai kal"* (Let not the mind think of tomorrow), always come to my rescue. The myriad contingencies are impossible to predict. I must learn not to project my fears onto the future, to stay in the space of relaxed unknowing, trust that the universe will send help as it has in the past. After Donald's suicide the strings of my life were cut loose, flapping in the wind. Yet some unknown power comforted me. Though I grieved long and hard, my hand was held by a hand that has never withdrawn itself since, though I often forgetfully let it go. Help was sent and will be.

Time to prepare for different eventualities, tame my fears that grow fiercer as my bodybrain's defenses erode with the years. The other day I gave Payson permission to find someone else if I go before him. But at night I fell into fear and despair that he would find another, bring her to our house, sleep with her in our bed.

I must think of the journey ahead with less fear and in the light of adventure. My life after Payson's death *will* be an adventure. There will be much to navigate and many challenges to meet.

Lingering and luxuriating in bed long past the time to get up and begin my day is my old-age luxury. The pillows, the sheets, and warmth from a heated pad and an electric blanket keep me in a cocoon of warmth. My relaxed body sinks into deep comfort and wants to laze about some more. I try to stay in the present, in the now, our bed, the deck, the colors of the sea and sky merged into one unspectacular gray with no gradations. I love mornings when there is no pressure to get up and begin the day with activity and routines, just a slow, almost timeless lingering in my increasingly favorite piece of furniture with my favorite person. They are not as frequent as I would like, but often enough to keep me satisfied. This is definitely a boon of aging.

Propped up on our pillows, Payson and I gaze out the sliding glass doors to the sky above the Pacific Ocean just beyond the prow of our deck and watch the morning drama of the vast western sky, the shifting palette of colors and clouds, the canvas gradually changing from an indistinguishable gray to pre-dawn hues of blues and pinks. Who has named all the blues and pinks our eyes have seen? Color names are convenient abstractions that somewhat convey what we mean.

This rectangular window of sky I consider ours has afforded us spectacular views of the many-colored sky and sea—sunrises, sunsets, the moon, planets, and stars—God's kaleidoscopic canvas.

Payson said the other day, "This is where I'd like to die. Propped up on these pillows, watching the sky before merging with it."

Though I rarely step out of the sliding glass doors, happy to watch the deck and the dawn from the warm comfort of our bed, my husband goes out frequently in the mornings and at night before going to bed. "It is amazing that little me is part of this whole spectacle," he says.

Most mornings, wet, cold, or warm, he takes his meditation stool and sits, eyes closed, his body wrapped in the shawl we bought in Almora, India, twenty-three years ago. On Sundays he meditates for an hour.

Twenty-three years is not exact. Time is measured in approximations in my fraying brain. Time has become a wide, boundless field, vast as the universe in which everything is connected to everything else, including past, present, and future in the simultaneity of spacetime. Snippets, tableaux, moments, snatches of dialogue spoken many decades ago, events caught in the net of memory, small memories within large ones, all make up my past and are what count now, not chronology. Some memories remain for a mortal forever while others have disappeared in the trash bin of time.

5
The Great Remembering

Our shawls from Almora are moth-eaten now. I recall vividly the hand-looming workshop where we bought our *jamawars*, modern versions of the antiques the word refers to, in what the West calls "paisley" patterns. I remember well the swarthy face of the middle-aged owner with gray hair and beard, the half-woven shawls on the looms, weavers threading the warp, the rhythms of the pedals, shuttles flying their colors through the shed, the sound of the reeds packing in the weft. I bought two, one in purples and greens, the other in browns and yellows.

But Payson continues to use the soft, cheap, synthetic one he bought from a street vendor to "spread the money around."

I had witnessed the dawn of a Great Remembering in my parents, the mind swiveling in its aging to the bittersweet past. Mummy lived in a past that has a way of being very present. Her memories were always circling in a vortex around the difficulties of her life after marriage. She was treated like a servant by her in-laws when her husband was stationed at borders where families were not accommodated. Stories of her mistreatment hurt my heart as it must have hurt hers then, and even now when I recall them. I was hurt at each retelling, endlessly iterated as the years progressed. Daddy, too, had hard times, his family plunged into dire poverty after his wealthy father died intestate at the age of fifty-two, and the miraculous moments where fate manifested to ensure his rise from rags to riches, from the ranks all the way to brigadier, a high-ranking officer. Mom's recollection of her childhood was of the love and respect she got from the extended family in which she was the first survivor after two other girls had died at birth. No, not all their remembering was about hardships; the dark cloth was threaded with veins of silver and gold.

Indian to my core, I feel time exists simultaneously. The present is what is in focus in that particular time. Sometimes the past is in focus and sometimes the future, sometimes that which has never been but exists somewhere on the vast and inexhaustible canvas of time. In *The Holographic Universe* Michael Talbot wrote: "It is the viewer's changing perspective that provides the illusion that it (life) is unfolding in time. The holographic theory suggests that the same is true of our own past. Instead of fading into oblivion, it too remains recoded in the cosmic hologram and can always be accessed once again. Time may be more like an endless sea, every drop of which we can instantly access, regardless of where we might be standing."

Payson, too, is at that threshold, repeating twice-told tales about his family, difficult childhood, youth, and college days, strung through with passion, suffering, delightful defiance, rebellion, *chutzpah* (Yiddish for boldness), perfect moments in nature, and a hunger to know the world and himself through long years of therapy, seeking through it all an orientation toward the spirit, toward home.

The Great Remembering has come upon me, too. Who says we can remain forever in the now? Who wants to? All this New Age business about living in the now. Why should we stay in one place when we are the inheritors of mansions of memories? To turn in memory toward, say, Binsar, near Almora, when we were younger and desiring an adventure in India, to which I longed to return after decades in the United States, is not that a part of this delicious now?

Payson's cheap, soft blanket. Binsar is a forested town near Almora in the Central Himalayas, the magical forests wherein black-faced white langurs swing on hoary, bearded oaks. Its dirt trails are lined with star moss, and on one of them we were adopted by a black dog Payson named Bhallu, the bear, that slept in our room in the funky rest house that was the best accommodation available in those days. We were on one of our many honeymoons after one of our many marriage ceremonies in the United States and India. The priest at the 2,500-year-old temple complex near Almora, Jageshwar, married us again when Payson told him we had just gotten married, and blessed us with a hundred sons. We laughed. We were already in our fifties, and childless through our many marriages to others.

We strayed in our wandering toward homes we liked and inquired from many groundskeepers if they were for sale. This was long before our dream began to flesh out in the Himalayas in March of 2003. That date is exact.

How perverse the psyche is, so torn between intentions and hidden desires. My hunger for India started soon after I became an American citizen, after our marriage and my commitment to Payson and the house in Del Mar. I couldn't rationalize the desire or muscle it away. Life happens despite our conscious minds.

Inner voices first whispered, then talked, and then, because I wasn't listening, screamed two urgent needs: quit my tenured teaching job and make a life in India. How energy- and time-sucking teaching was getting, but I was fearful of retiring: *What will I do with my time? Do I have enough money? I don't want to be old and poor.* My heartstrings pulled me toward my aging parents in India. I had spent half my life away from them, first boarding schools and colleges and then the United States, to study, work, and live. Now I wanted a life in India, the India in my blood, its food, sights, sounds, language, and more family. India is my charging station. Without it, my life force was diminishing.

Payson and I made a few trips to India at the turn of the century to look for a place to build a home. Panjab is flat like Kansas and Nebraska, polluted, and brutally hot in summer, which lasts for about eight long months. The farmland outside the city is dotted with chicken coops with electric wires overhead, marshy fields, attractive chunks of land with clusters of mango trees so old they produce no fruit, peacocks roosting on the hoary branches of a centuries-old Bodhi tree, and strawberry fields. I loved a lovely tree-shaded parcel of land, perfect for bicycle riding near the turquoise irrigation canal by the zoo. But then Payson saw a *mahout* (elephant caretaker) beating an elephant, and said, "Never!" Nothing clicked. My heart wanted to be near my parents in the plains; my soul longed for the mountains. The tug-of-war went on and on within me. Accustomed to the open vistas of Del Mar, nothing but the horizon where sea meets sky, we wanted open, uninhabited spaces in nature.

The Himalayas, the hoariest and youngest peaks of the world, still rising as the Indian continent continues to move northward into Asia, had entered my soul with their mountains and forests, and, of course, water. The two, the hardest of materials and the softest, are so tied as to be inseparable. But the high Himalayas are eight hours by car from Chandigarh, where my parents lived.

Mummy didn't want us to live so far away. Our fight over it hurts still. My words—"I am an adult, I don't want to live my life in your lap"—hurt her and hurt me now in the retelling. How harsh I was, a harshness I inherited from her. We always spoke our minds and hearts, sometimes too directly and without forethought.

How we hurt others by being true to our needs. I have, most of my life, been oriented toward myself, like my mother—prompting others, Payson included, to accuse me of being selfish. How much of my struggle has been a tropism toward and away from you, Mother! I am swirling in an eddy of regret. I think of your end and how I failed you by not being there when you died. I must remember now, before I proceed any further on regret and self-bashing, that as I age, I must exert some discipline while continuing to be very kind to myself. I say to my mind as it is drag-ging me to tortuous places and painful memories, *Stop! Don't go there!* I remind myself of my vow of self-compassion. I am gloriously worthy of love. How many times a day I say these words to myself: *I love you.* These are not words mouthed by my lips alone but arise from the inchoate, sloshy, heart-spring of feeling. I hug myself close, my nose nestled into my breast, and say, *There, there, it's okay, it's okay, my baby, it is okay.*

Where was I? My mind begins to meander. It frays like old tis-sue, strives fruitlessly to catch the disappearing tails of ever branch-ing memories and thoughts. Reason and chronology, which have and continue to hold my brain in a vise, begin to lose their hold. Language begins to have glimpses of something beyond its reach. I begin some-where and end up somewhere else, like the stories of our lives—tangled, nonlinear, braided with other tales. I must go where I am taken in this tapestry of words, reflections, concepts, memories, and emotions. This tapestry is an abstract design, yet all of a piece: coherent incoherence. I keep cultivating my thus-far intimate connection to language, align-ing the threads so as not to lose you, dear reader. This relationship is paramount now as I, an old spider weaving her webs, fearing becoming irrelevant and defunct, spin my tale in my solitary cocoon. Is it a womb or a tomb? Not wanting to face the question, I take a fiber of language and spin it into a mooring rope to the cleats of your heart. My lifeboat, though bobbing in the tide, is secure, safe, connected to you, to God, to Payson, and to our home. I dare not let it drift away entirely into the tumultuous sea that surrounds me, into the abstraction that awaits.

Before I return to the thread, an insight bears recording. The brain begins to lose things, memories, logic, words, coherence because it is weary of carrying the voluminous tomes of a life in its long trudge through life's endless by-lanes. In addition to endless to-do lists I am carrying desires, dreams, despairs, regrets, two continents, three homes, a beloved stream, the corpses of my dead parents, and the sick (soon to become a corpse) body of my dying sister, Mishi.

My words, "I don't want to live my life in your lap," hurt my mother. But they reached her. She withdrew, ceased to persist. Her objections undoubtedly came from her repeated prescience. If I had known then that she would never be able to visit me at seven thousand feet above sea level because of a heart condition, would I have . . . yes, I probably would have. I must accept it now though I have been incapable of it before. How much pain it gave me when she and Dad visited for just that one night and had to rush back home because her heart was beating 150 times a minute due to the thin mountain air. How destabilized I was by her departure, how off kilter with worry for their long trip back within twenty-four hours. I wanted so to be calm and peaceful, wanted to stay in my center even as I grieved, knowing she would never visit again. I felt attached in a fundamental way. Her brief visit left a thorn in my heart, and longing, unreasonable, immeasurable love in which my heart floundered. It was a pain of both attachment and severance.

How many days it took before I thought: *Go to the Hirab, she will wash away your pain.* She is the stream that flows right in front of our home in the Himalayas, the stream I worship and adore not only as metaphor, but in her flesh made of boulders and cold, crystal waters whose presence lends me the equipoise with which she flows through different terrains.

Let me just add, Mother, though you can't hear me—or can you?—I am sorry we did not live close to each other. After that one time you insisted we live near you, something I wanted, too, your own needs never superseded the necessities of my life, even for the nine years you were widowed. You thought about me before thinking about yourself. How many times you missed me when I was away for six months of the year, out of the country in the U.S., but you thought about how long and difficult the flight would be for me; how Payson would miss me and should not be left alone for long spells. Isn't that what love is? Thinking about the other, considering and condoning the other's needs?

One morning Dad summoned us into his bedroom, where he and Mother were both sitting up in bed, glasses of tea in their hands, and said:

"We are fading. Go where the universe is calling you."

You did fade away, Father. You had only four more years. Your death—how difficult it is for me to recall. I did not come to you when you called me to come to you before you died. Ah, there is a deep, dark well of pain here.

That story of shame, later. The demon of shame, too, must be faced, and defeated in the pages of this book. When the past becomes painful I arc away. Not the thing to do. Perhaps as these pages unfurl, I will become wise, as you always meant me to be, Daddy, wade through pain and regret, accept the way things happened, accept what Indians call *jo hona thaa*, or that which had to happen. Ineluctable. You would want me to accept and forgive my failings, metabolize the pain, even though I cannot now.

Fade. Fading. I had a friend long ago, Nibha Joshi, an art critic, long dead, who described a tapestry in a museum, her face lighting up as she uttered: "How beautifully it fades." Indeed, there is beauty in fading matter, including us. When Payson and I bought the Persian rug that we both love so much for our music/living room, I said to the Iranian salesman, "Our room gets sun in the afternoons. I hope it doesn't fade." His answer was quick: "You *wish* it fades." Antique rugs, faded to perfection, are rare and pricey. My mother's faded black pashmina shawl, some silk threads in its densely hand-embroidered border rubbed back to its dark field, fraying at the edges, is my favorite. I saw her maid, to whom she had given it "because it is old and fading," wearing it, and I had to have it. I took it back from her. She was happy to let me have the old one in exchange for three new shawls. I have a purple handbag faded to a plum brown that I simply adore. It is worn but intact, the soft, scaled leather almost like the crisscrossing web of skin on the back of my aging hands, patinaed, lovely, used.

Dad released us to our destiny, even though it meant more separation and distance.

At the end of March 2003, the day after Payson's birthday, we headed for the western Himalayas, to the state of Himachal Pradesh (the snow-laden province), of high snow-capped mountains and glaciers that are the springs of five perennial rivers and their countless tributaries, the five rivers that give the state of Panjab its name: *panj aab*, or five waters. They carve their way through rock from glacial heights creating fertile valleys, meadows, pasture lands, and agricultural terraces, as well as orchards of fruit: apples, persimmons, plums, peaches, pomegranates, pecans, kiwis, strawberries, and wild berries. Himachal is considered the fruit bowl of India, as Panjab is the grain basket. In 2003, 90 percent of Himachal was rural, growing wheat, corn, barley, and grasses for livestock on emerald terraced hills. Countless villages and hamlets perched on heights beyond the reach of roads and electricity.

Himachal is a rich reservoir of biodiversity: wildlife, flora, fauna, several conservation reserves, and parks, the greatest of which, the Great Himalayan National Park, was made a UNESCO World Heritage Site through the efforts of Payson and others. The Kullu Valley, the Valley of Gods as it is known, the place we were seeking to settle, is green, majestic, and wet, full of gorges, streams, waterfalls, medicinal herbs, groves and forests of cedars called *deo daars* (deodars), trees of the gods, looming lovely in their frilly green branches against dark bark and boughs, towering to the sky, their branches like wings, at once rooted and in flight.

Having lived mostly in urban environments I was struck by the many beautiful birds—the paradisal yellow-billed blue magpie with its long tail; the Asian paradise flycatcher, which swims in the sky and through the valleys like a white fish with long sleek feathers; and the loveliest of all, the blue whistling thrush. The first time I heard her ethereal aria one morning, I stopped everything to listen to her lilting, lyrical melody, glissandos of liquid notes strung together with phrases spiraling up the chromatic scale. I was surprised when I finally saw her, a nondescript black bird with an orange beak, clumsy on land. Her beauty is in her song and in flight, when her feathers, the angle of light being right, vibrate an electric Prussian blue.

Kullu, from *Kulant peeth*, or end of the habitable world, became accessible by motor only after Indian Independence, August 1947. The rural areas of the state are mythic, Vedic, unchanged since the seventeenth century, largely untouched by external influence, and that is true even today especially in religious beliefs, though it has changed drastically in many ways since we first arrived. Every village has its own god from Hindu and local mythology, symbolized by a mask of beaten gold. The gods, carried on palanquins by four devotees, congregate once a year during the weeklong festival of *Dussehra* in the city of Kullu, a teeming affair of music and dance celebrating the victory of good over evil. The five heroes, the *Pandavas* of India's great epic, the Mahabharata, are said to have spent part of their long exile from their kingdom here. There is a temple dedicated to them in a village east of our home.

Oh, but I get ahead in my tale. I speak of our home before we even saw or bought the land. The field of time extends in all directions as I age, and within it I move from where I am to where I am. So much of my job in telling this tale I am compelled to tell the only way I know how; the only way stories work, linearly, with some measure of coherence, is to scythe through the jumble of time in my head and let some of the jumble remain. I am compelled, as I move into the abstraction from which I was incarnated into matter, to free myself as much as possible from chronology, syntax, and structure; to flow like a stream, mindlessly within mind, take short cuts, cheat language, and free myself from time's tyranny while paying it obeisance. My sensibility expands out from the confines of logic and language's linearity to the country of indescribable images, of beings whose presence is felt, not seen; the country at whose border language self-destructs.

My first vivid memory of the Kullu Valley is bending low to enter a *gharaat*, which is a watermill turned by slabs of circular stones moved by "cools"—channels of water diverted from streams to activate the machinery; of wheat pouring grain by grain from a funnel into the shaft of the millstones grinding it into flour. Everything inside the small, low-ceilinged mill was white, including the gnome-like woman supervising the grinding. Flour had settled on her hair, eyebrows, and face, and on the webs in the corners of the gharaat, with fat, white, flour-dusted spiders at their centers.

Some friends arranged for us to visit various lands for sale in the Kullu Valley, away from the crowded town of Kullu. At the end of an exhausting day of driving on treacherous mountain terrain with perilously narrow winding roads that record frequent and major incidents of buses and cars tumbling into the gorges, our guide said, "There's just one other parcel of land up the road for sale."

"No, I've had enough," I said, and then on second thought, "Okay."

We stopped the car. One glimpse between blinks was all it took: green spears of wild iris blooming bluish-purple on the mossy deodar- and oak-lined banks of a youthful, sunny stream surging and bounding over boulders, its waters swirling and coruscating with liquid gold in the brilliant fading light of a vernal sunset.

"I want it." The words slipped out of my mouth with all the authority of desire and destiny. The arrow had struck home. I was in love at first sight. Our years-long search for a home in India was happily at an end.

That the universe was sympathetic to my desire—which simultaneously became Payson's passion—was proven just a few months later when the land, not a large parcel but bordered with forest land that would ensure for the most part that we would have no neighbors, was in the bag, and at an astonishingly low price. We bought it for a song.

The miracle of this can be understood in the context of land titles taking years and years to register; most land in the hills is in dispute by family members, not all of whom want to sell. The red tape for title is a hundred miles long.

I was still teaching in the fall of that year, having gone half time from my full-time job. Payson had retired from his business and without knowing the Hindi language, without knowing anything about building a house or the crooked ways things work in India, hopped on a plane. He bought a car, hired a driver, and found a place to stay, all with the help of family and friends, and made his first excavation on the land by our stream, our beloved Hirab. He traveled far to find stone, wood, and masons, and got all manner of miraculous help from all sorts of people. Even before the building began he named our home on the banks of the Hirab, Behta Pani, "flowing water" in Hindi. It is a name we take to heart. It is a reminder that there is never any cessation. The earth, the mountains, stone, our brick-and-mortar houses, our bodies, and the very air we breathe are all ceaselessly flowing and flowing away. How often I have forgotten it!

A few words about our very own stream before I continue. Hirab comes from a colorful character in Hindu mythology, at once male and female, hero and villain. I didn't know this when I fell in love and knowing it now only adds to my adoration and appreciation. I call Hirab mine, but who can own a stream? And yet, how often I have tried!

6
God's House

*L*ong before Behta Pani's foundation was laid, I had a dream. Payson and I were walking up a hill and we passed a small cottage. We looked through the windows into its cozy interior and saw a little round table with a red tablecloth, set for two. As we climbed past it a voice said, "This is God's house." We continued past it in my dream but I awoke with the certain knowledge that the cottage/house was Behta Pani. I also knew the house was a gift, to be experienced with all our love and attention, but that we had to let it go when God's arms reached out to take it back.

As we had to let it go in the summer of 2017 when toxic development came to the valley. And as we will undoubtedly have to let it all go, soon enough.

Because I do not naturally think of myself as being anywhere near old—though I still have prolonged phases of old age–like symptoms when I am sick or tired—I did not think I was anywhere near the Great Remembering. This morning, my mind straining toward the past, I know I too have arrived far nearer to old age than I know. And yet, I must not fall into the fallacy of time as a straight line, or think my health will start to decline steadily. The future is always flexible, unknown, and there are still miraculous moments and rare spells of vibrant youthfulness, always eliciting gratitude. How will I be when they cease, as they must? Will I be in utter despair, or can I prepare now to circumvent it, find other consolations? As in the arms of God, or sucking on her teats, as I often do when my body-brain is wracked by night fears as I toss in my little boat, obliterating waves towering over me, until I fall asleep, maybe this time forever?

Will I be able to complete this book? Stamina diminishes. So much of writing now depends on strategizing it. I must make writing, and my life, *easy*. This is the mantra to live by now. Because not much remains of life and energy, I must be kind to myself, selective of strokes, the broader and more abstract the better. I grow a little delightfully lazy every now and then, and it is good.

I tell myself: *Limn only in broad brushstrokes; scribble, cheat, find shortcuts that save labor and energy. Come away from abstraction, move toward it. In describing the past, resort to outlines, silhouettes of things at dusk when shadows begin to lengthen, then melt into darkness. The lengthening is the elongation of time, more behind me than ahead.*

I understand now that the devil is in the details. Details, like vampires, suck precious energy. And there is so much more of the past. Only the short end of this journey to the crematoria remains, the oven, which was the final house of what remained of the house-proud person I knew as my mother, that person who was here and who continues to live vividly in the house of my heart. Others, ghosts of people and animals, live here, too.

The Great Remembering must recall insights I forget at my peril.

I had not prepared myself for the loss of Behta Pani. We were oblivious in our happiness, enjoying our 3,000-square-foot Kullu-California kitsch house, designed in stone with wood interiors, surrounded by nature. The Hirab at Behta Pani is a very visible presence, glimpsed in its leaping, cascading, pooling from every window of our home. We had settled in as if forever. We acquired three dogs, went on hikes and picnics, and created our own little bubble where I wrote and Payson painted. We had not thought this experience would be temporary, like all else.

In June 2017 we lost our beloved Behta Pani, where we had been spending six months each year for fourteen years, to nearby development that made it impossible to stay there. When God's hand reached to take back our house, I clutched it. After all, the inhabitants of God's houses are human.

The state of Himachal is in a frenzy of road building and modernization. Over the years we had seen the state transition from rural to urban. Cell phones replaced the spindles of goat-herding women; trucks replaced donkeys; cows disappeared along with the goats that formerly scampered upon the cliffs. Several horse chestnuts, springing out of their brown trunks in luminescent amber leaves in spring, and many deodars, trees of the gods, were cut and quickly cannibalized for the aromatic wood, so rich and endangered; the gharaats disappeared. Where there were many only one remains, run by Gomti, our mythic gnome and her husband, always proud and straight in a very patched, many-colored homespun jacket made of wool from goats he has raised and shorn. His mother birthed him in the forest when she went to collect firewood and morel mushrooms, and named him Junglu Ram (of the jungle).

At that time an ugly and hazardous coal tar plant spewing carcinogenic benzine into the air was being constructed fifty yards from the pristine, crystalline waters of our Hirab.

One of our first experiences after moving into the house was two deaths on the banks of the Hirab, on a dirt path used by villagers from habitations perched higher up the mountain. A pregnant woman was brought down on the shoulders of her husband who was taking her to the only local hospital ten kilometers away. It was a breach birth and both mother and child died.

Payson and I, despite our aversion to the predation of the state by development, see the need for roads. But I am a NIMBY at heart: "not in my back yard." I occasionally sign petitions, donate to environmental and other causes, even saved a marvelous, magical, majestic horse chestnut tree once by hugging it when they came to fell it, speaking my mind to the authorities. But most of the time I prefer to live with my head in my own bubble.

Yet this battle had come to us and I had to fight tooth and nail for our home. Continuing to stay in it while the coal tar plant ran was not an option. Payson has been battling prostate cancer and I have CLL, a chronic form of leukemia. We are both immune compromised.

I amazed myself with a burst of uncharacteristic energy. We hired lawyers, approached high officials, engaged in verbal warfare, strategized, and mobilized support. I prayed passionately. There is nothing like desperation to make us turn to God. I believe in the power of prayer to solicit help from our higher selves, elicit our reserves of energy and courage, and establish a connection with the reciprocal world we inhabit. This time it didn't work. The villagers, who had not wanted the plant either, turned coat and not one member supported us. Money changed hands, the bribable were bribed. We lost. It felt like the beginning of the end of our life in Behta Pani and in India. My parents were dead. We were aging. There were no medical facilities near our village. After fourteen years God's hand was reaching for our home. I was angry, anything but submissive. I felt yanked away from a body made of trees and water on whose teats I was suckling.

Here we were, stuck in India for almost six months, having rented our home in Del Mar, and unable to return.

I clambered on a yellowish boulder with emerald moss and colorful algae in the middle of the Hirab, flowing over jeweled pebbles all around me in waves of liquid glass. I watched her cascading down in waterfalls into pools, and wept. I don't weep easily. It felt like a catastrophe.

The plant had to happen and I had to learn my lessons. One insight was worth all the sorrow. I had loved Behta Pani blindly. I had taken it for granted. I had thought I was going to be here forever. I had forgotten there are no forevers here, that the Lord giveth, and the Lord taketh away. In my hope that I would have Behta Pani forever, in my forgetting that anything and anybody can be taken from me whenever, I had not been fully present in it. I had not given gratitude for the fourteen years we lived in it. The sadness was as much for my ignorant way of living as for losing our home. I resolved that should God return our home to us I would experience it with gratitude and presence. In the meantime, I had to think of the loss as the will of the universe. We had to leave, sacrifice our comforts, find an alternate home in the area, and live in submission.

Though my prayers that the coal tar plant go elsewhere were not answered, we were miraculously rescued. Our royal friends from Rajasthan, descendants of a thousand-year-old dynasty of kings, King G and Queen P, who own an estate an hour away from our home, offered us their palatial and spacious guesthouse. As soon as they heard about our plight, G sent us a message: "Move it!" As we packed up necessary items, I reminded myself of the hardships of all those refugees we see on TV, and the many who do not even make it to the news. We loaded a funky rental truck with possessions and our two dogs, Foxy and Bhalli, and moved out of our home, accompanied by our helper Raju, who ensured we would lack for no comfort.

I sent G a message the morning of the move: "I feel like a refugee who has found refuge." His answer, "Think of it as a vacation!" G's sentences tend to be directives. I said *hukum** and followed his command. It turned out to be the best vacation of my life. As Shakespeare writes in *As You Like It*, "Sweet are the uses of adversity."

That is the thing. When we live in God's house, surrender our losses, surrender even to suffering, something beautiful resurfaces in us. Then all our suffering becomes our healing. Being human we forget this, and the forgetting causes and multiplies our sorrows.

And yet another prayer was answered. I hoped against hope we

---

*Hukum is a word used by servants of royalty. It means "What is your command?" In Sikhism the word refers to the king of all kings: God.

would be home again for my seventieth birthday. And operations at the coal tar plant proved to be temporary. Though the plant, a miscellany of engines, and other equipment remained, production was over. I was thrilled to return to our home after a year and a half and had a marvelous celebration with my sister and her entire family, both sons, wives, children, picnics, hikes, balloons, tinsel, gifts, and lovely diamond earrings from my sister. These I wear all the time.

But I, a mere human living in God's house, forgot, again, to live in presence and gratitude. I am reminded of it as I write here and will strive to do so again when we return to Behta Pani next year. The practice of living in the present, in gratitude, never ends.

7

Allies in the Adventure

*H*and in hand with the Great Remembering comes the great sifting down: emptying closets, trashing or donating items and clothing no longer needed, pitching photographs of my deceased ex-husband, Donald, held on to for twenty-seven years, and drafts of projects that did not come to fruition.

In all this casting away I have to decide what it is I want to keep in my closets, drawers, and shelves—clothes, cherished objects, legacies, books—and in the tote bag of my heart till the very end of this adventure.

My tote bag has many rooms, pouches, and pockets to organize my real and imaginary gear. Little difference remains now between the real and the imaginary. The thing becomes the idea becomes the thing. It is no ordinary gear I carry. In fact, I do not carry anything. It carries me. The heft of these possessions, preoccupations, and passions lighten my load, give life to my life.

The Great Spirit, the whole big multiverse, existing from before the time when the first blob of life became aware of itself and its thirst to worship, is in my bag. The One infused through multiplicity; the One with countless faces of humans, insects, fish, vertebrates, invertebrates, prokaryote, eukaryote—all the amazing diversity and variety of life, mineral and chemical, contiguous, dependent one upon the other. The One life of which I am a part—past, present, future to the edges of the unexplorable wholeness of existence—I carry in the pocket of my heart. If you have God in your heart, you can go anywhere in your journey and still be safe, at home.

God—not the institutionalized, sectarian God but s/he, not bound to any religion but manifest in all; who cannot be ritualized, contained, conceived, or comprehended; s/he who is not a concept, an idea, or a belief but a living experience, my highest, best, supreme; anthropomorphic, amorphous, visible, invisible. S/he is the God of my mother and father and all mothers and fathers of this earth since the beginning when time and space emerged from the womb and tomb of the Great Mother, Matrix, Ma, Amma, Uma, Mama. S/he, my beloved friend, companion, and support of my breath, who comes into relief the more my body disintegrates. Her hand is always in mine, though I don't always feel it when I am absent to everything but my pain, absent even to that presence which is my breath. When I move away from her I become a zombie—unliving, unfeeling. S/he is air, oxygen, without which my existence—and for me that means meaningful existence—is threatened, depressive as I am. Nothing else accounts for my long life but God.

The only journey is the journey to God's heart through rightful living and thinking, but most of all through love. Loving God, having this passion in life, is the privilege and solace of my aging, the rhythm to my dance of dissolution.

Of course, there is the voice that says, *There is no one there. You are worshipping nothing.*

I say to this voice, *It is not what or who you worship but the act of worshipping that bestows magical gifts. I know strong feelings of love are reciprocal; I am listened to, loved, as are all of us, having direct and immediate conduits to the Divine in our hearts.* When God appears to be absent from the picture, it is because s/he *is* the picture.

My tote bag is full of words, the words of my allies in the sky—my gurus, muses, saints, and poets on this journey that I am not undertaking, but that is taking me where I need to be from moment to moment of my life. Their words dispel my darkness when I am floundering. They show me the way when I am lost. My allies are my community, my country, my clan, my international tribe from every corner of the world. They are the gang of the Great Spirit, emissary angels who put their hands in mine and take me in the right direction.

When I remember to turn toward them, my allies never fail me. Their strength swells in my weakening muscles, their hand in mine steadies me when I falter and fall. Their words, made of air, echo in my ears and reverberate in my heart when I slow down enough to stop and listen. *Hear them, fool. Harken. They will defeat your demons, and you will never more be lost, though you are bound to be. Lostness is your destiny. You cannot find yourself without it.*

I keep my allies, who always steer me, when I turn to them, to the embrace of the Great Being, abstract and concrete, formless and with forms that my human heart-brain fashions into shapes I can access, hold, hug.

My allies tell me to embark on this aging adventure with trust. Though hope will play its part in my eternal hunger for more and more life, more and more health, more and more success, I must keep in mind Guru Nanak's words: *"Aasaa maahi niraas raheejai"* (In the midst of hope, remain without hope). This fleeting life is certain to end, and I must proceed without hope that I will even finish this book, or write any more; that Payson and I will be together for at least, dear God, another decade; that I will experience any more life than I already have.

My allies' words are my weapons. They are swords, shields, armor—instruments of offense and defense that are my gear in the battle that is life. They do not weigh me down but are light like breath, like thought.

My youth was given to passions, to finding the mate with whom my heart would find its home. Having found him—never forever, for who knows what losses are in store?—I would turn my face even more to my closest friend and ally, nearer to me than the skin of my heart. I would turn now to the Light of which I am coagulum, and into which I will merge when I am gone from here.

Let me not delude myself about any of this. Every relationship worth having is worth the conflict. Even my relationship to the person closest to me, Payson, is sometimes conflicted. Just this morning we had a fight. He wanted to give away my scarf and hat to a friend of his, and when I protested he grew angry and said, "But you have so much!" I probably do, but he raised my hackles by judging me, by not taking me into account. I recall Gandhi taking away his wife's jewelry for one of his causes, despite her protests; I think of him turning celibate due to some twisted idea that sexuality was not compatible with spirituality, without, I am sure, consulting his wife. And I grew angry for myself and for all the women in the world who have no say over their bodies and their things. Fights like these are ongoing. For being a feminist in my own home, where it counts the most, I have to butt heads with my husband's sometimes-patriarchal attitude. There is much to be said in his favor, but not now, not here. Let me stew a bit more in my anger. Oh, how perverse I am! I will tell a bit of that story because there is always so much to learn about ourselves from our conflicts.

My relationship with the Beloved is conflicted, too, though less so. I know now that I doubt her closeness or even reality when I am not getting what I want. How deep is this wanting and how it blinds me! I do not realize that this is at the heart of most of my unhappiness. Something in me is eternally greedy. My limbic hungers come from my earliest presence on this planet, when I was just a single-celled mouth.

But love and adoration return, as with Payson, given sufficient suffering, time, space, and humility. It is good to know this, to remember that everything is turning on the lathe of time. When I forget, I suffer.

8

Ariel

*T*he first piece of hardware in my tote bag is my new light and airy laptop. I call her Ariel.

Several years ago, before I began writing this book, I was unable to accept how I have aged. As I looked into the mirror and in photographs of yesteryears—my long white hair, much thinned since my youth, framing my face with its contours shifted and changed; my eyes far smaller than I remember them being, a little sunken and receding—and was maimed by misery, a thought lifted my spirits almost immediately: *Why not write about it?* Suddenly my age became grain for the mill, flour for my bread, words for my songs.

Ariel is the personified spirit of my angel, tangible matter I can hold, keyboard I can play, a material extension of my mind, fingers, thoughts, and emotions. Ariel's face is full of light and upon it I can etch my designs, remake my world with black print. Ariel's body, soul, spirit is what I carry in my real and abstract tote. When I become leaden with despair, I speak to her in my journal, dialogue with myself, objectify my pain, and she gives me wings; when I am dying she gives me life; when my heart is hurting she applies her magic balm. The universe will have to snatch her away from me before I consent to part with her. And who knows what the universe has in store, what is further, even a tiny bit further ahead on this road I travel, even as I lie in bed scribbling? A stroke, triggered by a fall—it happened to my mother—or an unforeseen accident, injury to my fingers, can end it all. There's never any stasis. Everything is flowing. This house, these solid walls of wood and cement, the sky, the sea, the twisted juniper outside our window, the rocky hills of San Clemente Island rising in the clear air above the waters of the Pacific this morning are eddies of fluid waves, like the whorls one sees fossilized in wood and stone. And I must flow along with it if I am not to perish.

Like the magician Prospero in Shakespeare's *The Tempest*, Ariel shall do my bidding, whip up storms and conjure calm. Shakespeare has been my ally in the sky since my teens. I have used his words as signposts when I am lost. I am no Prospero, however. He knew, as I so seldom know because I delude myself with hope, that something very important, like his lifeblood, writing, was happening for the last time. He was human enough to mourn the certainty that "our little life is rounded with a sleep." He knew "our revels now are ended." He actively gave up his gift, his calling, his livelihood, his karma that birthed him as the god of theatre, when the universe's hands were reaching for it. He made the sacrifice, consciously gave up the given.

Will I be able to, or will I keep on babbling incoherently way past my coherence and relevance? Will I know, as Hamlet knew, "There is providence in the fall of a sparrow"? I am weaker than my bravado sometimes imagines. I will take heart. Shakespeare, human enough to feel every known emotion, too, was troubled about renouncing writing. Prospero's words, "We are such stuff as dreams are made on," are immediately followed by, "I am vex'd; my brain is troubled." He feels weak and infirm. When he who was made in the image of God was disturbed by dissolution, who am I not to be troubled by the thought of giving up my love and passion for Ariel, who turns into wonder my despair at my diminishing energies?

In happy contrast to the god of theatre, I will keep on writing even though my mind is straining toward abstraction, less structure, less coherence. Weaving words is arduous work. If I had not the love and passion for it that sees me through almost all obstacles, that has wedded me to word, I might let myself become so widowed.

Words serve me still. I will work on this book as in a garden, a bit at a time, do it for the sake of doing it, seeing in whatever minor way a little improvement, a weed pulled, something thirsty watered. I do it for the hell and heaven of it. I do it because I still can. I am no Prospero but as I age, I am becoming a devotee of myself.

I will go into my future with trust in myself. After years of questioning, scolding, and denigrating my ambition, I accept it fully. It was Socrates' teacher, the priestess/philosopher Diotima of Mantinea, who gave me the words that set me free: "The struggles and sufferings of human life are all animated by the desire for immortality."

How should I alone, of all creatures who strive for immortality through children, or children of the soul, be without this struggle? Yes, I must remember to keep it in check like Plato's black horse, that "crooked lumbering animal, put together anyhow . . . of a dark color, with gray eyes and blood-red complexion; the mate of insolence and pride, shag-eared and deaf, hardly yielding to whip and spur." I will let Krishna remind me, "Do, act, for its own sake, mindless of rewards." Let Lao Tzu instruct me: "Produce without possessing; create without regard to result; claim nothing."

I know I will forget their advice.

Will you, Ariel, remind me when I forget?

9

Death and Music

$\mathcal{M}$y synthesizer is also packed away in my tote. It had its humble beginning in the harmonium. It's asking me to tell its story and I must obey, even though it's taking me where I don't really want to go, to the suicide of my former husband, Donald. In my case, death was the mother of music-making. Revisiting events and people, however painful, are part of this journey, part of the Great Remembering. Perhaps these thorny memories are sent to me to learn the lesson locked in them, then move on?

The roots of the harmonium lie in Donald's death. Who knows where the roots of that whole story lie?

As a writer I know details take too much energy. Having survived the suicide of a loved one, I know that even after almost twenty-seven years they are almost too painful to recall. Perhaps in the process of writing these reflections I will be able to express, embrace, and exorcise them. Perhaps. And then, perhaps never till judgment day.

For several months preceding his suicide Donald had been like a silent dark hole in the house. I knew something was wrong but destiny had thrown a veil on my sight and insight, and I was blinded by hope that whatever he was going through was temporary and would pass. When I asked him what was wrong, all he said was,

"I'm just tired," or, "Old and in the way." The latter, he told me, was the title of a song by *The Grateful Dead*. He was forty-six.

The bullet that Donald destroyed himself with shot me into a zone I'd never before encountered. My first experience of death catapulted me suddenly into unknown territory. I say "suddenly," though my soul had had premonitions long before the event. But that is another story, one I may never tell.

On the third day after Donald's suicide, an American Sikh acquaintance told me about an *akhand paath**** in the house of a woman named Satinder. Oh, so many unnamed allies in the guise of strangers and friends were sent by the universe in my hour of need. I'd never met or heard of Satinder, and though I had never attended an akhand paath before, I knew all are welcome to it. Volunteers do the recitation and cook food for everyone who comes to listen.

The concurrence of the akhand paath and my desperate need and other synchronicities still amazes me. Several months before Donald's suicide I had, what seemed like out of the blue, started to pray before going to sleep, and the prayer was always, "May your will be sweet." When Donald and I first reconnected in 1988, after a gap of almost sixteen years, suddenly a love for *kirtan*, holy hymns sung to classical ragas, was rekindled in my heart. Even though I didn't understand all the words, their sounds resonated in my genes; it felt like I had arrived home. I listened to it incessantly, and it prepared me for what was to come five-and-a-half years later.

I drove in a daze to Satinder's house an hour away, and collapsed before the Sikh holy book, the *Granth Sahib*. I lay there for three days and nights, half comatose, the reassuring honey of sacred recitation pouring into my ears. The message of the *Granth Sahib* is supremely optimistic: suffering has a purpose beyond our knowing. It is sent by the power to purge and heal us, and the more we surrender in the spirit

---

*An uninterrupted, relay recitation of the Sikh holy book, the *Guru Granth Sahib*.

of sacrifice to that energy that gave us everything we have and are, the more fruitful sorrow is. Remember this energy, face it, turn to it with love, praise, adoration, and prayer. Call to that energy by whatever name or gender you choose—God, Goddess, Durga, Nature, Allah, Khuda, Ram, Yahweh—and your path will be made easier.

Even though I couldn't understand all the *Gurmukhi** words, they poured their basic message of all rightness into my ears. The paath went on for long enough to seep like rain into my burning, charred heart.

About a month later Satinder came to my dark house bearing a gift full of light: a tiny, portable, foldable harmonium. "Somebody is selling this for $300. Give me the money and take it." She said it with so much authority that I had to obey.

From then on my days were happily taken up by the almost puerile exercise of finding notes to *shabads* (hymns) I already knew. From here I graduated to the synthesizer, composing my own simple melodies and tunes using words from the *Granth Sahib*. It gave me hours of sweet occupation, focus, and healing. I have since taught myself some ragas.[†] Music—listening to, composing, and singing—is salve. Kirtan is a marriage of music and meaning, ointment for the soul and cognitive food. The magic of music-making, however humble, was gifted to me.

Twenty-seven years later I have not progressed enough to perform in public, though chutzpah made me do it several times, once to an appreciative audience of five hundred at the Asian Art Museum in San Francisco, at the 2015 launch of my book *The Singing Guru*. But performing is not why I play and sing. Singing is a direct conduit from heart to heart. It makes me one with the One I address in my longing. I soar on the wings of songs in those rare moments when I am singing to the best of my ability, the best my lungs and energy allow.

---

*The Panjabi script invented by Guru Nanak and his successor, Guru Angad. It means "from the mouth of the guru."

†A raga, meaning "color" and "love," is a melody of prescribed notes used for improvisation and composition.

I can only describe the spin-offs of the little bit of music I do regularly. It keeps at bay my chronic bronchial condition that graduates to asthma and pneumonia, conditions that killed three of my father's siblings, and which I and my siblings have inherited from that side of the family. The complicated Indian classical rhythms please my rhythm-loving, rhythm-making heart. My fingers stay nimble and exercised; my heart, honed on the whetstone of sound, stays connected with the Great Spirit that is becoming the solace of my dusking years.

I will always be a student of music, always far from mastery. If all I do on low-energy days is scales for the rest of my life, I will be content with my progress. Its value far exceeds the value of an audience. It gives me something fun and soulful to do, something that opens a gate to a connection that is ultimate and total.

My cherished Sankyo silver flute, purchased forty years ago from the House of Woodwinds in Oakland, is part of my gear for this journey. I graduated to it from the humble recorder. Though I play it amateurishly, having taught myself to read music, it gives me enormous occupation and pleasure, and beguiles many a moment with joy. I carry my flute back and forth from India and the U.S. each year in my carry-on bag. Whenever I take it out of its walnut coffin and assemble it, I find myself at the bottom of the musical ladder, refreshing my memory and rarely moving beyond the basic scale of C. Just getting the fingering, the sound, the notes right and playing a riff on it is enough. Just ten minutes a day, or a week, sometimes even a month brings sweet, healing music to my life, melodies that spring unbidden into my mind. Its value lies in far more than whether I play it well or not. As I grow older I eat metaphors, and my flute serves me a major one. It saves me when my heart congeals with attachment—to things, people, desires, disappointments, discouragement, despair, loss. And the following story of the flute is the metaphor by which I try to live.

I have had only a few flute lessons, but I remember one of them vividly. The instructor said to me, "Don't hold your flute so tightly." She tried to pry the instrument from my hands as I held it under my lip, but she had to wrest it from me. I was clutching it.

She took my flute and put it below her chin, preparatory to playing, and said, "As I play, take the flute away from me." She played a lovely ditty that I didn't want to interrupt but reached for the flute as instructed. There, mid-melody, mid-note, utterly obedient to my intention, the flute fell into my hands like a ripe fruit anxious to be plucked and eaten.

I still feel the amazement, these many years hence, at how easily her flute fell into my extended hand. She was not tense about her song, she was not striving anxiously for mastery, she was not fearing "it is made of silver, it is expensive, it may fall and break." It was a lesson in letting go.

I would be terribly upset if I lost my flute. I am aware of the irony of the flute being my metaphor for detachment. I think of her instruction when I need to remind myself to hold things, people, dreams, that lightly. Should you lose it, break it—all of which is the universe's way for asking for it back—let it go; sooner rather than later after the inevitable sorrow and hurt. My dearest desire is to fall with such surrender into Death's hands when he reaches for my life.

The next time the word "lightly" came to me was in my father's voice when I phoned to tell him, "Donald is dead. Donald killed himself." After a long, shocked pause, he said, *"Beti* (dear daughter), take this lightly."

The word stayed close, nestled in my ears, within easy recall in the succeeding years, and kept me company even as I wandered in the dead of night from room to room of the unlit house we had bought together—my first home at age forty-three—keening and howling.

I did not know I was capable of so much sorrow.

I don't think I'll ever be able to take lightly the deaths of the beings in my life. It is humbling and releasing for me to know that I will weep and mourn each time. That grief is inevitable and holy. But the light the word "lightly" casts around me will help me survive my mortal condition to the best of my ability.

10

My Friend Cookie,
the Healer

*A*h, and I carry Cookie in my tote, Mother Cannabis, the green goddess I eat. I call her Cookie so she sounds more like the friend she is. I also call her Cookie from the time when she was taboo, and I dared not use any of her many names—weed, dope, marijuana—for fear Uncle Sam, who had made it illegal till recently, was tapping my phone. I did not want to live behind bars. I personify and glorify this goddess of the green hair, thrusting her hands out of the earth in invitation and welcome, taking me to other realms right around and within here, intensifying the moment, plugging my waiting receptor cells with her strains, transforming my reality, deepening, heightening, and altering my experience of existence. Cannabis plugs me into my life. Yoga, writing, cooking, gardening, walking, and even lying about become deeper, more vibrant, and more meaningful. It makes me a material being when the amplitude of my senses and my appetites decreases. It makes my house a treasure trove of things I love and enjoy: my colorful demitasse cups in which I drink my chai, my Spanish tea tray, my paisley throws spring alive to my eyes.

When I am inclined to forget during suffering that my life is an adventure, Cookie picks me up and puts me squarely on the path again.

When I am moping, discontent, lost, unable to get moving or deciding what to do with my time, she whisks away my depression and malaise and makes my life purposeful again.

Life coevolved with cannabis. Even in the first amoeba, the first emerging of sentience from the soup of chaos, a receptor cell was waiting and hungry for this herb to spring from the soil. It is sustenance, aid to the greening of consciousness.

Cookie is the comfort of my old age, and of many other oldies like me. Whenever I go to the cannabis store it is filled with older people like me. It is because Cookie works magic. She can also help with sleep, many times a challenge in later years.

Cookie has been around for a long time. In Pazyryk, a valley in a high plateau in Siberia, archaeologists discovered an ancient burial site from thousands of years ago. It included the oldest pile rug in the world, mummies, chariots, votive figurines, and cannabis seeds. These nomads roamed with their sheep, smoking the weed that was found everywhere and still grows like a weed in India, making their lovely carpets. They knew what a gift this herb is, taken in moderation. It makes all places home.

How demonized Shiva's healing herb has become in the very country in which the gods smoked, ate, and drank it. How hypocritical the governments that blindly ban her for our "good." Don't they know that if they legalized it, made it available at every *dhaba* (roadside food shack) as well as in high end restaurants, not everyone would smoke and eat it? It is, like many other things, not for everybody. The world is divided into two (for simplicity's sake): those who drink alcohol and those who don't; those who smoke/eat cannabis and those who don't. I never drink liquor, though it is easily available and legal. It is not my thing.

I don't want to do without Cookie now. She was in my ancestors' blood in the form of opium and *dodas* (poppy husk), and I inherited the gene and receptor for this intimate relationship. It is one of the elements in my body now.

This is not to say there are no fears associated with the relationship. I worry it is making me tired, lazy, laid back. I worry it is distorting my perception of myself, making me think the writing I produce is better than it is; or that I will lose my balance and fall. After my last fall eight months ago, the pain from damage to my shoulder and head is only now abating. I worry that it is destroying my short-term memory, melting my brain, killing off cerebral cells; I worry it is damaging me in ways I do not know.

But my worry is only a goad for me to live in a healthful way, maintain and exercise my body with yoga, meditation, weights, and walks. I am healthier for my addiction to Cookie. Also, I like what Cookie does to my brain, weakens it in ways it needs to be weakened. I have been its slave, but Cookie is freeing me, day by day, bite by bite, of the tyranny of the left hemisphere. Oh, I know! The practical must be taken care of, logic honored. I cherish the part of my brain that makes me pay close attention to my safety. I live mindfully, anchored to reality.

Old age is about making moment-by-moment momentous, life-enhancing and life-changing choices: Eat a treat or abstain? Surrender or control? Work or rest? Travel or stay at home? Cookie or no Cookie? God or no God? I choose to err on the side of rest, treats, Cookie, surrender, staying at home, and God.

I try to make my choices fearlessly. I choose Cookie because her benefits to me far outweigh the negatives. After a lifelong, conflicted relationship, I have fearlessly chosen and married her.

I know I cannot abuse her. I cannot nibble on her more than is good for my health, cannot take large bites or get greedy. She will fight back. She can cross my wires if I lean on her too much. Then we have to separate for some time. If I stay away for too long, thinking I am going to be oh-so normal and live as others live, however I imagine that living to be, time lies heavy, my life lacks intensity, and living from day to day becomes a grind. Though I do the necessary, I am not engaged, not plugged in to my vitality. I skim the surface of existence instead of diving into it as far as I can go. Food loses its taste, sleep becomes coquettish, my gaze turns outward, and I start whining: *Why don't I have more friends? Why doesn't anyone call me?* With Cookie my gaze turns inward and I am my own best friend.

When I honor Cookie by eating her with attention and intention, as a sacrament, she honors me with her many gifts. She gives me the key to that interior castle with magical spaces where I truly live.

One day my tote bag with my favorite things in it will be taken from me. Everything, including my body, will be in it.

11

The Benefits of Denial

*B*ecause aging is imperceptible, like the changing of seasons or the coming on of day and night, without a break and with no discernible endings or beginnings, it is easy to deny. I see others' denial, but not my own.

Larry, Payson's brother in New York, won't admit his brain is deteriorating even though he doesn't know who the United States president is, what the date and year is, or birthdays of anyone in the family. Alzheimer's runs in their family: mother, aunts, grandmothers, granduncles. One of our friends, a Shakespearean actor with a Ph.D. in Shakespeare, doesn't recall the name of her favorite role or play; leaving the apartment to go outside in the snow, she is agitated, looking for something. When asked what she is looking for, she says, waving her hands, "Fingers, fingers," meaning gloves. She is slipping and sliding down the memory slope and refuses to acknowledge it or see a neurologist. The only time she agreed to do so, she ran out of the doctor's office when he asked her such simple questions as: When were you born? Where were you born? What was your mother's name, your father's? What was your profession? What year is it?

I, too, have been in denial of my aging, which is another way of saying unconscious. Whenever I meet people I know after a long stretch of time, I think, "My, how he or she has aged." I do not turn the mirror on myself, and think, "Wow, I must have aged, too." Even as I see children in my sister's family grow up, I do not realize their growing up has anything to do with my own aging. I think I alone will live forever.

I asked Payson to take photographs of me. I needed them for publicity for one of my books. I have older photographs that have worked in the past, photographs I am attached to because I still look relatively young and vital in them, but I wanted something more current. I didn't like any of the photos he took. It took me a while to admit why. I didn't like them because they didn't reflect me the way I think I look: aging, yes, but prettily so. I wanted them to reflect how I feel inside, attractive to others and myself, but not old. These photographs showed my chin beginning to sag, my neck in folds, my eyes, once so big and beautiful, now crinkled, crumpled, squinty. I deleted the photos. My many aging faces, seen fleetingly in mirrors and photographs, were lies, promptly forgotten.

The hardest thing for me to accept is that my brain, too, is fraying. Some weeks ago I woke up one day feeling rested and excited to go to work on my new Ariel. I had been kvelling to myself about my dedication to upgrading my brain with a new laptop and software. Because computers are intimately tied to what I do and because what I do is so intimately tied to who I think I am, I had gone to my upgrading project with excitement and dedication. I had been painstakingly copying everything from the old laptop to the new one.

I was not prepared to discover that the folders and files on my new machine, and my old one, too, were helter-skelter. For three hours I tried to re-create, make sense of what had happened, my poor brain utterly flummoxed and in panic: first, at the fear of losing my precious material; and second, the fear that I was losing my mind. I have experienced this confusion in the brain before, mostly in tired, hurried moments. The more the brain panicked, the more it feared losing itself, the less it was able to perform. The sheer terror of it took me to the very edge of the abyss where the egg of my brain fell into the darkness below and cracked upon the rocks. This wasn't anything like walking into a room and wondering what I came for or misplacing my glasses; this wasn't anything like sitting at the computer unable to form a sentence or even edit one. This took my fear to a different elevation altogether.

I, prisoner of my melted brain, floundered for several hours before deciding on a brisk walk. I keep in mind what Diogenes, the beggar-philosopher born in 412 BCE, said: "It is solved by walking."

I walked demonically, images replaying themselves in my mind: my maternal grandmother taking a dump on my mother's new bed-cover, my mother's eternal repetitions, Payson's mother's vacant eyes. I was flooded with compassion for those who are experiencing, and have experienced, the terror of losing their brains. "Fingers, fingers" was no longer an abstract experience that was happening to someone I knew; her panic was now my panic. I kept reminding myself, as I have tried to remind others through my many stories, *Live as one dead if you want to be free. Give up everything before it is snatched from you.* It didn't help. The panicked brain was telling itself it was okay for it not to be, and was failing miserably.

But exhausting myself by the pace of my walking worked its magic. Exercise exorcised my demons. It never fails. Go out for a walk when you are agitated and depressed, and you return home a new person. With tiredness comes a certain degree of calm. Calm is a wide-open, horizonless space. My dread at the loss of my identity, my being, my ego, became an infinitesimal point surrounded by infinite space and geologic time. Two words came to my rescue: *"Let go."* The Great Letting Go is right around the corner.

But how will I truly feel when my brain and body begin to go? Where will I be when this mass of tissue that is the consistency of raw eggs goes AWOL (absent without leave)? Does my knowledge define me? Who am I when my body is wracked by pain, my mind with terror, all my wisdom flown out the window? Who knows? Who the hell knows?

Denial rules because it is so comforting; because nature and our ego cushion us when we are incapable of looking clearly into the future. Who can? What can one do when there is no recourse?

It is just as well denial rules. Denial is human. Life, pulsing life, here, now, this *mater*, material, mother, matrix, earth from which springs the tree of life, matters to us more than we know. More than we allow in our spirituality and philosophy. So many gray beards forbid an adoration of matter, of the body—Plato and his sage, Socrates, and Rumi, for example. It is an illusion, we are told; just reflections on the walls of a cave inhabited by blind people.

Despite spirituality that tells us to wean ourselves of the deception, adore life we must. Hell, we are meant to love life. That is why we are here, that is why we were brought here from God alone knows where or even how, despite science's authoritarian claims. There is some hubris in thinking we can fully know the hows and whys of things.

Life matters. Slumped in my chair after four days of a twisted body, the head, neck, shoulders, and back tight, pains here, pains there, I look out my window. Ah, beneficent windows, windows beyond the windows of my eyes, multifold prisms that receive light and refract it to sixteen million colors. The spreading fig tree unfolding its translucent spring leaves like palms facing up, its many branches like arms spread wide to receive, to give, matters. The yellow, red, and white tulips, freesias, violet bearded irises and narcissus, blue hydrangeas not yet unfurled, the green composter in which red worms are working to digest death to make nutritious soil for our garden, matter. The material world, God's *lila* (created from bliss), theatre, entertainment, sorrow, suffering, tragedy . . . it is all "wonderful, wonderful, wonderful!" says my guide Guru Nanak. God's creation is true, holy, and good, he affirms. Life on earth and all it affords by way of body, mind, spirit, food, friends, family, and beauty is a marvelous magical miracle, so overwhelmingly inspiring as to have no descriptions, just the exclamation of wonder and awe, *wah*, an outbreath mimicking the outbreath of the World Spirit exhaling the multiverse. Guru Nanak can utter wah because he has learned to die to life as we know it, and set his sights and heart, while he was young, still strong of limb, passion, and desire, on that love that transcends all our other loves that live in its light.

Oh, I know I will have to bid goodbye to this thing called my life. In my dreams and fears I have seen Geras, Greek daemon of old age, one of the malevolent spirits spawned by the goddess of night, the magician who transforms people and faces from stage to stage of their lives, over before a blink. He has been following me faithfully since my birth, though I have denied him, over and over, distracting myself with a thousand things. I hear his footfall, see his face in mirrors, his puffy, gummy eyes, his distended body, some fat of life still clinging in pouches on the belly, skin moth eaten, like my cashmere sweaters.

Geras will make me disappear, I know, take away the bag of my senses, and this earth, this life I love so much, my brain, my mind that I marvel at, its flight wings together with its snake pit of thoughts. My brain is indeed the best part of me. I love what it can do, how it keeps me safely anchored to reality, how mysteriously it works, manifest to me in my writing, which has a life of its own. It is a being, a wizard, a guide, a God, with whom I am in constant struggle, like Jacob wrestling on the banks of the river with an angel.

Before the parting, let me pause awhile at spring. Ah spring, how mixed with death you are! Hush, thought! Let me stay awhile longer, inhaling this breath outside the window of budding new life.

12
Night Sea Journey

*P*erhaps the moon, in reflecting our shifting selves, is a material manifestation of the human psyche. But its many phases are nothing compared to the many-layered facets of our experiences. Our phases are not visible but assuredly are recurring, though not predictable.

Time spiraling around the axis that is me brings me to old places that I perceive as new due to the failure of memory. I have been in this darkness before, many times. It is the dark strand of my life that runs invisible and parallel to my conscious existence.

Out of the blue I take a downturn. Perhaps because I have been trying to live deliberately; perhaps because I am tending, as I age, toward order, organization, decluttering; perhaps because I delude myself that living with awareness makes me immune to the vaster shifting matrix of internal and external weather and circumstance. "No matter how much we make conscious," C. G. Jung says, "there will always be an indeterminate and indeterminable quantity of unconscious elements, which belong to the totality of the self."

Chaos happens periodically but consistently in life as well as nature. Who knows why? It might as well be the flapping of a butterfly's wings in Shanghai that causes a storm in my soul. It might as well be a shower of neutrinos sending cosmic intimations from beyond matter, from the very edges of the universe, billions of light years away.

Last night, like the last many nights, unable to sleep, watching Payson sleeping peacefully on his side of the bed, his back to me, the phrase "Your solo journey begins" forms itself in my mind.

Nobody can accompany me when I am, against my will, embarked on my night sea journey. Togetherness falls apart. Payson in his own uncharted dimensions of sleep, I in my own abyss, and nary a bridge between us.

At night when all my cognitive defenses are down, I am dunked into painful emotions I have deluded myself into thinking I have overcome. I become an infant in a cradle swirling uncontrollably on a gale-lashed sea. None of the skills and techniques, the breathing and prayer that I have painstakingly taught myself over a lifetime to tide me over such periods, help. Only the sensation remains of being sucked down to the depths of my unconscious mind and memory where all those I have lost—mother, father, husband, nanny, dogs, cats—swirl, alive and present; death feels bone close as I circle the dark hole of professional and personal failures.

I will never complete another book; my flute will be snatched from me in the middle of a mediocre melody; I will die a nameless unknown, sink like a pebble into obscurity.

I feel the knot of ego in my heart called "ambition." I let it be, incapable of unknotting or cutting it, so interwoven is it into the plasma of the cells that make up my "I." I live scenarios of dreadful illnesses and think, *I will take myself out if that happens.* I think of my solitary librarian friend, Tom Goonan, rabid atheist and hermit extraordinaire whom I befriended because of my predilection for curmudgeons. He belonged to the Hemlock Society and took himself out when his colon cancer recurred. It took him twelve hours to die, time enough for him to be discovered and taken to the hospital, a rosary clutched in his hands.

I live in the boiling waters of failed relationships that once mattered to me in a dark sort of way, and do even now. My brother and his family, who preferred greed to a sister's love; friends I love, for whom the relationship is less important than it is to me; people who have disappointed me and people I have disappointed, the worst of which was disappointing my father who gave and made me all I am today, who gave me unconditional love and freedom. I did not go when he summoned me to him before he died. I was too enmeshed in my ambition, being "someone" after the publication of my first book, *Ganesha Goes to Lunch*, intent on leaving a mark, stroking my ego. I blinded myself with the hope that he would survive till I got there a month later. And you, Mother, who implanted yourself like a fetus in my heart, birthed yourself like my child in your old age as you lay like an infant in a coma. Ah. I must pause here and feel the pain, though my heart doesn't want to reexperience the anguish of remembering the details. *Later, sufferer.* Know there are many abrasive grains of sand in the oyster's shell that never turn to pearls. You will never fully extirpate regret. Some consequences of bad decisions will quake in you till you are incinerated in the awaiting oven.

In the morning when Payson awakes—he has slept through my journey through hell—and returns from wherever he has been in his own world and dreams, I ask him, "Will you help me take myself out when I am ready to go?"

"Of course," he replies reassuringly, stroking my arm. "I will do whatever you want. But you don't have to think about this right now." I heed the wisdom he offers. In its light I see how false my fears are, even though they seemed so very real.

13
Stupidity Has a Purpose

*L*ast night, again, on the verge of getting uprooted in a vortex of worry, I reached for the Indica gummy that the sweet young man at the cannabis store recommended for sleep. Instead, it propels me out of bed with an urgency to return to the teats of Mother Language. If I can write about it, however poorly, I am well. But I am not allowed that relief. My left forearm is spasming and the mind is twisted into a knot around the sore node in the body.

Though I have been telling myself over and over a thousand times that I must, must, must listen to my body when it talks to me; though I have even dared somewhere in my writings to be a glib and hypocritical sage by writing a commandment to "Listen to your body when it talks to you," there is in me a basic lack of wisdom when it comes to that which is nearest to me: my body.

My knowledge doesn't always control my emotions. I ignore it till it begins to scream, "I am tired! I am hurting!" Why do we have to suffer to learn? Because we are essentially stupid and suffering awakens us. We don't value something till it is gone; because suffering is the prod, the goad, the two-by-four on the head.

I know the exact moment I injured my forearm by not being present. I am a bit ashamed to tell of it, because I finally got what Payson has been accusing me of all along, that I am a clothes horse. I was standing on a step stool in the room we call our library, because there are many books in it, but primarily it is the room where we put everything when we are decluttering the rest of the house. While taking handfuls of clothes from a plastic bin in which they had been stored against mold when we were in India for six months, and dumping them into a laundry basket, I knew at once something had happened in my left forearm. Despite that certainty I kept overworking my hand and arm for the rest of the day. In the interests of doing, of taking care of business, of being productive, I injured myself for months of suffering and incapacitation. I didn't see a doctor. I suffered for weeks and weeks hoping it would just go away. When a friend said he had had the same thing that lasted for three years, despite physical therapy and medication, I panicked and felt hopeless. Why should I try to do anything?

But that is not the way to think. Hopelessness is carcinogenic. I determined to be attentive to the messages of my body. Paying attention to the voice of the body is a cardinal rule of aging. At Payson's insistence I went to see my doctor. He gave my condition a name, *tenosynovitis*, and sent me to physical therapy, which helped enormously.

The important lesson here is to sift down further, get rid of, give away. I have recently packed two black garbage bags full of clothes to give to Disabled American Veterans and Goodwill. It feels so good to have some empty shelves in my closet.

Another stupidity: for five or six weeks something has been going on in my Achilles tendon. It has made walking difficult, but I have not remembered to tend to it. I have been limping about without stopping to think that something is going on and I need to do something about it. At best I tried a few ointments. Instead of doing something about it, I grumbled about getting old.

I allow myself moaning and whining every now and then. They are healthy expressions if not taken to an extreme. Whines help. Donald used to say, "A whine is a terrible thing to waste." My mother didn't hold back from making her pains bearable by crying out, *"Hai, hai, hai"* in Hindi. Dad, on the other hand, never ever uttered his pain. She survived him by nine years. Did whining have something to do with her longevity? Did blabbing out her heart, something she never shied away from, sometimes to the point of hysteria, help her to survive?

I was weaned away from moaning by Payson, who said, "Enough with the whining already." At its best marriage acts like a mirror when your own vision is fogged. He downloaded some videos from YouTube for fixing Achilles tendonitis, and I did the exercises in the spirit of doing the universe's work. Taking care of myself is no different from taking care of the universe, of which I am in indissoluble part.

I want to gab some more about my stupidities. They help me see myself, and sometimes even remedy my ills. They also make me laugh. When I sleep badly, like these days, I snack a lot. Though I try to eat consciously, in a controlled sort of way, a few evenings ago I lost my consciousness to the potato. I ate chips, and they ate my awareness and my digestion. One episode of bad digestion can last weeks without my knowing it, the only symptom being that I'm feeling terrible and I wonder if I'm dying. Will I be able to remember the mind-gut marriage in the future, or continue to be a fool?

Like my father, I am a bit of a hypochondriac. A tickle in the throat is cancer. A sneeze harbingers pneumonia. A cramp in the belly is a malignant tumor. Gas is an impending heart attack.

It is this readiness to jump all the degrees between an ailment and death—to be kept in check from becoming too serious or comic—that helps me to rehearse for my demise. I lie down in the *shava asana*, the corpse position, and say to myself, *You're dead. Nothing concerns you, nothing matters.* Dying is a wonderful way to relax when I am not afraid that dying is actually happening. But I push through the fear, surrender even more, and usually slip into sweet slumber. Death is wonderfully renewing. One day I will, or will have to, go all the way with surrendering.

Not remembering I had not slept well because of chip-induced insomnia, I mistook my restlessness and irritability as a sign that I should be doing something. On days I don't know whether to rest or do, I foolishly throw in my lot with doing. The sunshine outside gave my body signals to conform to the imperative of a sunny day: go out. I ran errands till I couldn't anymore. I couldn't settle into anything, nothing at all interested me, nothing. But still the demon of doing pushed me. *Eat something? Drink something?* offered my Jewish inner host. *Shouldn't you be cleaning the kitchen counters, or put this and that away?* scolded my inner critic. I distracted myself from my need to rest by the many little things that always need to be done, my arm in a brace. The orchids I got for Payson were wilting and needed to be fed. The mourning doves were hovering on the neighbors' melaleuca tree, giving me the feel-guilty eye. I put bird feed into the trough I had made specifically for the purpose and perch it in the arms of the fig tree. Some of the succulents looked dry and I began to fill watering cans, adding fish emulsion for the fuchsias, orchids, and two miniature potted roses I gave Payson for Valentine's Day five years ago that survived and thrived in the soil. Watering and feeding the succulents that P and I planted on mounds of dirt several years ago to cut down on watering during our ongoing California drought, I marveled again at the beauty of these fleshy plants that are so prepared and adapted for dryness. They change their appearance, color, and size according to how much space they have to grow in, how much water they get. The tiny green ground cover—I don't know its name—becomes red or pale green with lack of sufficient water. Succulents thrive on deprivation, use it to create beauty by becoming miniatures, but given enough space they grow to gigantic proportions.

Well, I did too much. The next day was a zero day. On zero days I am unable to get going, not even to remove a used tissue from my desk or the floor, or put the house phone back in its cradle. Nothing at all gets done. I console myself with the thought: *I have more energy than dead people. They can't even blink their eyes or lift a finger.* But zero days are anything but restful. Instead of resting I vitiate them with agonizing brain chatter and worry about my paralysis and lack of stamina. I resist, fight, think all sorts of unproductive thoughts, such as *I ought not to be feeling this way, why am I feeling like this,* and on and on of needless cogitation.

I fail to see the connection between doing too much and zero days. I realize I have taken an inordinate time, decades, stuck in the tween stage of youth and age, striving to maintain the one, struggling against the other. I have done anything but aged with awareness, grace, patience, and acceptance. I have aged like a fool.

But some good has come from my folly. I have learned to listen to the voice of my inner angel when she says, *Dispel the worry! Silence the chatter! Take charge!* With her help I push aside the inner legion of troubling thoughts with one mighty movement of the arms of my mind, opening a space for myself to do what I need most to do: rest.

Resting is the way to negotiate the turmoil of aging. Resting is divine because God is in it. Whenever I stop, become still, quiet, God pays me a visit. I have taught myself to rest guiltlessly, luxuriously. Some days it is enough that my heart and my lungs do the pumping and breathing for me. I remedy my tiredness by renewing myself with days in bed, with or without a book, listening to music or not, napping or just lying about, letting my mind meander where it pleases in the vast field of time, or disappear into blessed vacancy. I have come to accept my limitations. I do not force myself to behave or act younger than my age. I make do with what I have; I cope. With resting. And coping is everything.

But I do set myself minimum tasks on zero days: brush teeth; take care of body hygiene; ten minutes of yoga and a meditation, even five minutes of walking. It makes me feel the day hasn't been entirely lost.

Today I know with clarity that with zero days and downturns in my health and sanity, stupidities will recur. Knowing this I will have to come up with strategies to deal with them, cognitive tools to handle them with equanimity. I don't want them to catch me unawares and fretting.

I shall expect, then accept zero days, knowing they will recur, probably in greater frequency. Instead of the endless search for causes for my tiredness, I shall trust my body's increasing need for repose, not question it. When words fail me and there is just the tourniquet of unnamed fears around my heart, I will strive to remember that it is God's hand doing the squeezing. S/he churns the ocean that I am, uprooting my hold-fasts, dredging up long buried lees. It lasts a long time, it lasts till I admit my helplessness as I whorl in turbid waters, till I cry out to the Great Spirit for help from the depths of my anguish. Then my tiny little boat stops rolling and plunging and begins to sail on calmer waters again. When I actively submit to the storm, it rolls over me.

And when I act foolishly again (I know I will), without awareness, I will remember that even my stupidities have a purpose—to keep me humble. I need my folly to learn my lessons. If we weren't stupid, we would be gods. And the Greeks were right about gods waiting in their clouds, lances pointed toward those who dare to scale those heights. Look at what happened to poor Psyche because people considered her more beautiful than Aphrodite. But even Psyche's travails had their purpose: self-awareness. She would not now be married to the god of love without them. If I can't avoid my stupidities on this adventure, I will be grateful for them.

14
Memory Is the Root of Wisdom

*B*ut of course, I keep forgetting my lessons. Remembering. Ah, remembering! How much lostness before remembering to remember on this journey. Forgetting causes most of my insanity and disasters. It causes, the guides tell us, most of our suffering. Forgetting that we are one with God, one with each other, one consciousness manifesting as different entities and bodies is an illusion called *maya* in Indian mythology and philosophy. Our quest is to tear away the veil of this illusion and see that we are gods dreaming we are beggars.

One of my favorite stories from Norse mythology is about Mimir, "the rememberer." The wise one. Mimir was a giant who guarded and drank daily from the well of memory and wisdom that sprang from the roots of the world ash tree, Yggdrasil, the center of the cosmos. Odin, the god of magic, poetry, and death, wanted to share in this wisdom and asked Mimir for a drink from it. Mimir named his price: one eye for one draft of water from the well of wisdom. Odin thought the sacrifice well worth the reward. He paid the price and became the one-eyed god of wisdom.

Somewhere along the myth, Mimir was decapitated in a war. When Odin saw his head, he picked it up from the battlefield and cradled it in his arms with love and worship. He chanted prayers and sang songs while embalming it with precious herbs. He wanted to preserve it, to treasure it above all gold. Mimir's head was the voice that counseled him throughout his days. The one-eyed Odin is a god because he sees the value in things, especially the value of memory, the tap root of wisdom and insight, more important than eyesight.

If Odin had been a Buddhist, he would have drunk from Mimir's skull. Buddhists and Hindu Tantra practitioners drink out of beautifully carved, gem-encrusted human skull cups to remember the most important thing we need to remember on this adventure: death.

Memory is pivotal in all cultures and mythologies. Mimir's name comes from the Indo-European root *(s)mer*, meaning "to think, recall, reflect, remember." It is connected to Sanskrit *smarati*, *smarana*, and to the Sikh concept of *simran*, to remember God by the repetition of his/her name. In ancient Hindu texts Smara is another name for the god of love. When the *gopis*, the cowherdesses who love Krishna, accuse him of cruelty for deserting them, Krishna replies: "It is not from cruelty that I cast a veil over myself. It is so you can remember and yearn for me during separation. As a poor man always recalls and yearns for the wealth he has found and lost, I want my lovers to remember me always." Memory is an important part of spirituality in the Indian system, called "*smarna marg*," By remembering, God is known. Memory bridges separation and union.

Memory, Mnemosyne, is a powerful goddess in Greek mythology. She is the daughter of heaven and earth, consort to Zeus, inventor of language and words, mother of the muses. In Greek mythology people who forget are reborn to learn the lesson of remembering; those who remember are sent to the Elysian Fields to live in uninterrupted peace and bliss. The word "mnemonic," techniques of remembering, comes from Mnemosyne. In Plato's *Theory of Recollection*, all wisdom is remembrance of things we have forgotten. In Hindu mythology even gods forget their divinity in their enmeshment with life. Vishnu becomes a boar and lives the life of a pig. When he is immune to Shiva's reminders of his true nature, Shiva lets fly his trident and kills him. When the dying Vishnu despairs that this is the end, Shiva says to him, "Remember who you are! Remember you are spirit, Vishnu, the undying energy of the universe. You are formless light, the eternal, undying flame."

The striving to remember in the morass of forgetting who we are must be relentless.

15
Letting Go

Another thing we encounter on the aging adventure is loss, the falling away of dear ones. It is expected, but difficult to accept.

I have been hyper-speeding because I don't want to think about the information I received through WhatsApp after waking from one of those healing sleep-ins that rarely happen these days. Perhaps it's because I don't let them, loving, in the best of times, to wake around 4 a.m., take a long time to wake-up, do the necessary, meditate, yoga, drink tea, write, lengthen the precious day. This is the kind of sleep-in that infuses me with peace. I had an hour of it before I turned to the phone and read a message from my brother-in-law, Kuldip, about my sister, Mishi. Her ovarian cancer has spread to her stomach over a course of seven years: "CA 125 has increased from 287 to 1100. Value should be less than 35." She has survived her cancer for so long that I had forgotten she would ever die.

No preparation could shield me from the sucker punch this news delivered. Just a few days previously, one of my young friends told me her mother-in-law had died of an identical cancer. After my mother's death in 2016, Mishi and I bonded intensely. We became each other's mothers, staying in touch regularly, caring, concerned, and loving.

I tried calling India but both Mishi and Kuldip's phones were switched off. My 8 a.m. was their 9:30 p.m. I locked down in an emotional spasm.

On our walk at Torrey Pines Red Ridge Trail last week, Payson said, "Nature brings us into the now effortlessly." Today I know that disease, disaster, and death do the same.

On our return I asked Payson to hold me as I lay on the infrared mat but as he came closer to me, I saw the cholesterol deposits (xanthoma) around his eyes and recalled again the news he had told me two days ago about his LDL cholesterol and PSA (prostate) levels climbing through the roof, and my anxiety spiked, the fear of the loss of my sister multiplied by my fear of losing him. I touched his deposits, and he said, "Don't mix things up." I heard him, talked myself out of it, and let him hold me in silence.

When Payson was done holding me and went off to do his thing, I found myself focusing in my agitation on his artwork and sculpture that fills our music room. I was particularly drawn to his totems above the piano made of iron, wood, and bronze, and the painting hanging on the north wall, an abstract image of a fountain of water contained within a circle, rippling out of it concentrically. Energetic circles and spheres appear in almost all his artwork. How soothing and safe geometry is: circles, spheres, mammary glands, wedding rings, terrors circumscribed, blessed borders between us and chaos. Circles are healing because they evoke a fixed center, always the object of our desiring; because they remind us of our longing for some place safe in this turning, shifty world.

But when I got up from the mat to begin my day, I had the jitters. I moved about aimlessly, agitatedly, unable to plug into any activity, doing things without attention or focus. Even the yoga I did under the breezeway by the pool in the sun was a hurried affair. Bend my neck, one-two-three, bend to the other side to a count of whatever, hurry through the neck exercises, rush through warrior pose, pick a weed from the flower pot, go inside, make myself a cup of tea, force myself to wait for the water to boil, put away a few things on the counter. Keep checking the water, spill it as I pour it over the tea bag, spill some cream, too, and return outdoors where Payson is doing his yoga calmly, taking his time with his stretches.

It was time to eat my friend Cookie. She calms and slows me down, draws my eye to beauty, makes my hours okay and sometimes rapturous, transports me to a higher level of existence from where I can see my way. Till she kicked in I was like an uprooted plant. I fetched the timer and told myself I must sit in half-lotus pose for twenty minutes. I could barely make five, but even those five minutes worked their magic.

What a magnificent tool meditation is! What an essential, crucial tool for this journey; how beneficial to our physical and mental health. Twice it's saved me from madness, and many times, though I have been an erratic practitioner, it has come to my aid to energize or calm me. This just sitting, reclining, or lying, doing nothing, being still and silent, is the highest activity of all. This vacancy, void, is the very ground of all activity.

I got up, went outside, the sun bright and warming, and sat on the edge of the wicker chair. My eye was taken to the rippling reflection of the sun—that golden glowing sphere, circle in our dimension—pulsing in the pool.

Cookie kicked in and my mind segued seamlessly into greater intensity, another perspective, another layer of experience. Guru Nanak's words flowed into my brain, "Who weeps for another? We all weep for ourselves."

Our world reflects who we are. When we fear others' deaths, we are only fearing our own; our entire response to life, to our world and the people in it, is self-referential: "Me, me, me, me." What will happen to *me* when Mishi dies? I will lose my closest family connection. Our love and connection has given me some anchoring after my parents' passing, and the consequent loss of my brother's side of the family, due to—what else—property disputes.

Before I knew it, I had brought out the little blue bucket with my gardening gloves, hat, implements from the shed, and a set of children's tools—shovel, trowel, rake. Just my size, now. As I was cutting off the dead heads of the roses I was thinking to myself that I must untangle this knot of grief, not only to survive without crippling sorrow, but to live even more vitally in light of Mishi's imminent death.

How often serving a garden has saved me. How much more plants give back than I give them of love and care. I think I am taking care of my garden when it is taking care of me. It helped me survive a husband's suicide back in 1993. I was sitting on the front lawn a few days after Donald's death so I could feel some human connection with people in cars driving into the cul-de-sac, so I wouldn't feel all dark, desperate, and horribly alone in the house. My eye turned to the red roses Donald and I had planted. They looked wilted, their canes full of cankers, the brown edges of the too-tight bud petals browning and fraying, the leaves infested with black, yellow spots, and powdery mildew. I got up and began to tend them. How many doors opened with that little gesture of turning to something other than myself and my sorrow! And the gardening gave me healing images and metaphors for the long poem I wrote for Donald: "As a Fountain in a Garden/ The Gift of Grief." Mother Nature herself came to live with me in my grief. I spent most of my days outdoors to do her healing work. I bought new trees: apple, nectarine, macadamia, fig, lemon, star pine, and liquid amber; more roses, and passion fruit and jasmine vines. I added lettuce, broccoli, chard, kale, and tomatoes, planting them in the raised redwood beds Donald had made. I also bought two bird feeders to have feathery visitors to quell my loneliness and make my house a home again.

In the throes of the imminent loss of my sister, I availed myself once more of the many gifts of the vegetal world. Bending over to pluck the broccoli head that the squirrel had been nibbling, the squirrel whose presence I love in the garden even though it is destructive of my labors, the pressure of the morning found release in the words, *Let her die then. We must all die. Let her die.*

One way of dealing with a painful situation is to see it through to the end, and consent to it.

"Consent." What a word, what a concept. It comes from the Latin *con* (together, in agreement with) and *sentire*, to feel, discern. The heart aids the brain aids the heart aids the brain. They are commingled.

I resolved not to let my sister's condition steal my day. I must live my own life, even when my heart is breaking.

I thank Cookie. I thank the garden. For how long, dear God, will our garden continue to suckle me? My stamina is failing. I fear I may trip on the flagstones that I accidently wet while gardening. I tripped yesterday. Some fear is creeping in, and I must beware. Dylan Thomas cautioned, "Do not go gentle," but I do not want to go fearful into that good night. My angels speak to me: *Know that fear comes with the message: caution. Do your balance exercises. Know, too, no amount of caution will come to your aid when it is time for you to fall. Live fearlessly. It is time to pay attention and embrace your destiny, whatever it may be. Falls and all. Take it all in the spirit of Hukam (God's will) and like Nanak, you will walk carefree, your arms swinging.*

The damn thing about wisdom is how shifty it is. As Socrates said, "True wisdom is the property of God." Even as he said this, he himself did not rest, nor let others rest in their march toward whatever small amount of wisdom we fools can acquire through ruthless self-examination.

Socrates was wise because he knew he wasn't wise. The rest of us just bumble along from wisdom to folly and back again. "The same person is foolish and wise," said Nanak. This ricocheting back and forth reminds me of how laboriously dyers dye fabrics in India. They soak them in the dyeing vat, then hang them out to dry in the sun, to fade. They keep dyeing and allowing the fabric to fade till the color shifts from fugitive to fast.

My resolve to consent to Mishi's death did not penetrate all the way to my unconscious layer. It kept me from sleep and calm. Anxiety returned. A talk with Kuldip the next morning did nothing to make me feel better; the doctors have given her three months. Cysts have begun to form and they had to drain four liters of water from her abdomen, which leaches out protein and minerals. Without chemo, which she is refusing, water is going to continue to accumulate. We discuss palliative care.

"I am seventy-five," Mishi said on the phone. "I have lived enough. Life with chemo is not a life. I am okay with it." I cried, she cried, we cried together on the phone. I recall the day I crawled into bed with her during my last visit to India, when we hugged each other and sobbed. I think of all the dead since the first man or woman died. I think, all the moisture of our planet is the stuff of tears. I think of my mother's words as we sat together in the garden in the warming winter sun: "These eyes have seen enough; my tongue has tasted enough. It is time to go." I hear my father say, "It is time to make the big leap." Will I be as stoic and ready to go when it is my time?

Wisdom could not touch the place where I suffered. Ariel could not help. As I went about my chores, I found relief in howls and barks. All day I was in the kind of darkness in which my future collapsed upon me. One loss blew its bugle and resurrected all my dead. I was maimed and mourning all day, pre-experiencing all the losses to come: my sister, Payson, and God alone knows who else will be felled during my lifetime. And of course, what I invariably forget in my fear of the loss of others is the loss of my own self.

It is just as well I forget my own death. I recall the terror of it one morning, sitting on the pot, scrolling through the news on the phone, checking my email. My neck had been talking to me in tweaks, squeaks, and pops. Whenever I am under stress, working too hard or too foolishly, worrying and anxious, the first thing to go off is the narrow stem of my neck on which my brain blooms. Suddenly I felt a shooting pain through my temple and down my neck. My brain went crazy with an unnamable, unutterable terror. I was gripped in the fierce claws of feral thoughts and my unchecked imagination let loose: *I am dying of a ruptured brain aneurism.* I recalled someone I knew who had screamed and screamed from a monster headache, had a stroke, was paralyzed. Now it was happening to me. Either that, or the whole edifice of my bone architecture—my spine that holds me up, the discs like cushions inside my vertebrae stacked on top of each other—was imploding like a high-rise collapsing in on itself. I was spontaneously combusting. Payson would find me in a heap of ashes and smoke in the toilet.

I remembered in my tunnel of terror to turn to my tote, to the holy words that never fail to rush to my aid, sirens blaring. A prayer, a *shabad* by the fifth guru of the Sikhs, Guru Arjan Dev, came to my rescue: "*Meharban, meharban, sahib meharban, sahib mera meharban.*" (Merciful, merciful, my beloved is merciful, always merciful.)

Go on, admit it. I *am* afraid of death. Which of us isn't, except for those moths, like Donald and other suicides, who fly into what Sylvia Plath called the cauldron eye of death? It is this fear that keeps our otherwise more dangerous highways, for the most part, functioning in order; that makes every creature on the planet scurry to safety at the slightest threat.

Death is not a maybe but a when, as real as it can be on this side of the event horizon. Genetic mutations in the DNA of my cells that produce blood in the marrow of my bones are producing abnormal blood cells. It is a condition called leukemia. Fortunately, mine is chronic lymphocytic leukemia (CLL). The internet says I have at least another four years before CLL takes me out. I, however, choose to believe I have much more time than that. I have learned not to take a medical diagnosis too seriously, though I have taken my sister's numbers to heart. I choose to live with hope in the safe pockets of medical unknowing, of the mystery of survival and death, which exceeds every physician's skill, no matter how experienced and accomplished. Kuldip was given a year twelve years ago because of stage four prostate cancer that had metastasized to his hip bone. I know many people who go to hell and return. A friend's mother, admitted into hospice four years ago, is hale and hearty, enjoying her beer and her life. And another friend's mental and physical health had deteriorated so much she had to be institutionalized due to amnesiac spells in which she couldn't recognize anyone, but after all had said their goodbyes she sprang back, like a dying tree with new growth.

Which is not to say I don't also have some very pessimistic spells, deducing from night sweats and low energy that the cancer is advancing. I have been resting these days due to a conjunction of several little ailments. All I want to do is lie in bed, scribble, and read. Actually, this feels wonderful. If I could only get rid of my worry that my low energy level is becoming chronic and wondering if I will ever feel normal again.

Anything is possible at our age, at any time. We have heard from our friend, T, a good friend of Payson, that his wife, younger than he by ten years, has just been diagnosed with a fatal cancer. Doctors have given her a few months. Though some beat the odds, others succumb. And yet I cannot, at least not this morning, accept my death. Perhaps I won't till, in poet Kabir's words, *"Jam kaa dand moond may laagai khin may karai nibayraa,"* roughly translated as "death's club hits her over the head and everything is over in an instant." I do not want to cushion myself with hope of more and more life—mine, Payson's, Mishi's—but acquaint myself with loss. It suits my purpose, as I lie in bed from a sudden drop in energy level, to contemplate death. The preparation for loss, the letting go, must begin now. My downturns are the best times to prepare. Nothing like illness to take some time to befriend Death instead of fear him. The illness becomes more tolerable when I see it serves the important function of rehearsing. It is preparation and play-acting before opening time, the performance of the most important act of my life: the disappearing act.

Often I forget death entirely and think myself immortal. How rare those moments are now, when I let fear slide and go about the business of living, thinking it is not imminent. I am not Shakespeare's Hamlet on the threshold of death, saying, "If it be now, 'tis not to come; if it be not to come, it will be now; if it be not now, yet it will come; the readiness is all." I am not ready, though my practice of surrendering to it is ongoing. Will I go gentle into that good night or scream, reverted to a little girl in her unpreparedness and inability to surrender, "I don't want to die! I don't want to die"?

Isn't death always something that happens to someone else? The word and experience "death" is only for the living. Our experience of death is always someone else's death. Who knows what we experience when we are the ones doing the dying? There is much freedom in this unknowing. We can make things up as we go. In seeing death as an adventure, I hope to make it one. I also believe the accounts of the near-death experiences (NDEs) recorded in Raymond Moody's book *Life After Life*, and his subsequent titles. The journey carries on, I console myself.

I go for a walk in the gray darkness of a lusterless dawn. The flowers blooming cheekily in people's well-tended front gardens are an affront to my suffering. Beauty lies dead and dying around me. Suddenly I see a heron's white wings glimmering in the budding blue and gold light of morning. I think, I will use the color of my suffering as I weave my book. I even admire the phrasing of "blue light budding into day." I doubt the genuineness of my sorrow. I care more for metaphors and phrasing. I survive all my sorrows, translate them into words. I go on. I will go on. The ego will ensure it.

16
Preparing for Death

*I*f Death must be, and I know in objective moments shorn of desires and denials that he has already staked his claim, why not look forward to the meeting? Why not turn Death into a lover instead of a foe? Nanak says, "Think of the summoner when the summons comes." He talks of death as the wedding night.

The thought of turning Death into a lover, a groom, excites me. Excitement is rare these days, getting rarer as I age. Excitement comes to tell me I am on the right track.

To prepare for the union, I have bought myself a cartload of books.

Two in particular have stoked my excitement about death. I have already devoured Eben Alexander's *Proof of Heaven*, about a neurologist's experiences in a coma. It was a fascinating read, the kind that keeps your ass in a chair or in bed. Even a few years ago I would not have read a book with a title like that. My hyperrational mind was not open to anything my senses couldn't endorse. My many mystical experiences I dismissed as coincidences. I was skeptical of everything that breached the laws of physics and gave me a glimpse into mystery. The hackneyed word "heaven" still does nothing for me, though intimations of something unknown have begun to filter into my open mind. "Everything possible to be believed is an image of truth," William Blake wrote. Intimations of my own death have made me ripe and receptive to mystery.

"We can only see what our brain's filter allows through. The brain—its left-sided linguistic/logical part, that which generates our sense of rationality and the feeling of being a sharply defined ego or self—is a barrier to our higher knowledge and experience," Alexander wrote. More than his words, I was persuaded by the tone and excitement of Alexander's voice. His insights are the insights of the ancient Indian *Vedas:* "The (false) suspicion that we can somehow be separated from God is the root of every form of anxiety in the universe, and the cure for it is the knowledge that nothing can tear us from God, ever."

I have also devoured Elisabeth Kübler-Ross's *On Life After Death.* It is, as with Eben Alexander, her voice that elicits my trust. I appreciate her use of the metaphor, so close to my heart and the heart of humankind, of metamorphosis: "The death of the human body is identical to what happens when the butterfly emerges from its cocoon," she wrote. Like the cocoon, the body is "only a house to live in for a while."

I have experienced my own periodic molting that has wrought all the changes in me since infancy, no less dramatic than the changes from larva to butterfly. I have only to see my photographs over the years, and the faces of my old friends juxtaposed with my memory of their youth, to see time's magical transformations. Death is the price we pay for becoming everything we become. Parts of us die—science calls the process "apoptosis"—so other parts can live. Without it, nothing would be. Form emerges from death. Our limbs are sculpted by death. Take the digits of our hands. So many cells have to die off in the webs our hands are in the womb for them to differentiate into fingers.

I need to have a model of someone who died consciously, cheerfully, joyously; someone for whom the movement toward death, and death itself, was an adventure. Who better than Socrates, who showed us how to live and die?

Being a philosopher and a lover of wisdom above all, Socrates befriended death for his entire life. When he was condemned to die at seventy by the Athenian court for his free and radical thinking, for "believing in gods of his own invention" rather than the traditional gods of Greek mythology, he defended himself eloquently, as he always did, through dialogue and debate, not for its own sake, but for the principles he adored, espoused, lived for, and taught: beauty, truth, goodness, moral virtue. He refused to betray them to escape death. After his attempts to convince his accusers failed, he did not try to evade his fate, even though his friends presented him with exile as an alternative. Socrates, who had lived in complete obedience to the will of God, wanted "to follow the course, since God points out the way." He was reconciled to and ready for death, the unknown adventure that lay ahead, believing that, "No one knows with regard to death whether it is not really the greatest blessing that can happen to us."

A happy coincidence kept Socrates from being executed immediately after his trial. Each year a boat with a flower-decked prow was sent to Delos to honor Apollo, and till the boat returned to Athens, no one could be executed. Fortunately for us, we have the story of the three days leading to his death that he spent in prison before drinking hemlock from the chalice; three days to die consciously, bravely, without fear, imparting to posterity insights we would do well to live by today: "The really important thing is not to live, but to live well." And by living well he meant consciously, with awareness, without which, all our sages say, life is not worth living.

Socrates, humble Socrates, knew he knew nothing; that real wisdom is the property of God; that to be afraid of death is only another form of thinking that one knows all there is to know. A wise man knows he knows nothing.

The boat from Delos arrived, and it was time for Socrates to say goodbye to his life. Holding high the chalice of poison, he said, "We can and must pray to the gods that our sojourn on earth will continue happy beyond the grave. This is my prayer, and may it come to pass." He drank the hemlock, readily and cheerfully, with trust that "The soul is immortal because it can perceive, can have a share in beauty, truth, and goodness, which are eternal."

As the poison crept to his heart, his last words to his friend Crito were, "Crito, we owe a cock to Asclepius." It was a Greek ritual following recovery from an illness to make a sacrifice to the god of health. Socrates believed his death was the cure for the disease of life.

Ah, perhaps this is too optimistic a version. Perhaps it does not include the dark side of things. In all the paintings I have seen of Socrates's death, there are mourners. The sheer sorrow and anguish in their averted gazes tell us that for them death is terrifying. We are the mourners who weep and doubt and continue to grieve far beyond the time allowed by gods. We are not the enlightened ones, but we are meant to get past death, leave behind mourning, and give up sorrow for the song of hope.

And hope there is, even beyond death, hope by which I love and live. My most intense and primary love is my deep, bloodroot, earthy attachment to my parents. I am joined to them with a ligature that will never pass. This love, at once abstract and concrete, like air, like a golden bridge made of light, spans abysses of space in an instant. I write "Mom, Dad" and they are here, not just as traces of a memory, faint echoes of voices long lost, but palpable, their ghosts snug in my arms.

And here is another story that I would like to live by, from Chuang Tzu. I am happy to discover him and adore the title of his book: *The Inner Chapters*, translated by A. C. Graham. The book was given to us by an Englishman, Simon, who lived in a remote village in India for ten years. He unexpectedly showed up at Behta Pani with three boxes of books, just the kind I read and re-read. Though I have always been drawn to Taoism, I had never heard of Chuang Tzu. I had Payson to thank for pulling it out of the stack for me to read as I lay sick in bed one day. I go through periods where I'm quite lazy and don't want my brain taxed in any way, and then I must set myself tasks/goals: *I'll read just one chapter, or even one paragraph, of this or this book.* I read Chuang Tzu and was hooked.

The Inner Chapters articulated for me one of the ways in which I want to live in the last part of my life, with fluid and shifting goals. What does this mean to me? In a simple sense, listening to my body-brain and acting accordingly. *Now I want to do this, don't want to do that, that feels like too much work, this is the perfect thing to do now.* It is the greatest way to be. Chuang Tzu calls it "roaming freely in the cage." He recounts the following parable.

Three men, Master Sang-hu, Meng Tzŭ-fan and Master Ch'in-chang, were talking together.

"Which of us can be with where there is no being with, be for where there is no being for? Which of us are able to climb the sky and roam the mists and go whirling into the infinite, living forgetful of each other for ever and ever?"

The three men looked at each other and smiled, and none was reluctant in his heart. So, they became friends. After they had been living quietly for a while Master Sang-hu died. Before he was buried, Confucius heard about it and sent Tzŭ-kung to assist at the funeral. One of the men was plaiting frames for silkworms, the other strumming a zither, and they sang in unison,

"Hey-ho, Sang-hu! Hey-ho, Sang-hu! You've gone back to being what one truly is, but we go on being human, O!"

Tzŭ-kung hurried forward and asked, "May I inquire whether it is in accordance with the rites to sing with the corpse right there at your feet?"

The two men exchanged glances and smiled: "What does he know about the meaning of the rites?"

Tzŭ-kung returned and told Confucius, "What men are these? The decencies of conduct are nothing to them, they treat the very bones of their bodies as outside them. They sing with the corpse right there at their feet, and not a change in the look on their faces. I have no words to name them. What men are these?"

"They are the sort that roam beyond the guidelines," said Confucius. "I am the sort that roams within the guidelines. Beyond and within have nothing in common, and to send you to mourn was stupid on my part. They are at the stage of being fellow men with the maker of things, and go roaming in the single breath that breathes through heaven and earth. They think of life as an obstinate wart or a dangling wen, of death as bursting the boil or letting the pus. How should such men as that know death from life, before from after? They borrow right-of-way through the things which are different but put up for the night in that body which is the same. Self-forgetful right down to the liver and the gall, leaving behind their own ears and eyes, they turn start and end back to front, and know no beginning-point or standard. Heedlessly they go roving beyond the dust and grime, go rambling through the lore in which there's nothing to do. How could they be finicky about the rites of common custom, on watch for the inquisitive eyes and ears of the vulgar?"

Chuang Tzu, *The Inner Chapters*, trans. A. C. Graham

Yes, I will look forward to Death, but like a coquette, I will keep him at bay. Like Scheherazade of *One Thousand and One Nights*, I will tell enchanting tales. I will take my time, linger in my stories, stretch out the yarn, mix up stories, even repeat myself if I can't improvise. All tricks are in my manual of flirting with death. I do not fear he will turn away by my lack of total availability. We both know the ineluctability of our union. I think he enjoys the play, too, but expects me to take him very seriously, to be utterly surrendered when he does finally wrap me in his embrace. He lets me know the marriage is unplanned, that he can play master and come, for that final meeting, like a groom, whenever he wills. Any time the Divine Will commands.

17

Dance of Kali

I participate in the universal *Tao*, the path of life, the absolute principle underlying the universe. I *am* the Tao—yin and yang in harmony with the natural order. How wonderful it would be if I identified with neither, but rather with the circle that contains both—up, down, happiness, depression—looked at my life with Shiva's third eye that sees beyond the conflict between the two, or aligned with Guru Nanak's "One." Though I strive, without much success, it is my ongoing endeavor.

This morning I was awakened out of a prolonged depression by the singing of my angels: *Enough of death! Get up and get going, kiddo!*

Magical downturns and upswings of my life happen beyond me. Yang energies climax and return to the yin phase, and vice versa. Clearly it feels this morning that my internal weather has changed as I move into a new, yet familiar country in my being.

Having slept through several days, I have revived after another long spell of body-mind chaos and illness. Clouds of insomnia had obscured my gods and brought out my demons. Sleep, a long cozying up with death, is the elixir of life.

What a blessing these days are. I relish sleeping well, waking, falling asleep again, lying about in bed for another couple of hours, getting out of bed, moving slowly, taking even more time to fully awaken, sometimes hours.

So very many reasons to sing hallelujahs of gratitude. Getting out of bed in the mornings is the greatest reason for rejoicing. I know many who didn't; I am still here. I won't let the shadow of the future deprive me of my today. Has the time come for Mishi? Goddess of the ample breasts, give her, as you are giving me, some more time on this planet!

My prayer was heard. Mishi has decided to try chemo again. Ah, we will meet once again on this plane.

Looking out at the roiling Pacific, past the bleached whale vertebrae Payson lugged home from Baja that now sits in the prow of our deck, at the bands of soft, smudged light in pinks, blues, and grays above the horizon, I think how blessed life is. Everything we need is here.

Until recently I have not allowed myself to think of a future or to hope for one. Yin had me in thrall, a dark heaviness in the body-mind, a leaden stuckness from a bad back, a broken arm, a lack of quickness in the brain, something gray and ashen around the heart. I have been in the thick of thunderheads of ill-health, doubt, turmoil, unknowing, and lostness—death-hugging thoughts. I wondered on the trail to North Torrey Pines—a hike I persuaded myself into because I have been utterly incapable of physical movement, the body creaking and groaning at every step—whether I was talking myself into dying. One can talk oneself into anything, living, dying, or any story the mind concocts out of fear or trust.

In hindsight I can see the pattern of my cycles. My downturns are a syndrome. The same complex of symptoms swirls in each of them, the same descriptions encapsulate them.

First, I feel desperately, dreadfully lonely, isolated, exiled, cut off; no emails from anyone, no phone calls, no anchoring in the external world, no job I want to go to or have the energy to do. All my life I have been an exile; even in Behta Pani, which we *chose* for its isolation, I feel isolated. Isolation is the fruit of choices made along the way: America,

American spouses, no offspring, not many friends because of my "passionate preference" (to borrow from Robert Frost) for solitude, though I have a few dear ones I speak with regularly, whose presence in my life is healing and helpful.

In my yin phases I feel locked inside my skin despite having an incredible partner who offers togetherness—closeness where it matters most, and everything a human could ask for by way of health (at my age), money in the bank, beauty outside our windows, beauty and comfort in our home, vegetables growing, flowers blooming, and fruit ripening in our garden. Even Cookie doesn't come to my aid. Even God, whom I endeavor through music and prayers to keep close, flees.

As we come to the end of life, we become aware of all that remains unfulfilled. My professional failures loom large in the syndrome. What I consider my *magnum opus*, titled *Malini in Whirlwood, Book of Potentiality*, forty years in the making, has been rejected by publishers again and again. I despair of getting more success with my writing than I already have, which, from the pit, looks miniscule.

The dark veils have lifted. I have remembered. I am a queen dreaming she is a beggar. My head has risen above the clouds, my eyes have seen in the sunlight what riches I possess. No one can take away from me the passionate engagement and sheer fun the writing of *Malini* gave me. Labor, lovingly done, passionately engaged with, is the highest award and reward.

Yesterday on our hike I saw, momentarily, a sight that surprised my dull and dimmed eye with beauty: our blue Pacific, viewed through groves of charred, beetle-blackened, and some still green Torrey Pines, rolling in long crests of wave upon wave of shimmering light.

In the lifting of the veils I see that isolation is a call to connect. So much of being connected is *feeling* connected. Isolation is a state of mind, a failure to feel the connections that I do have. Hell, I can be connected to anything, everything. We cannot have pets because of our dual countries, but we have birds that I feed, mourning doves that mind-link with me, finches, hummingbirds, mockers that sing to me and populate my world. They bring *rawnak*—"a teeming sense of enlivening and belonging"—into it.

Only I can fix my problems. God has equipped me with all the power and strength I need to live a full life. I call friends and connect with them; I make chai and invite Payson for a tea party in the music room. I catch a glimpse of myself in the mirror in the hallway, going to the party for which I have prepared, using my beautiful tiled Spanish tray, wearing a colorful scarf and lipstick. I applied it in the dark and it has spilled the boundaries of my lips in a most comical way. My hat, too, is awry on my head. P says I look like a drunken old lady. I laugh aloud in joy. He and I sit, schmooze, drink tea out of our colorful coffee mugs, eat baklava. Then I put my head in his lap as he sits on the couch, reading news on his phone. In my hunger for connection I want his undivided attention and ask him to lay aside his phone. I want to plan small changes in our home and garden. A new stone wall, Baja pavers with yellow and red hues in the walkways, an outdoor porch, lighting in the garden. How peaceful it is to imagine an extension of our life together, here in our home in Del Mar.

Now I am planning to return to this book. My peace is not peace without laboring on it; beauty fails to please; nothing excites. My old age project has much to recommend it: something to wake up for, to look forward to, with which to be deeply engaged.

So much of writing, like everything else I do, is dependent upon right thinking, self-motivation, persistence. Cosmic vectors turn me toward Ralph Waldo Emerson, author of *Self-Reliance*, who has rescued me frequently from the bog of self-doubt. "To the persevering mortal," he quoted Zoroaster, "the blessed immortals are swift." He counsels, "Trust thyself." And, "Every heart vibrates to that iron string. Accept the place divine providence has found for you."

Cleaning my desk in a state of dejection and overwhelm about my deteriorating brain that is producing abundant, uncontrolled, and uncontrollable material, I am rescued again. I come across, once more, McPhee's article "Tabula Rasa, Volume 1" in the January 13, 2020, issue of *The New Yorker*. McPhee describes Mark Twain's old-man project—his autobiography—as "only seven hundred and thirty-five thousand words long. Repeatedly, he (Twain) tells his reader how a project such as this one should be done—randomly, without structure, in total disregard of consistent theme or chronology. Just jump in anywhere, tell whatever comes to mind from any era. If something distracts your memory and seems more interesting at the moment, interrupt the first story and launch into the new one. The interrupted tale can be finished later."

McPhee offers another lifeline to my drowning self that fears this book wants to become books; it will never end, for I am spinning out my ever-unfolding life in these pages. McPhee, on a bicycle ride with his friend Joel Achenbach, "whines" that his project begets a desire to publish what he writes, and publication defeats the ongoing project, the purpose of which is to keep the old writer alive by never coming to an end. Achenbach advises, "Just call it 'Volume One.'"

I will not get hung up on endings, give myself every freedom to flow exactly as I am flowing, produce as much as I want, get lost as much as happens, please myself alone. I will make my writing sectional, anything can go anywhere, and not get hung up on transitions or too tight an organization that hurts my brain.

I tell myself I have time to complete this book. I tell myself I am still capable of invention. I will return to the notes I made and if nothing else, read them. In however small a way, I will return to that which is my life, that which makes the whole of me cohere.

Even as I plan changes to the house and garden, changes to my way of thinking, a cautionary voice whispers, *Don't get attached to the scenarios created by your desires. One never knows.* It is a sobering voice; much wisdom in it, in not knowing. What is given must be given up without a thought when the Universe's hand reaches out to reclaim it.

But today let me hope. Who knows, the Universe that grants all wishes may yet allow me to complete a volume or two of the books of my life.

Finally getting out of bed, doing the necessary, I climb down to the kitchen with the intention of nourishing myself with soup. I have parsnips, turnips, yams, broccoli, spinach, and tomatoes. I don't bother chopping anything, it feels like work, though I do wash the vegetables, cut off their ends, put them whole in a large pot, pour broth into it, set it on the stove, add ginger, turmeric (always turmeric), black pepper, and salt. Later, when it is cooked and blended, I will add walnuts, pumpkin seeds, and, oh yes, some cream and a tad of butter. Putting the lid on, turning on the timer, I pick up the large knife and do the dance of the fierce warrior goddess Kali, slicing through the demons that had me in thrall.

I clean the kitchen and the music room, straighten the blankets on the infrared bio mat. Having lived a life of litter and clutter all my life, I can think of nothing more difficult and joyous than organizing. Finding things in their right place is a question of comfort as much as a strategy to circumvent the frustrations of a declining memory.

I don't want any agendas, just an amble through my day like a mature river on the plains, broad, wide, open under the skies, past its agitated midlife descent from its source after so many responsible struggles to stay within its shores, straying aimlessly in whichever direction the flow takes it.

I have had a lifetime of rushing here and there, pinching minutes and hours in the service of being productive; "I have measured out my life with coffee spoons," as T. S. Eliot laments in "The Love Song of J. Alfred Prufrock." Having deprived myself of many of the simple pleasures of life—the luxury of doing just one thing at a time, sitting on the pot for as long as necessary, being idle, doing nothing, lying about, watching TV, hanging out with friends—I avail of the supreme gift of aging: slowing down.

I don't delude myself into thinking I have learned the art of slowing down once and for all. I will fall into hurry again; hurry has a way of catching up with us. But slow is the tempo where my heart is. The very word "slow" sends pulses of peace throughout my body. Slow is as close to eternity as I can get. It is to this utterly at ease, leisurely adagio pulse that I make my chai in the spirit of the Japanese tea ceremony, each activity given its due and fruition of time. I sit in the patch of sun on one of the small chairs upholstered in raw silk that we brought from India, munchkin chairs that fit our size so well. I take in the beauty of that bit of petrified wood that serves for a coaster on the tiny table made of an irregular piece of olive wood, a slice of a tree trunk. I take a minute to admire wood transformed to stone, and drink my creamy, honied chai.

Oh, let me not tell how long it has taken me to *allow* myself to slow down. I have imposed myself much too much upon this work of art called life. I have pushed, pulled, squeezed, and stretched my mind-body this way and that. I resolve to give myself ease, let myself be. Ease moves us into the whole circle of yin and yang, into Shiva's third eye, into Guru Nanak's One. I will strive to move in the stream of time like a queen rather than a slave, allowing each activity and chore to take whatever measure of time it needs to unfold like a flower, without hurry, without shortening or lengthening any part of it, like a musical note taking all its time to express its playful, variant fullness within the rhythm of the whole piece—the day.

18

Mummy, My Mummy

Twice a year the center of the sun passes Earth's equator and results in the equinox—a day with light and dark of equal length, the sun rising precisely in the east and setting precisely in the west. It is the spring equinox today.

Even as a part of me thrusts toward light, my root digs deeper into sustaining darkness. Death is the rhizome from which I and the earth spring again and again. A time will come, soon enough, when I will not return, but the earth will renew itself. Though we don't know what happens to us after we are dead, here on Earth spring and rebirth are assured.

Spring always heralds death. It is the beginning of the end, as is all birth.

You come today, my Mummy, out of invisibility from the land beyond my senses like a visible ghost. Suddenly, you are here.

I realize why I have been thrust again into sorrow. The body remembers even when the mind forgets. It is the equinox on which you died four years ago. I wanted to be with you when you died. I wanted you to die holding my hand. But death doesn't wait, nor take our desires into account. You died the night before the morning I was to fly to you. I was relieved my brother and his family had cremated you before I arrived. I didn't want the trauma of seeing you that way. I am squeamish about death. Life has shielded me from your and Dad's deaths. My only death up-close was Donald's, finding him in our secret spot in the oak and cottonwood forest by a seasonal stream, slumped on the limb of an oak tree.

But let me stay with you today, Mummy.

You moved out, stretched into the wave, into that abstraction—midwife to our first screams and howls—from which everything comes. My aging brings me closer to the mystery from which I manifested, the mystery to which you returned, Mother. Being is an interlude between two non-beings. Are they different? Are they the same?

Victor Frankl in *Man's Search for Meaning* described how real absent things can be, how they can help us tide over hard times. In the Nazi death camp of Auschwitz he clung to his wife's image, her smile, her looks. "Real or not, her look was then more luminous than the sun which was beginning to rise." In the hellish isolation of the concentration camp, Frankl's spirit entered another dimension in which they were together. He didn't know if she was still alive—she wasn't; she had been exterminated—but her physical existence ceased to matter to him. "Love goes very far beyond the physical person of the beloved," Frankl wrote. This was one way in which his inner life sprang alive, amplified, and ultimately saved him. He understood then that "the salvation of man is through love and in love." The remembered image of a person can have as much impact on the senses as the thing itself.

Mummy, I, too, have experienced the healing, nurturing properties of love at unimaginable distances, and turn to absent things that are very present in my life: you and Dad. The other night you both came to me in a dream, all the way from India to America, to our new home somewhere in this town. The house was not complete, the fridge was almost empty, and yet I managed to make a meal for you. You were tired and jet-lagged. You wanted milk in your chai and I had only coconut milk. You weren't happy with it. Milk materialized out of somewhere and I made you a good cup of chai that you slurped with pleasure. A sticky liquid goop that resolved into a silken web flowed out of me, as from the spinnerets of a spider's abdomen, and covered both of you. I knew I would never let you go, that we were connected for eternity.

I have orbited around you most of my adult life, Mummy, the soil in which Daddy planted his seed to make me. You have left behind not just memories but a large part of yourself in my life. I see you in my face, my mannerisms, in the way I scratch my head, wash my hands, my way of keeping house, though it is nowhere near as perfect as yours. You are in me even as your soul moves through space-time and all the dimensions beyond it that death has released you into.

My own death sometimes seems imminent, Mother. My energy plummets for unknown reasons and I collapse. How often when I have lain in bed, my friend/my enemy, Death has come, breathing through my breath. I have fought with him furiously and desired his embrace. Yes, I think of Death as a he, not because I am male-identified, which I probably am in some ways, but because I envision him as Daddy, who nurtured me more than you, Mummy. I see God as male, too, someone who lifts me up, holds me close to his heart, the way Dad did when I was little. My masculine God is kind, loving, all-accepting, not harsh, patriarchal, demanding obedience, threatening me with punishment, and ruling me with fear. Yet fear is certainly here. When I am cast adrift in periodic night sea journeys, I cower.

My male God transforms easily into female energy when I need the sort of nurturing infants need, a warm, soft body with cushy teats of the Great Mother who suckles and soothes.

I didn't get the image of a female god from you, Mummy. My need and desperation invented, perhaps discovered, her. For how long, if at all, did you suckle me? When did you begin? When end? Why didn't I ask? Would you have remembered? Unlikely. You were always self-absorbed. As I am.

But you did love me. I heard from Dad and Mishi how you, so

phobic about dirt, held my soiled clothes to your breast and wept when I left for the United States that first time. I wanted you to hug *me*, Mother, not my clothes! But it was evidence of the love you were unable to speak and express. Why is it so difficult for some people to express love? Perhaps there are many expressions of love that we don't count as expressions? Food, for instance. You were always good with that, Mummy. And when we were children, you were good with clothes.

My habit and desire for touch, cuddles, and expressions of love came from Dad's physicality. Am I capable of giving it because I got it, or did I just come into the world needy of touch and physical closeness? If I had to choose, I would say the seed of my father's prayers and desires brought me into being. He prayed for a person like me when you were pregnant with me, and we fell in love with each other from the start. But I have dreams in which this is not so, in which he is distant, not loving me as I would have liked. Then there are other dreams in which we meet and I jump into his arms like a child and he carries me, hugging me close all the while.

But Daddy, you have to wait your turn till it is your death anniversary, a week from now. This chapter belongs to Mummy. I have so many chapters devoted to her in my books. She was, as Dad so often smiled and said, a character, large, loud, with a presence that filled the house, so full of drama, theatrical in the scenes she created to get what she wanted because that was the only way she could communicate her hidden material and emotional needs.

I recall my first dream after your death, Mummy. I see you and Dad coming out of the front door of a house, holding hands and crossing the street. You are both old, yet vital in that dimension outside of time in which everything coexists at the same time. I run to you, and you collapse on the curb when you see me, weeping copiously as you say, "You didn't come! You didn't come!"

I am in the dark, hairy claws of regret today. I changed countries, lived in India for six months, not in your city but eight hours away by car. I visited you once a month for a week of quality time. But even then, I was busy running errands, buying things we could not buy in our little village near Behta Pani. You couldn't visit me because of your heart condition. I think of all the ways I failed you. How often you asked me, during the nine years you survived Dad, "Sleep in Dad's bed by me." I tried. But you slept with all the lights on and were up dozens of times, hobbling to the bathroom with your cane, calling out, *"Hai, hai, hai."*

What kind of an old woman will I make? Some days I unconsciously imitate your gait. My hair is silver, like yours. Will I be widowed, as you were? Will I sleep with the lights blazing? Will I check behind each curtain and under the bed for intruders before going to sleep? Will I keep a big stick by my bed?

Your father and his fathers included *hakims* (physicians), healers, teachers, and opium addicts. Guru Nanak, 550 years ago, was the first of the healers, and his perennial spirit springs and buds to this day. Nanak's business was to heal souls and hearts with love for the Divine. I count Guru Nanak, founding father of the Sikhs, as my first ancestor. My mother and her siblings were sixteen generations down from Nanak. The parent tree having spread its seed wide and far, many Bedis—surname and caste of my matrilineal line—know him as their ancestor.

I need no proof that I am his genetic descendent. I own him as my own, and that is all the proof I need. That and family legends, stories passed down orally, pride in him as ancestor, the existence of ancient *granths*—ancient holy scriptures—in the family's possession, handwritten, leather-bound volumes embossed with gold that my father bequeathed to libraries and *gurdwaras* (places of worship; literally, "the Guru's door"). My father, who had thought more of the community than I do, was far less possessive than I am. I have one small granth in my possession, and the colorful story behind my acquisition of it tells me I was always meant to have it.

I was ten years old, vacationing with my grandparents in my mother's ancestral village. They had built a new house, made of brick and cement, when electricity came to the village. The old house made of mud and straw was at a distance from the new one. I walked to the old premises one day. The house had crumbled to the ground, though a few freestanding walls stood here and there, defining the vanished. Sunlight poured into the roofless rooms, empty spaces curved around window frames, and wild grasses grew where floors had once been. A doorframe stood stubbornly firm without any walls supporting it, and upon a crumbled portion of a wall, a small, closed cupboard stood intact, with two blue and white dirt-encrusted ceramic knobs shaped like flowers. I opened it and found several little treasures sitting there, waiting for me.

A pressed glass aquamarine plate, chipped at the edges; a large white conch shell, double lines etched parallel to the spirals, dirt in its whorls; tumbling stacks of manuscripts bound in red cloth; and a small, rectangular, handmade *gutka* (holy prayers from the most holy text, the *Granth Sahib*) that I have treasured most of all. The other manuscripts were in Urdu, and Dad, who knew how to read and write it, said most of them were herbal recipes and secret formulas for traditional Muslim *Unani* medicine with ties to Greece that my ancestors practiced. I have kept several of these, too.

The gutka is a roughly six- by four-inch rectangular manuscript that I will bequeath to family. The thick burnt-sienna leather front cover, featuring a gold medallion surrounded by a border, is detached from the body. Some of its tan handmade sheets have been nibbled here and there by generations of silverfish. The back pages, rain-stained, utterly smudged and sticking to each other, are missing a cover. The binding where the back cover came off was mended at some time by an ancestor (was it a woman? a man?) who had tried to preserve the cover by stitching it with a double-twined, madder-red thread that has preserved its color despite its age. The calligraphy, handwritten in straight lines, is certain, without flourishes, a simple, clean, matter-of-fact script so well-proportioned as to be beautiful.

Engraved in it is the *"Japji,"* the central prayer that opens the *Guru Granth Sahib*.* The words run together without breaks, pauses occurring only after each stanza, called *pauris* (steps) in Panjabi. It was written for readers who already knew the prayer by heart, and knew where the pauses and breaks naturally occur.

The *Guru Granth Sahib* is worshipped by the Sikhs as a living incarnation of our gurus, eleventh in line from Nanak. Our guru is a word; words, lovely words, worshipable words, sounds, manna to our ears from long ago, manna from the mouths of all the Holy Ones of our planet. "You uttered one word, and hundreds and thousands of rivers began to flow," Nanak said. The entire created world is a word, he said, more than four hundred years before another of my favorite bards, William Butler Yeats, put it in "The Song of the Happy Shepherd."

> *The wandering earth herself may be*
> *Only a sudden flaming word,*
> *In clanging space a moment heard,*
> *Troubling the endless reverie.*

My maternal ancestors, mainly the men, were lotus eaters. They ate opium and drank a brew made of poppy husks, called *dodas*. They were dreamers who had lost their land and wealth to their addiction but still had enough to be privileged, hiring people to work in the field and in the home. I attribute my habit of cannabis to my ancestors, all but Nanak who was high on God's name. We know that his son, Sri

---

*Sikhs believe their holy book is an extension of the Sikh line of human gurus, the manifest body of the eternal living Guru. It is a composition of the teachings of six Sikh gurus, one Sufi Muslim, and fourteen Hindu saints in ragas set to rhythmic Indian classical music.

Chand, was often high on hashish. I believe his other son, Lakshmi Das, whose descendant I am, also took it. Anyway, that is how I justify my cannabis habit: it is in my blood.

My maternal grandfather was stoned all day and spent most of his time sitting around in the sun in winter. His sole concern was to move his four-footed hempen cot, his *manji*, from sunny spot to sunny spot, his only worry that he may run out of opium.

There is no account of any women in the family eating opium. They had too much to do: feeding and milking livestock, making dung patties for fuel, washing clothes by the village well, sweeping, mopping, cooking, spinning yarn on the spinning wheels (*charkhas*), making butter and buttermilk from fermented cream, and always, the care of children and grandchildren.

But they had fun, too. I heard women in the village sing lyrical, soulful, loud, bawdy songs to the rhythms of the churn and the spinning wheel, percussion of mortar and pestle—and laugh with a laughter that echoed in the stars.

You, too, were a hakim of sorts, Mother, informed about herbs, spices, and natural remedies. You, too, had knowledge about the nature of food: which was warming, which cooling; the many manifested symptoms of coldness and hotness; what to eat when. You were never taught it, or anything else, because you were female, considered fit for only marriage and breeding. You imbibed the art through your pores, watching, absorbing. Oh, you were sent to school as a child till the sixth *jamaat* (grade). How often, and with how much pride, you had told me the story of your teacher coming to your home, your fear at seeing her there . . . Had you done something wrong? Had she come to complain? But she had come with a request: "*Bedi Saab*, don't withdraw her from school. She is very bright. I know she can get a scholarship to go to college. I will see to it myself."

But Mother, didn't you feel enraged at your father's answer? "We Bedis observe *purdah* (seclusion of women). We do not allow our women to study." Never once did I hear you express anything but love for him. Your memories were all about how much he loved you, how you were his favorite, how he and God Himself ensured, even during lean times, that your rotis and daal were always lubricated with ghee.

There is that story about the time you refused to eat your meal because there was no ghee. Just an hour later a Sikh arrived at the door with a small earthenware jar, a *matki*, full of ghee and said, with folded hands, *"Bedi saab, sadee majh sooee seee taan meh pehla ghee tuhaadai laee lyaya haan."* (Our buffalo gave birth and this is the first batch of ghee from her milk.) Yes, the Bedis, descendants of Nanak, were revered. People would genuflect to, and kiss the feet of even the infants and children of our family, you told me.

Purdah in the house of Guru Nanak? In the house of one who reveres and extols women in his *bani* (writings of the guru)?

Your father's reply may not have angered you, but I am still angry at him for denying you schooling. What a blind, unconscious descendant of the farsighted, women-honoring Guru Nanak!

My anger also stems from the time he saw me running through the gully of the village and reprimanded me in the harshest of tones for being too old to run. I was eleven years old. Patriarchy! I have no use for it.

As I go about my day, I see you again through the hospital window after your stroke, hooked up to tubes. It wasn't visiting time and they were strict. I didn't want to go home. You were on the ground floor by the window and I could see you, but not as I had always seen you, strong in yourself even as you grew old. I saw someone else through the window, not you, with a vacant stare. Not you, and yet, my Mother. After the stroke your always fine-featured face collapsed into a mass of sagging flesh. Beneath the greenish hospital gauze cap on your head, your lips drooped in a way I had never seen before, your closed eyes sunken into the folds of your cheeks.

The windowpane was too separating. I longed to be with you, near you, touch you, kiss your hand, kiss you, though you had already, except for brief spells, passed on to that other land where communication with the living falters and fails. Was anybody there? Where were you when you were in your coma? The question fascinates me. There has to be a place we go when we are neither here nor there but in a limbo between life and death, another place that teases with its mystery. I myself trust the first law of thermodynamics: energy is never lost. Ovid, who demonstrated the magic of transformations in *The Metamorphoses*, wrote: "Everything changes; Nothing perishes."

I need to make my life intentional. I don't want to stay in the tourniquet of regret today. I need to ritualize anniversaries, to self-reflect. When Payson asked me when I turned seventy, "Does your seventieth birthday hold any significance for you?" I replied, "I choose to invest it with significance. It is a turning point, and I want to embark on the adventure of aging consciously."

There is something serious in anniversaries. Even when we do not remember where we are in our annual cycles, the body, in its silent protests, laggings, illness, remembers. Anniversaries occur on the same spot on the spiraling gyre of time.

I recall your snake story.

For decades during every monsoon your neck broke out into an ugly rash. Always on the exact same spot of the gyre of time each year. The doctors were confused. But your uncle, a healer, figured it out and cured you. He asked you, "Did anything traumatic happen to you during the monsoon?" And you flashed on that time when you slept naked on the mattress in the muggy weather—the bed had not yet arrived at your new house in Assam, was it? You woke Dad to say, "I feel something cold on my body." Dad said, "You must have spilled the glass of water." You felt around in the darkness and the glass was upright. Dad turned on the light and you saw a black snake slithering up the whole length of your body, up from your groin, your belly, between your breasts, hissing as it reached your neck, spewing poison from its fangs, then gliding off your neck.

Dad killed it, but each year your body's memory relived the incident and burst into a rash where the snake had sprayed its poison. The cycles of our bodies are no different from the movements of our suns, planets, satellites. They move in annual orbits fixed by the gravity of experience.

Isn't there hope in knowing that making a bodily memory conscious takes away its sting? Didn't your sudden illumination about the hidden cause of your rash make it disappear? Your death has darkened my springtime. Can I turn it around now, knowing the secret cause of my sorrow?

I will relive some good times in my rambling remembrance of you, bring out my bundle packed in mothballs and wear one of your shawls, the purple one. Your bestowing that shawl upon me is one of my happiest memories.

I was in India for a visit, and you had been wearing that shawl a great deal that winter. Unlike your other heavily embroidered ones, this was a plain, textured, soft pashmina. It looked beautiful on you. Secretly I coveted it. You and Dad came to see me off at the train station when I left for Delhi to fly to the United States. I was just about to board the train when you took it off your neck and put it around mine. It was done on impulse, and the smile on your face told me you had surprised yourself by your gesture. You loved me in that moment, touched beyond the touching that was so hard for you. I have treasured the shawl ever since.

Your shawls have stories associated with them. During the Indo-Pakistan war of 1965, Dad was the station commander in Srinagar in Kashmir. He was sending his family back to the Panjab because it wasn't safe for us in the heart of Kashmir. He withdrew money from the bank and gave you a large chunk for expenses. You, Mother, had a different and, in retrospect, brilliant idea. You knew the shawl merchants would be selling off their stock cheaply during the war. Beautiful shawls were your love, as they are mine. You summoned the driver and off you went to buy up as many as you could. You had to bear Daddy's wrath, but you got your loot.

Your intricately embroidered shawls, Mother, were the inspiration behind my love for *jamawars* (antique paisley shawls) and embroidering, an activity that is calming me these days. I highlight in contrasting and similar shades the outlines of paisley patterns in newer, but nonetheless lovely versions of jamawars available in the Indian marketplace. It has been a happy occupation that has saved me from many a depression. I call them my "desperation shawls."

And then there was your all-time favorite shawl, a madder-red *shahtoosh** embroidered in greens and yellows around its borders, embroidery so fine from both sides that one can barely tell the difference. The back side has no knots! One day I am going to take a jeweler's loupe to it and go on a knot-finding mission. They have to be there, even though they are invisible. The shawl is so fine it can be pulled through a ring.

I remember the exact spot where I was standing in your bedroom when you hobbled over to your closet and brought out your precious shawls tied in a white cotton bundle. You placed the bundle on your bed, opened it, took the shahtoosh from the stack of other shawls, shook it, then faced me and ceremoniously put it around my shoulders. It pleased you enormously to give it to me, and it thrilled me to receive something you had so loved and worn frequently.

You had a genuine love of lovely things, jewelry excepted. You knew this was beyond your range. But later in life, when Dad earned better than in his army days as the proprietor of a petrol pump and gave you gold and diamonds, you loved and enjoyed them, too. I have inherited, together with dozens of embroidered Kashmiri shawls, some of your

---

*Valuable wool woven from the neck fur of the Himalayan ibex and Tibetan antelope. Shahtoosh shawls are now banned because these animals are endangered species, and older ones require government registration.

prized jewelry, chief among them a diamond pendant on a gold chain. "Wear it near your heart when I am gone," you said.

There are many good memories. Just lying about on Dad's side of the bed after his death, hearing your stories, pretending I was hearing them for the first time though I knew every word you were going to say, what the climax of the story was, where your voice would modulate and how, where the pitch would change, the expression on your face when you came to a particular point in the story. How often you prefaced your stories with, "I have to tell you something that is very, very important," or, "Did I tell you about the time . . . ?" And I would say, "No," because I knew your stories were so important to you, you had to tell and retell them. Our own stories are of infinite interest to us, for we have inhabited them and continue to do so in our memories. How often I found you, sitting cross-legged on your bed, happily telling your hundred-times-told tales to anyone who would listen, usually me, the cook, the maid, the gardener, or the driver, who sat on the carpet beside your bed.

How often you woke me as I slept on hot summer afternoons on Dad's side of your double bed after he was gone, saying, like a girl, conspiratorially: "Let's eat fruit!" We would cut up mangoes, melon, pears, apples, whatever was in season, peel lychees, and sit on the bed that had become your home in old age, eating and gossiping like girls, you repeating your stories over and over so that they are etched in me till forever lasts.

As you aged, we got closer. You let me hold you, let me put my hand on your flabby belly. "My Mama," I would say, caressing your head, "My Mama." My hugs were never returned. Perhaps our relationship set the tone for my female relationships. I give more than I receive. There is some hurt in this, but because I do not like to stay with hurt I think, "It is my karma to be a *data*, a giver." As Dad taught me, giving is its own receiving. In accepting my hugs, Mummy, you gave me a gift. And toward the end of your life, you returned my touch. It was no more than a finger on my hand, or your hand on my leg as we sat on the sofa together, but it was enough.

Your body, except your belly, was collagen rich, like mine, and firm even into your nineties. Up until your stroke, when your life as you lived it went all to hell, you bathed daily, took great care of your hygiene, brushed your teeth manually for twenty minutes each morning as you sat on your stool by the sink. You died at ninety-three with most of your teeth, though some front ones had begun to crumble.

Strong-willed Dragon Lady, you were not touchy-feely but independent, very defended. "Even my mother didn't know how to love," I can hear you say. You were sometimes such a terror and a tyrant. Whenever I came to visit you, I couldn't do much of anything else. Visits to Mishi and her family were interrupted repeatedly by calls from you: "You're gone too long!" Even if I went while you were asleep, I had to be there when you awoke. What a hard time you gave me for my messy room, my inordinate love for my niece-in-law and her children. You were jealous of them. I indulged you, Mother, most of the time, though I took what I needed of time to have fun. And I was very upset with you for projecting the family shadow onto Mishi. You disowned her because she rebelled against your controlling nature. Nobody could question anything you said or did. Not even Dad. You disliked criticism of any kind. You were so fortified that any questioning threatened your defenses.

I see your faults, and they do not keep me from loving you. Daddy told me that when I was an infant, you would kiss me by sticking your tongue into my mouth. Ah, there was love there! A love beyond conflict and conditions. And there was that time I called you from America and said, "I love you, Mummy." There was silence on the other end. "Do you love me?" I asked. It took another silence before you said in that deep emotional voice of yours, "I love you very, very much."

Let me celebrate you today, Mummy. I will stay with love, the Arch

Healer. "Love," as Rumi says, "is the physician of all our ills." I will become my own hakim, reclaim my spring.

Flowers. You loved them, loved your garden, loved it when people stopped before the house to admire it and take pictures. Your garden was your work of art. Fall was the time for planting for spring, and the driver drove you to every nursery in town so you could collect your treasures. How happy I am to remember that on a strong impulse I went to the nursery a few days before you fell and went into a coma. I bought a jeep-load of flowers in pots. It was fall and the gardener was planting seedlings in the flower beds. I thought, "She shouldn't have to wait four months for flowers." How happy they made you! The next morning you awoke, excited as a girl, and said to me, taking my hand, "Take me to the verandah, I want to see my flowers!" They were your final experience of beauty.

Our umbilicus, though severed, is existent still. Like two neutrinos, though galaxies apart, move to each other's movements, we resonate to each other wherever we are. We are quantum entangled.

And, Mummy, we *will* meet again. It is one of my most joyous fantasies.

19
Loving Myself

"*Energy* is eternal delight," wrote William Blake. Today I do all those blessed things for which I have had little energy. I turn on some music, invariably classical kirtan (Sikh devotional music) in ragas, and the heater in the bathroom, take a long, slow shower, and shampoo and condition my hair. I had not realized in my younger days how tiring showers are. I never thought about towels. A towel was a towel was a towel. Now I am thinking of something soft as well as absorbent for my drying, thinning skin. I will look for it on line where I do all my shopping now. The body must be pampered in every way. It is nearing the end of its days and deserves utter protection, kindness, and gratitude.

I sit naked on the olive wood bench, bought a few years ago in preparation for old age. Looking in the mirror I recall a dream fragment: I am looking at my face, which is also someone else's face. I see the sockets beneath her eyes into which her skin has sunk. I trace the contours of her face with my hands, then kiss my fingers. I was the other, whom I loved.

I plug in the small rice cooker in which I keep my concoction of oils: coconut, lavender, lemon, hemp, hibiscus, walnut, almond, and aloe. It gives me relief from occasional itching. It moistens my dry skin, which drinks it in and absorbs it. I am full of regret as I rub myself down with oil. Why didn't I make it for you, Mummy, you who were plagued by itches, rashes, and boils toward the end of your life? Neither of us realized they were allergies. You thought something was biting you, perhaps mosquitos from your neighbor's vines. In your dotage you projected everything that went wrong in your life on neighbors. It was somehow all their fault.

How many times I offered to oil you down, Mummy. You stubbornly refused. I could never get you to do what you didn't want to do. It frustrated me that your mind was so closed, that you thought about things—"the clothes, the sheets, the bedcover, the chair will get stained"—rather than your body, your skin, your comfort. I wear clothes that can take stains: socks, underwear, undershirts, mainly black, that have interacted with a lot of oil and show no signs of it.

Mummy, I would have loved to nurture you in so many ways. You asked me many times in an urgent voice, "Bathe me when I am dead; powder and perfume my body, clothe me in the yellow, printed silk suit your Daddy liked on me. Promise!"

I failed you, Mother. You were cremated the day before I arrived in India. Nobody bathed and dressed you before putting you in the oven. My brother and his family were in charge of the arrangements, and nobody bothered. They were happy to see you go after your long ordeal in a coma; now my brother thought he would finally get the house and the rest of the property he felt entitled to by virtue of being male. When I landed in India the day after your cremation, none of that side of the family was happy to see me at a religious ceremony for you. The nieces I had loved so much did not greet me, looked through me as if I weren't even there. I was the troublemaker who would ensure the house be equally divided among the siblings. What a long court battle, what a heartache it has been! I established domicile on the floor on which you lived, Mother, while the battle is still being fought. How much solace it has given me to stay in what I continue to call your house, with all your furniture, rugs, lamps, items that you loved so much that once in your dotage you asked if you could take your garden, your house, and everything in it, especially your shawls, with you, or put them in storage to return to in your next life.

"Mummy, remember Duni Chand?" I asked you.

"Of course I know who he is. Who was he?"

"About the golden needle that Guru Nanak found?"

You looked blank, so I told you the story of the Golden Needle, first published in my book *Into the Great Heart*, which you told me when I was a child, embellishing it as I went along to make it relevant for you. You listened wide-eyed, like a child.

In his travels Nanak met Duni Chand, a rich merchant. Duni Chand's wife, Savitri, was the source of his wealth. She did exquisite embroidery on shawls in purples, violets, blues, and indigo, embroidery so fine you couldn't tell the front side from the back. She used well-crafted gold needles and silk threads on the finest of woven pashminas and shahtoosh, not a stitch out of place, everything part of the design so beautiful you couldn't take your eyes off it. From small beginnings, embroidering her own clothes that received a lot of envy and praise, she expanded to employ a hundred embroiderers from Kashmir in her factory.

Her customers were the royalty of the country and rich merchants and businessmen who could afford excellent quality and high prices. Their home was a luxurious palace surrounded by Moghul gardens that Savitri had personally designed with the help of the best architects and renowned gardeners. It boasted fountains, miniature rivers of paradise, geometric designs, flowering bushes and trees with different colored flowers, and trellises upon trellises of roses, mulberries, and fruit trees.

When Nanak arrived at their gate, Duni Chand received him

wearing cream-colored silk that rippled and shone in the light, and one of his wife's pashmina shawls, embroidered all over in intricate patterns of paisley with the loveliest of colors.

Duni Chand gave Nanak a tour of his home, gardens, and stables, enthusiastically showing off his Kabuli horses and European buggies made of silver. He loved his home, his garden, and his clothes. On the way to the building that housed the embroiderers, Nanak stooped and picked up something from the dirt. It was a needle made of gold. It caught a beam of light and shone brilliantly.

"This is Savitri's favorite needle! She has been looking for it everywhere! She will be so happy to get this back." Duni Chand exclaimed, eagerly reaching for it.

Duni Chand was about to run back to the house to tell Savitri about the happy recovery of her needle when he stopped and said, reluctantly, "But Guru Ji, since you found it, keep it. My wife has others, I know, because I got some more made from the goldsmith and she loves them."

"I don't want it," Nanak said.

"I insist," Duni Chand said magnanimously.

"Alright," said Nanak. "But keep it for me for the time being. I will take it from you in the afterlife."

Comforted by the thought that Nanak had confirmed his own desire for an afterlife that was a continuation of this one, Duni Chand took it and pinned it to his shawl for safekeeping. Later that evening, Nanak was about to retire for the night when Duni Chand returned, accompanied by his wife, Savitri.

"Thank you, thank you," she said, falling at Nanak's feet and kissing them. "Thank you for opening my sewn-shut eyes," she said.

Duni Chand explained in a confused sort of way, "I took the needle to her and explained how you had found it and how I had offered it to you and you had said, 'I will take it from you in the afterlife.' Her jaw dropped, her eyes grew wide, and she sat totally still for a while. 'What's the matter with you?' I asked her, and she cried, 'You fool! You fool! Don't you understand that we cannot take anything with us? Not even a needle? There are no pockets in shrouds, nor in our bodies?'

"'I'm not a fool,' I replied. 'I know that.'

"'No, you don't!' she cried, casting away the shawl she was embroidering, and ran to you."

"You're a wise, enlightened man," Duni Chand continued. "Guru ji, please show us a way so we never have to part with our wealth. Look at all these expensive things I love so much! If I put them in storage before I die, could you ensure that when I reincarnate I can have them back?"

"You can take untold riches into your next life, but not these baubles," Nanak replied.

Duni Chand fell at his feet and prayed to know how his wealth might accompany him. Nanak answered, "Give some of it away, feed the poor, nurture the sick and the feeble, and that portion shall accompany you as light."

"Guru ji," Savitri said, "Give us your understanding and wisdom. Teach us how we may live well in this life and in the next."

Nanak took out his rabab (stringed instrument) and sang two songs: "Ka<u>dh</u> kasee<u>d</u>aa pahirahi cholee <u>t</u>aa^N <u>t</u>um^H jaa<u>n</u>hu naaree" (She alone is known as the Lord's bride who embroiders her gown with the name). The other translates to, "If a woman becomes virtuous and turns her heart into a thread, the Beloved will string himself on it like a priceless gem."

You knew the words, Mother, and sang them in your deep, throaty, off-key voice. The story must have gotten through to you. Shortly after, you began to distribute your jewelry. After you had given away good pieces to my sister and sister-in-law, I got the jewelry that was your favorite, the one I insisted you wear till the very end because I was in no hurry to get it.

Now I have to remember the lesson you learned: become less attached to my things. But oh how I love your shawls and the jewelry you wore! I am not ready to give any of it away. It is a good sign. They ballast me to life.

Where was I in my story before another story intervened? Toilette. Oiling myself. I resolve I shall not wait to have my body oiled and perfumed till after I am gone. I will nurture and anoint my vessel while it is still quick.

Starting from my feet I oil every inch of my skin with warm gobs of oil. My skin glows a rich walnut brown. I recall my paternal grandmother oiled her body with ghee, and plan to add that to the mixture.

It becomes clear to me as I look in the mirror that I am at once alive and dying like a manzanita tree, part dead bark, part live limb. My body has the brittleness of age. I see the crinkled skin web that contains the universe that is me. My face looks thin. I have lost weight. I am pleased.

My hands that have labored greatly in many fields are worn by countless movements in the service of life and living, giving and receiving. Rarely manicured, earth-colored brown knuckles whorled with folds of skin, they are the much-used hands of an old woman, adorned with diamond and ruby rings. The backs of my hands are wrinkled with crisscrossing lines forming stars in some conjunctions, with rivulets of veins, varied in size, shape, texture, some fat, like worms through skin tunnels.

They've served me very well, cooked for and fed me, played the synthesizer to bring music into my life, made jewelry to adorn my body, drummed sense into my life by beating on the keyboard of the computer, taken me on so many journeys into the world the internet has opened up to me, and countless other things. I'm glad to have my old-woman hands, quite written upon by destiny, move and work still. I honor them on the cusp of their extinction. So many little things are breaking down in them and elsewhere—arthritis in some knuckles, knees, sacrum, neck, wrists. They, too, are destined to burn as I burn, sans rings, unclutching everything, who knows where, in which oven or open fire? On which continent, country, or in-between?

I look at my fingers with their horny nails with soft, thin, whitish cuticles encroaching at the base. These wrinkled things have worked for me all my life and will, if all stays well, for a while more. I have not stopped to thank them for all they do for me. I must take a break from typing to say truly and mindfully, "Thank you." I do. They thank me in return for giving them life.

Even though I know all parts of me are one, a whole, it's love-promoting to see and appreciate them as separate, life-giving entities, as all our body systems are. Is that how the whole God thing works, too? How foolish we are with our separations: divinity from human-ity, humanity from nature, freedom from bondage. Everything is one seamless, border-free skin, Indra's net* with silken strands, each point reflecting every other point. We are all part of the web; connected. We forget this oneness because there is something sweet about separation. Gods in Hindu mythology leave the soup of Oneness and descend into individuality and separation to experience its sweetness and terror.

After oiling my fingers, each one individually, including the nails, I apply balm to my aches. A generous dab on the left side of my sacrum, on the tendon of my left arm, on the right knee. Who knows whether it works or not? But there is something very self- and body-loving in tend-ing to my aching parts. It is a message to them to say, "I am listening. I care. You are my mount, my house, my mare, my vehicle, my infant."

I am not only in touch with my "inner child," as they say, but with my inner infant. I have to be both infant and mother at the same time. I travel through my days with my invisible infant who takes on differ-

---

*Indra's net is a Hindu myth that symbolizes an infinite web of interconnectedness. At each crossing of threads in the net there is said to be a perfectly clear gem that reflects all the other gems in the net.

ent forms, my own and sometimes that of another. Lately I see her as a tiny African American infant with curly hair, cute as a button, the one I saw in a show called *Babies*. I watched it to get a hit of oxytocin, the "love and cuddle hormone" secreted by a pea-sized structure at the base of my brain. She morphed from being a few days old to three years old in a day. How real this nonreal companionship and mutual nurturing! How comforting to have the invisible imagined right here in my arms in my aging, solitary cocoon.

I cream my face, make a French braid, put on earrings I made from amethyst and peridot (light ones, getting lighter), define my eyes with kohl, apply lipstick, put in my hearing aids so I can hear the birds twittering on the fig tree outside. I dress up for Payson and that person in the mirror I am learning to love more and more each day. P always notices when I am wearing something nice or new, and compliments me on my jewelry. I let each activity take its due of time. It is the closest I can get to timelessness.

Age has many advantages and on top of my list is precisely this: meandering, puttering; having time to listen to the needs of my body-mind-soul; sitting silently in the dead center of my life; choosing willingly, with open arms, accepting and surrendering to whatever internal or external circumstances I encounter in my revolution; and loving myself throughout it all. This is my hope. This, my prayer.

20

Sending Daddy to the Milky Way

*Y*our ghost visited me, Daddy, in yet another recurring nightmare. I am at a conference with colleagues and acquaintances. I recall with a jolt in the middle of giving a speech that I have not visited you in the hospital for years. You have been waiting for me to come. I must sit by you, hold your hand, tell you, "I am here, Dad, I am here." After hellish attempts to get to you, airplanes, busses I miss repeatedly, I arrive at the hospital and am told by nurses in hazmat suits that family is not allowed to visit. I try to claw my way in, screaming and shouting, "I *must* see him, I must. You don't understand. He is waiting for me! He is all alone!" But they bundle me off to a waiting room. Your sister walks in, looking sad, and says, "He is dead."

Propelled out of sleep by the thudding word, *dead*, I lay on my back in some nameless dimension between dream and waking; here, not here, my body like stone, unmoving like the ancient dead, my heart convulsing in the stone sarcophagi I have become, entirely alive in my death to the terror and regret that has no name and cannot be described, unable to move, to speak, even if there were someone here. Payson was up and doing his thing downstairs. Then, unexpectedly, I heard his steps on the carpeted stairs. He is so attuned to my needs in that soundless, wordless plasma we share that whenever I need him most, he is there.

"I had a nightmare," I said, almost inaudibly. He got into his side of the bed, put his hand on my chest and rubbed gently. Though he asked me several times to tell him my dream, I couldn't. The experience of the dream—yes, dreams are experiences no less than our waking life—had swallowed all expression. Haltingly, reluctantly, repetitively I whispered, "I am somewhere," and after a long hiatus, "I am somewhere." Words, as they tumbled out, broke the spell, the coffin cracked, the dream story poured out of me. When I came to the words "He is dead," the sobbing began, arising from somewhere deep below my navel, heaving and pulsing up my body and through my throat.

You died thirteen years ago today, Daddy. The heart knows no time. The painful and pleasurable past, future hopes and fears, all co-exist here, jumbled and inextricable.

My nightmare is rooted in my most active regret. It has taken me thirteen years to articulate it, to give the gnarled feeling a name: shame.

For months before you died you asked me to come to you. Months? Weeks? I forget how long. Perhaps it was just that once; but shouldn't once have been enough? I was in the United States, in the thick of unaccustomed publicity for *Ganesha Goes to Lunch*. "Come, I know how my body is feeling," you said. On your eighty-eighth birthday, twenty-three days before your death, you distributed *ladoos*, sweet, syrupy yellow balls made of chickpea flour, to all your employees. You said to me on the phone, "It is my last birthday." During our last visit with you, you said to Payson, with whom you would have long walks and conversations, "I am getting ready for the big jump."

I did not see the signs. I was blinded by my ego, my ambition. I did not come to you, you who made me everything I am, who loved me unconditionally, always encouraged me to be independent of you, to experience to the fullest my own life, my own way. Though your heartstrings were tied to mine you left me free, sent me to America, let me marry whom I liked, let me break every rule you expected me not to break as a good Sikh girl, and continued to love me.

I spent large chunks of time away from home. At twelve I wanted to attend the best boarding school for girls in India, even though you couldn't easily afford it. I recall sitting on the steps of the admissions office with my suitcase on the day you left me there, crying my eyes out. And you, Dad, hugged me and laughed, though you had tears in your eyes, too, "But you wanted this!"

My college life, too, was spent away from home in a dormitory in boarding school. You let me go to a university in America when the possibility arose, even though you had just retired and didn't have the funds for the looming responsibility of building a house and weddings of your three children. It was radical for a father to give his daughter her dowry money to get an education.

I always looked forward to coming home for the holidays. The thrill at seeing you and Mummy was a physical sensation, a spasm in the region of my heart. I felt it each time I landed home from wherever I was, school, college, the States. For how many years, Dad, you made the journey from Chandigarh to the airport in Delhi to welcome me home from America. And when you grew feebler, you sent the driver with a cooler full of drinks and fruit, and always a letter that began, "Welcome home!" You arranged for the food and drinks, not Mummy. After a lifetime of taking care of others she was taking care of her own needs to be free of domestic chores. And I didn't mind, but often, when my own need for love from her bumped up against who she had become, I accused her of not loving me.

You longed for my visits, too, Daddy. That time I landed in India, walked into the house, excited about surprising you, and was amazed at your reaction. You were angry at me, refused my hugs because I had deprived you of the pleasure of anticipating my visit.

Remembering you today, I see your six-foot frame slumping a little as you aged—you always had exemplary posture—sitting on the stool upholstered in maroon tapestry before the mirror of the dressing table, the one you shared with Mummy. On one side of the table lay her lipsticks, hairpins, perfume, combs, and brushes, neatly arranged; and on the other, also neatly arranged, your brush and comb with which you combed your long, curly hair and beard that remained thick even after it turned gray. I see also your bottle of hair fixer with which you dressed your unruly beard, a long silver stick shaped somewhat like the sticks women use to apply kohl to their eyes, for tucking your beard, a small container with headpins for your turban, and finally your *thathaas*, two long ribbons of cloth you used to fix your beard and moustache in place with the hair gel.

I see you in your white *katcha*, the long, loose underwear most Sikh men wear, bare-chested in summer except for the blue strap of your *kirpan*, a small sword.

You were a Sikh through and through, following your guru's instructions in the way you dressed and lived. Guru Gobind Singh, the tenth guru of the Sikhs, enjoined his warriors in the Sikh initiation ceremony during the spring harvest festival, *Baisakhi*, in 1699 to wear the "five Ks," *kesh, kutcha, kanga, kadaa,* and *kirpan*. These were mandatory articles for men to live and sleep in so they would be prepared for battle with the Moghul* forces at all times. They were to keep their hair kesh, uncut and natural; wear knee-length underwear, kutcha; a small wooden comb, an article of toiletry tucked into the top knot for grooming even on the battleground, a kanga; an iron bracelet, kadaa, a wedding ring to God, which could also serve as a weapon in hand-to-hand combat; and a small sword, the kirpan, worn on a holster across the body.

You twisted your beard into a roll, wrapping it in black thread to braid it, tucking the end of it into the pocket of hair under your chin.

---

*Members of the Muslim dynasty of Mongol origin founded by the successors of Tamerlane, which ruled India from the sixteenth to the nineteenth century.

You combed and brushed your long, curly hair, tied it into a knot, a *joodaa*, on top of your head, and affixed the small wooden comb at its base. Then you began on the turban, a six-yard-long piece of muslin which a servant, or sometimes Mummy or I, held one end of while you rolled it into layers. Fold by fold you tied it on your head, tucking in and fixing the loose ends above your forehead and neck with headpins. When you were done, not a hair was out of place.

Your grooming was evidence of a deep self-respect and a bit of vanity. You knew you were good looking, *a puer aeturnus*, or eternal boy, elegantly dressed, youthful till shortly before you died. You were attracted to other women but never acted on it. I know you were attracted to Mom's Nepali maid. She really was lovely in all ways. And she had, we later learned, slept with her last employer when his wife was away in order to wangle a job for her husband. You would not have. I know because you said to me once: "Do you know, I have never slept with any woman except your Mummy?"

You were very handsome, and knew it, too. I often saw a pleased look in your eye when you looked at yourself in the mirror. When you came to visit me in the girls-only college, the guard outside the gate of the compound often would not let you in because you looked too young to be the daddy of a college-aged girl. He once accused you of being a boyfriend pretending to be a father.

On Sundays you washed your hair and beard, and while it dried you turned into a wild, gray-haired sadhu, the kind I have seen living in caves in remote regions of the Himalayas. I loved the wild you. You were so contained and controlled most of the time. Your craziest with me was coming home one day after your retirement and saying, "Let's get drunk!" It was out of character and endeared you to me. You had promised your guru not to drink, though I have known you to break that rule a few times.

Did we get drunk? We should have. I so enjoyed the only time you, Payson, and I drank sweet *Crema de Membrillo* liqueur together in

1997, when you came to America to visit me in the house I had bought with Donald and to check out P, whom I was dating seriously. We sat around the small dining table after dinner, drinking, sharing, and talking. When P asked you if you were okay with your daughter marrying an American and living in America, you spread your arms wide, and said, "The world is ours!"

Payson and I looked at our photo albums and I found one of you and me, Dad. We are on Torrey Pines beach facing the ocean, you in a white shirt with your black pants rolled up above the knees of your tall, lithe figure, your seventy-eight-year-old face youthful despite a graying beard. I am in a colorful bathing suit and tan shorts. Your right hand and forearm are cupping my face; my right arm is around your waist. We are holding each other close against sienna sand cliffs, our faces glowing in the warm yellow light of the setting sun.

I put it in a large wooden frame together with Mummy's photo, she dressed in a silk *salwaar kameez*, her silver hair in a bun, leaning back on a sofa, laughing with her whole being. I don't have any pictures of Mummy and me hugging and close, though there is one of her, Mishi, and me with our arms around each other's waists. I frame and display that, too. As I put the framed photo of Dad and me on the beach on the windowsill of my desk, Payson climbed down the stairs into my *zenana*[*] and said, "There's something very Oedipal about this picture of Daddy Ji and you. Or Electra or whatever."

Freud articulated what we have always known but fail to admit, even to ourselves, so taboo it is. The male child is prepared for his relationship with a mate by his mother, and the female child by her relationship to her daddy. When I was a girl, I wanted to marry my Daddy, as do many other little girls. Sexuality is involved in these cross-gender dynamics. Freud called these the "Oedipal and Electra complexes."

Freud drew on two ancient Greek myths from fifth century BCE to

---

[*]A room or section of the house for women only.

name these complexes. In Sophocles's play, *Oedipus the King*, or *Oedipus Rex*, Oedipus unknowingly kills his father and marries his mother; in Aeschylus's trilogy, *The Oresteia*, the roles are reversed. Electra kills her mother, who has killed the father she adored. These plays are tragedies because the essential dynamic between children and parents of the opposite sex has not been brought to consciousness by the characters.

It has taken me a while to fully acknowledge this dynamic in my own life. As a child I slept in your bed with you, Daddy, whenever you let me. On days I was not allowed to, I sleepwalked to your side of the bed and looked at you with my eyes wide open as you lay by my mother's side.

I stopped sleeping with you after I got my period and my breasts began to bud. My body recoiled from the closeness. But once, when I lived alone in New Delhi in my late twenties, we slept together again.

I was in emotional trouble. My apartment-mate had stolen my boyfriend. I had been sitting alone in my room, drinking and smoking. The doorbell rang and there you were, Daddy, unexpected, standing tall, slim, handsome, clean looking, the kind of clean that comes from wholesome living and thinking. I reeked of tobacco and booze and had cut my hair, yet again, even after it hurt you so much when I cut it the first time. Any other bourgeois Sikh father would have slapped his daughter around. But you were too real, too genuine, too gentle to be patriarchal.

You said nothing, just went into the kitchen and drank some water. You sensed I was in trouble. You stayed the night, slept with me on the queen-sized mattress on the floor, just a bit smaller than the room itself. I awoke in the middle of the night to find we were hugging each other as we had hugged when I was a child, chest to chest, heartbeat close. I must have turned to you in my sleep, seeking comfort.

Today I think of the song written by Cole Porter, sung by Marilyn Monroe: "My heart belongs to Daddy . . . 'Cause my Daddy, he treats it so well." You have been the male model in my relationships, too. I have wanted, after chasing romantic *fata morganas*, responsible, practical, loving, sympathetic, supportive men with a strong spiritual bent.

When I was in Mummy's belly you prayed to have a child like me, a warrior with spiritual leanings, generosity of spirit, and grounding in the Sikh faith. I did not follow the precepts of Sikhism, broke all the rules, cut my hair, smoked tobacco in my youth. I am, however, a Sikh in spirit. I have never been attracted to the institutional side of religion. I follow Guru Nanak in this: I have no more religion than wind and fire. I follow Guru Gobind Singh when he says in his *Dasam Granth* that God is beyond religion, though manifest in all of them.

I learned to self-examine, to dive deep, from you, Daddy. As a child I recall reading and remembering a sentence you had underlined in *Reader's Digest*, something like: Don't scold a child for breaking a cup. What is more important? The cup or the child? Sometimes a simple sentence can change your life if you have a receptor for it in your heart. "Don't focus on the thing; focus on the person."

And then there are events and character traits that act as precepts. You were teaching me to drive when I was a teenager. Turning a corner too fast, I plowed into the back of a bullock cart, smashing the front of your new car. No one was hurt. You paid the owner of the bullock cart a generous sum for damage to his cart. I sat in the driver's seat feeling paralyzed, unable to drive. I asked you to take over, but you refused. "Be grateful for the lesson learned, and carry on. If you get too fearful now, you will never drive again," you said.

Pushing through my fears and lack of self-confidence has been my ongoing struggle.

I also learned a great deal about how to treat people that day I bought you shoes for Father's Day. The salesman paid us no attention, and when he finally attended to us, he wasn't listening, kept getting the wrong size and color shoe. It was a hot day in June and tempers were running high. You blew up at the salesman. He paid attention. We bought what we needed and came home.

But you were restless all day. You told Mom how you had yelled at the salesman. The next day you went back to the store, apologized to him for hurting him with your anger, and hugged him.

You were a true Sikh, Dad, knowing and practicing the Sikh precept, in class and caste-bound India, that God exists in all.

Mummy didn't self-examine. Far from it. She was too defended to ever ask, "Have I erred?" She simply was the queen bee whom everyone had to serve and obey. Hadn't she done it in her own time, served and obeyed? She wanted none of it. She went wrong in going a little too much the other way into dominance. When it comes to balance, very few of us get it right. I do not fault her. I fault the system that did not allow her an education. Not that education ever makes us self-reflective. In fact, education is no guarantee against ignorance. Nor is lack of education a hindrance to spiritual and worldly success. You used to laugh, "I failed high school!" Your riches to rags story, the dire circumstance in your childhood home, a widowed mother of three children and a stepchild eking out a living by teaching in the town schools, too many mouths to feed, made you drop out of school and run away from home at age fifteen to join the Boy's Company in the engineer corps of the army. You were largely self-taught. You taught yourself to write by reading a lot. You became good at it. After you retired from the army you wrote articles and essays that were published in well-known journals and newspapers.

Hardworking, responsible, with a lot of integrity, you were soon spotted by a British colonel who sent you to training school for officers in Dehra Dun. From then on your fortunes rose, and you achieved the once glorious wealth of your father.

When I think of you, I pair you with Mummy. I think of you together. In the nine years she survived after your death, she would frequently cry like a child, "Where did you go?" It reminded me of the developmentally challenged gown-up son of a neighbor who would stand in my driveway for weeks after Donald's suicide and cry in his twisted, thick voice, distorted by his disability into an anguished howl: "Why? Why?"

Have I not marveled at this sudden disappearance of people I knew so well? What does it mean, to die? Where do they go? Sudden disappearance from our material, sense-bound world—and all disappearances, even when expected, are sudden—has a bit of mystery and magic to it. Here today, gone forever tomorrow. Forever? No, I know from your reappearance in dream that you return. As Groucho Marx said, "Gone today, here tomorrow."

I pray in your next life you and Mummy are together again. It is what Mummy longed to have happen. "I will eat dried bread, become a beggar without a roof to be with you." She frequently addressed you. I unite both of you within me. Both of you, together, make my life cohere.

As I begin to wrap up this journal essay, I have a dream about you. I see you in the next room in a house I don't recognize. You are interacting with your son. I am a little hurt that you are not engaging with me, and just as I am about to walk away, you come to me. You are hurt because I am not engaging with you. You are looking very unlike I remember you. Even that time in the hospital you wore your clean white pajamas, your hair tied neatly in a *patka*. You did not look like an old man. In the dream you were rumpled, your gray hair askew, your shorts ragged and dirty with holes in them.

Who knows what it means? I interpret the dream thus: You had always wanted me to be a writer. Once, sitting on a chair looking dejected after a fight with Mom, your body sunk into itself, you cheered up suddenly and your eyes sparkled with light as you said, "Perhaps God has made us characters so you can write about us?" And I did, in many of my books.

The hole in your shorts in this dream was saying "You have not written about the rents in our relationship." You would want me to be more honest as a writer, Daddy. Yes, we had fights, arguments about God and Sikhism, and once when the whole family was sitting at the table I said something you didn't like and you shouted at me, something about cutting my hair. I was silent. You so rarely got angry that I was amazed and pleased at your anger. How beautiful it made you look, your beard fluffed out, full, wild, like a lion in a rage.

Cutting my hair—the ultimate Sikh apostasy. How often we argued about my defection from the fold. Once after an argument I boarded a bus to Delhi, where I lived and taught. A short time later you told the driver to drive you to the bus stand so you could hug me and tell me everything was okay, but my bus had departed. "He looked very upset," the driver told me later. You never brought up hair again. Think about the child, not the hair.

You would also get on my nerves because you were quite feudal about expecting your wife to take care of the kitchen, though as you grew older you would make tea in the mornings and bring it to Mom in bed. You always made *karaah prasad*, halwa made of semolina or flour, sugar, and ghee, on holy days, on the birthdays of gurus, and on our birthdays. But most of all you got on my nerves for being weak with Mom, letting her get away with verbal abuse. She never forgave you for not running interference in your mother's domineering ways when you were newly married. And you, feeling responsible for it, knowing she was right, absorbed it all. This self-knowledge of your own mistake, for which you never forgave yourself, made you weak in the relationship.

Even Mom disliked your weakness. If you told her something you felt ashamed of or hurt about, some slight or feelings of inferiority or depression, she judged you for it. You were being vulnerable, something she never allowed herself to be. She never let you unburden yourself with her. She couldn't just listen, couldn't communicate because her ego was so fragile and defended it could not take any words that sounded like criticism. Above all she hated any weakness in you because she herself had done everything she could to mask her own. Except that time after your death when all her insecurities came pouring out. In some context she screamed from the depths, where all insecurities reside: "I'm not pretty, I'm not educated, I'm not rich!"

I hugged you to my heart, Mummy, and let you sob out your feelings. I tried to make up for the education part and my destiny helped me to pursue it till it failed to serve me, right before my Ph.D.—a sore point with you, Daddy. Still, I heard you boast to some, "My daughter has a Ph.D.!" I didn't correct you. I had to fail your dream to pursue my passion for writing, something you also desired for me. The higher goal was realized so I have no regrets on that score.

I have other insecurities, however. There was always some social shame that my mother did not speak English very well, that my family was not as educated as other families I knew. My dark skin, too, has often made me feel unbeautiful in the past, and sometimes still does. I have allowed myself to be a victim of the norm, ingrained in us for centuries. It has been my work to experience and look at the world from the inside out, to self-affirm my own beauty.

I have strayed far in my memories of you, Daddy. How intermingled everything is! Teasing it apart is one of the greatest challenges of writing. But after much combing though, some tangle from the heart must remain for the story to be true.

I have been in bed all morning reminiscing, allowing myself to mourn your disappearance from the many layers of my life, Daddy. The Lakota Indians performed ceremonies to welcome life and send their dead to the heart of the Milky Way. I, tribeless, have no ceremony to send you on your journey. The umbilicus of undying regrets ties me to you.

But as I get out of bed and go about my day, I hear your voice in my head saying conspiratorially, as you often did: *"Chalo, cha peeyai,"* or, Come on, let's have chai. You loved your chai in the mornings, sitting up in bed together with Mummy, dipping biscuits into it, talking. I will celebrate you, your presence in my heart with chai and a shot of Membrillo quince liqueur today. It is time, having waded through the scalding waters of regret, to forgive myself my lapses and stay with the love. Oh, there was plenty of that!

I smash some ginger, cardamom pods, cloves, cinnamon, and peppercorns in the mortar, boil the spices in water for at least ten minutes, add tea leaves, boil them a bit, add some fresh cream and a generous gob of honey: just the way you liked your chai, creamy, smooth, sweet, strong. My delicate stomach will punish me for it, I know. I make some halwa, too, which you loved, only it is oatmeal with nuts and maple syrup. We will eat together today. You will eat through my mouth, and we will have ourselves a party. Afterward, I will send you off to the center of the Milky Way where you live with Mummy and from where you both come, riding a beam of light into my heart.

21

I Am a Many-Patterned Kaleidoscope

An old recurring pattern, with permutations, is playing out again in the kaleidoscopic configurations I am, the battle between my child and writer. Payson is leaving for New York for two weeks to spend time with his brother, Larry, who is in serious cognitive decline. My inner child has been whiny and afraid of being alone. P and I have grown accustomed to each other. My solitude is not disturbed by his presence, but somehow deepened by it. He is an artist and loves his own. We are the marriage of two solitudes. This is not always true but holds as a bold generalization.

I project a fantasized loneliness on the days ahead, have ridiculous forebodings of dying in his absence, having a stroke the way Mom did. Payson would return and find me lying desiccated and stinking on the bathroom floor. To control my anxiety I make a long list to keep myself busy in his absence: who to call when I grow desperate for connection, tasks I can occupy myself with, shelves and drawers I can clean out, things I can go out and buy.

Though I have thought of accompanying him to New York, I don't want to go for several reasons. For starters, it's cold in New York. I spent weeks during three brutal winters on a writing commission with the New School and do not want to subject myself to it again. But it's mostly because I don't want to become like the woman I met at a dinner party who was still devasted from her husband's death several years earlier. "Utterly lost, don't know what to do with myself," she had repeated. My compassion for the woman was mixed in equal parts with an unvoiced reprimand: "How can you give yourself away so entirely? Why didn't you keep a part of yourself for yourself?"

I believe it is incumbent upon us to be our own people in marriages. When my inner child is in the wings, I am guilty of the opposite pole: I want to keep a large part of myself for myself alone. This probably lends some truth to P's accusations during our fights that I am selfish. It is true, he is far more giving of himself to the people in his life than I am. I am jealous, above all, of my time, my space, and now of that precious, precious thing, energy, which I defend rabidly. What some writers crave most—and everyone does to varying degrees—is undisturbed solitude. I sacrificed life as others know it, severed ties to parents, siblings, clan, religion, country for this passion. My cells knew my true needs and spontaneously aborted two fetuses—one, ironically, on Mother's Day many decades ago—and hence neither of my pregnancies, somewhat desired by my biological clock, came to term.

My writer has always wanted solitude in her unconscious and conscious choices. I knew I didn't want a traditional arranged marriage or a life in a large joint family, or even a nuclear family with too many children and house guests. I didn't want to deal with a mother-in-law's expectations of a good daughter-in-law, or a father-in-law telling me what I should think, and what I should and shouldn't write. It seemed to me like a version of hell: to not be able to call your time or space your own. I have been a hermit all my life, except for those rare phases where I have felt isolated and sought out friends. I don't like to go out for concerts and late dinners because they interfere with my sleep and digestion. The ambit of my life is decreasing as I age, and I am glad of it. I accept and welcome my arc toward more and more innerness.

When I am alone I am compelled to write more, fall back on my own resources to keep sane. Aloneness produces a sort of desperation and an angst that is cured by writing. Misery makes us produce. Writer George Eliot wrote in a letter to a friend: "Every day's experience seems to deepen the voice of foreboding that has long been telling me, The bliss of reciprocated affection is not allotted to you under any form. Your heart must be widowed in this manner from the world, or you will never seek a better portion; a consciousness of possessing the fervent love of any human being would soon become your heaven, therefore it would be your curse." Though I am widowed from the world, I am not that strong and brave. I prefer a partner in my solitude.

Not going to New York is part of my preparation in the event Payson dies before I do. I must catch up with myself. Who am I when I am not in a relationship, when I am physically alone? Future scenarios of each other's loss have begun to enter our thoughts. The psyche prepares us for eventualities so we can plan, strategize, not be caught unawares.

I sometimes hope I die first. I don't want to go through the harrowing suffering I went through after Donald's death; I don't want to miss P dreadfully, which I know I will. We are like each other's limbs. Death is also a lot of work for those left behind, and I don't have energy to deal with it.

If Payson predeceases me, I have images of living like an eccentric hermit here in the States, should it happen that way, or preferably in India where I have family, emotional connections, domestic help. I want my own space, a home in India so I can make the transition easily. I want to furnish it to my taste, without P's interference. Payson and I have radically different tastes in décor. When I moved into his house from the house Donald and I had bought, I did not resonate with the white Berber carpet and white leather furniture. My previous home was done up exactly as I wanted, without any objections from Donald. He had let me do my thing and liked what I did. It was my very first house with a partner with whom I hoped to end my days. I spent all I earned from my first permanent job ever at the age of forty-three, along with my savings, adding four skylights in the kitchen and bathrooms, and in the two-winged dining and living areas, just above the fireplace. To furnish it we made runs to Tijuana to buy colorful Mexican sinks and tiles, a very bourgeois king-size cedar bed with posts and matching dresser and bedside tables. We bought sofas, loveseats in a smudgy floral pattern of browns and burgundies, carpets, stained glass lamps, and a dark blue leather rocker recliner for him.

After prolonged battles over territory for decades, Payson and I have both made accommodations, perhaps he more than I. The institution of marriage predicates compromises, sometimes not happy ones. I frequently itch to furnish our home my way and buy a sports car, of which he has disapproved. He won't let me buy rugs for the wood floor in the rug-less TV room because he likes to look at the wood in the wood floor. Or the bedroom, which continues to be white. It is his holdout of self-assertion. I like cozy, heavily furnished interiors, perhaps because I have *horror vacui*, or fear of empty space. A marriage is like a garden: prune off parts of yourself to fit in. I coexist with P's preference for white (because, he says, his painting studio is always a mess, and because he wants no distractions in the rest of the house), and he with my Persian rugs on his white carpet in the music room, called so because his Yamaha piano is there. It is the room we made music in with our wedding party for many nights. The mutual compromises have created an interesting, somewhat kitsch interior. I always remind myself that the disagreement is confined to decor, and not principles and values.

I hope, should he die first, I will adapt to my circumstances and even find some comfort and freedom in them. But who knows, if he should die first, how old I will be? We want lives post our partner's death, but what life will remain in me at eighty? Eighty-five?

When my father died, my eighty-three-year-old mother wanted a life. After Dad's death she splurged on an expensive, magically patterned *kani* shawl, beautifully woven using small wooden sticks. It frequently adorns my neck now. She also indulged in some new furniture and the car she had wanted, but which Dad thought was a waste of money because they already had a functioning car. But after the first flush of freedom paled, she collapsed in sorrow at her loss and at the loneliness that followed.

My resolution to be strong in P's absence is undermined by my childish self. I ask him to lie with me on the Vita-mat, hold me, stroke me to rest before he leaves. He says, "I'm busy." I sulk and wish I had a more obedient husband. He has, however, changed with age; earlier his busyness would go on for the whole day or days and I would just have to take care of myself. Most of the time I have no trouble taking care of myself, but as I age, I want frequent connection and togetherness. He *is* paying more attention these days to my needs. My CLL has hit him harder than it has hit me. We are both aware of the loss of the other. I started paying more attention after Donald's death, becoming more aware of the temporary nature of togetherness. I owe the success of this marriage to that awareness. Donald's death highlighted my awareness of sudden loss, and I am present with P the way I have never been with someone before, because I bear the burden of knowing I played a hand in Donald's death.

I had meant to talk about the battle within myself between the child and the writer. I am tangled in the intertwined threads of my existence. I must stray away into another narrative of a painful and eventful part of my life that must be expressed, learned from, embraced, come to peace with before resuming the theme of this chapter. Pruning parenthetical stories and thoughts is becoming my greatest challenge as I age. Perhaps it is not a disability but an inclination, a welcoming, even, of associative flow from feeling to feeling, thought to thought, story to story. Besides, it is time for me to wade deeper into myself, discover my shadows, confess.

22
Shadows

*R*egret. Shame. Shadow. I must confront them all on this adventure.

I can divide my life and personality into a gradually evolving and distinct before and after Donald's suicide. The clash of the shadows that resulted in his suicide forced me to embark on a much-needed path of self-questioning, reflection, examination of the many layers of my psyche, to whatever degree I can.

I met Donald in graduate school in 1971. He was my office mate, doing a Ph.D. in English literature on his GI Bill. He had recently returned from Vietnam. Our rocky, passionate relationship spanned nearly two decades off and on, and then from 1988 to 1993, the year he killed himself.* Somewhere along the way my subconscious, that deep, dark ocean beneath awareness where one knows without knowing or articulating, picked up on Donald's destiny of suicide. Not wanting any part of it, I ran away from it, had other relationships and marriages. Sophocles was right when he made Oedipus run away from his destiny only to run smack into it. When other divorces and abandonments left me without an emotional anchor in life, the time was right for Donald's

---

*That story is told at length in an unpublished, semiautographical novel, *The Autobiography of Saint Padma the Whore.*

return after sixteen years. Our reunion was conflicted and joyous, dark, and terribly high. It was a cosmic romance fueled by sake, marijuana, music, and poetry. Already tending that way, I fell into Donald's cyclothymic rhythms of bright shining highs and dismal lows. I discovered from his papers after his death that he had been diagnosed bipolar in 1980. Throughout our four-and-a-half-year reunion, though I kept hoping things would change, Donald kept binge drinking, a habit he had developed in his teens after he'd been sexually abused. He never said by whom, only that it was a man. He was loving and sweet when he was drunk, but it still made me angry. I wished he would stick with genial and healthy cannabis instead.

I was driving home from college on August 18, 1993. I planned to open the door and instead of our usual "I'm home" sing "Birds do it, bees do it, even educated fleas do it, let's do it, let's fall in love." Opening the door, wearing a hat with a feather in it, singing in his beautiful voice I so adored, was the sort of thing he did often. Once in the early days of our reunion he came in singing a blues refrain he had composed: "I'm your garbage man, baby. I've come to haul away your ashes." Opening the freezer he would sing, "I've got the chicken cordon bleus." He had been depressed for months since his failure to get a job at the college at which I was tenured, and he an adjunct. He wasn't singing or making the music that used to fill our house with life and jubilation. I would stop all chores when he was inspired, take tokes on his already smoldering joint, lie on the cushions on the floor, and enjoy the concert into which he interjected comedy with his inflections and improvisations. He was a one-man band he called *Donald and the Outfit* since the days he had sung in bars for a living after graduate school. He had kazoos and harmonicas on stands within reach of his mouth, pedals to beat the drums, a guitar strung over his shoulder.

He had been withdrawn, noncommunicative, silent, brooding. It depressed and estranged me. I missed the Donald I knew who could shake his depressions and return. I wanted so to rekindle our fire. I wanted us to fall in love all over again, the sort of love we felt when we reunited in 1988. The honeymoon was prolonged, though even then there were signs that all was not well.

When I arrived at the door of our home, rang the bell, got into a singing stance, he opened it with the sort of grin that told me he had been drinking. My song froze on my lips. His drinking always pushed my buttons, perhaps because I was brought up in a very bourgeois household. Dad rarely drank. Donald's background was like mine, but his experiences of life were different. He did not go into details about his sexual abuse in childhood, nor did he speak about his experiences in Vietnam where he had been a medic, except to say there was always a stash of marijuana in his backpack. Only after his death did his journals reveal to me the depths of his fear and anguish.

I went into the kitchen; the sink and counters were piled high with dishes. Somehow that made me even more angry. It was his day off and he could have done that. My shrew, my Kali self, came out. I got angry with him, took his can of beer and threw it at him. I disrespected him. It was absolutely the wrong thing to do to a man whose self-esteem was badly damaged by his sense of failure. Mine was the fatal blow that finally made Donald, after half a life of suicide ideation and several attempts, pull the trigger. I discovered later from his many journals that Donald had attempted suicide several times before. After one time with an overdose of pills, he had written, "Next time, a gun. No mistakes." This discovery went a long way in assuaging my guilt, though I still feel my responsibility in being made an instrument of his destiny, a destiny intimately intertwined with my own. He had to die. And I had to learn my lessons.

My anger at him sent wires sparking in my brain. I felt out of control. I tried to meditate. I saw Donald come out of his study with a bag slung over his shoulder, the bag I now know had the gun that I didn't even know he owned. He opened the front door and walked out. I ran after him, sensing something was not right. I pleaded with him as he was about to get into his red pick-up truck not to go anywhere. I was afraid he would get into an accident because he was drunk. I tried to restrain him physically, but he hit me, something he had never done before, got into the truck and drove away. Agitated beyond measure I tried to meditate again but couldn't. Shortly after Donald left the house in a fit of rage, after a fatal lapse of time—I do not recall how long, but long enough for him to have reached our spot and done the deed— I jumped into my car and knew the first place to look for him. Our spot was a place by a small creek overgrown with cottonwoods and oaks where we picnicked, spoke our hearts, and sometimes sang together.

I found what remained of him after he had sat on a low-lying limb of an oak tree and shot himself through the mouth. His body was draped backward on the limb. There was no doubt at first sight that he was dead. My immediate, instinctive thought was to take the pistol where it lay in the pool of his blood and use it on myself. But I didn't. I thought, *Who will take care of the cats?* Nor did I reach for it or even touch it.

I screamed, over and over, though there was no one to hear me. I bushwhacked out of the spot—we didn't have cell phones back then— saw a man on the trail, and said, "Please help me. My husband has committed suicide." And immediately after that—or was it the first question I asked—"Is this real?" I think the man was confused at my question. He wasn't experiencing the dreamlike, nightmarish quality of my experience. He went off to make a call and I returned to Donald's body in a daze that blurred the distinction between dream and reality.

I don't know whether it was the first thing I did on finding his body or when I returned from my encounter with the stranger on the trail, but I lifted his left hand to see if he was still wearing his wedding ring. He was. I was deeply relieved. We were married still. Our fight had not severed the thread, one end of which he had taken with him into eternity.

My first words to the emergency crew that arrived were, "I have killed my husband." I heard one man in a bright orange vest say something to another, some code number for murder, I would imagine, and felt the cold clamp of handcuffs on my wrists. I was taken away and locked in the back of a police car. An armed policeman stood by the window. I was very thirsty, extremely so, and begged the guard to give me some water. He ignored me till I managed to catch his eye and stared into it for the longest time. It wasn't just a ploy to satisfy my thirst. I needed desperately to connect with another human being. I don't think I have ever looked so nakedly, with so much raw emotion and revelation into another's eyes, ever since. And yes, he gave me water. I thanked him over and over for his kindness. It meant everything to me at my time of crisis.

They kept me handcuffed and locked up for hours, first in the police car and then at the police station. I couldn't even pee without the presence of a female guard who pulled down my pants. I was so distraught they may have feared I would kill myself. I was certain jail was my destiny. The police would go to our house and see the marijuana plants Donald and I had been growing in our shed. But they didn't, and when they checked my fingers for gunpowder residue and found none, they let me go after I made a factual instead of emotional statement about everything that had preceded his death.

Though I had not pulled the trigger there was no question in my mind then, and sometimes even now, that I had, in fact, killed Donald by the fight I initiated. I have often wondered: Did my subconscious engineer the fight to free myself of him because I was getting weary of his months-long depression, the dark, dense black hole our home had become in his abstraction from it? It was sucking my energy, draining me; I couldn't write or sleep.

Jung says, "What we are not conscious of, comes to us as fate." I have learned from that experience to become more aware of my inner workings, though I still remain ignorant of my deeper depths. Who knows what other shadows lurk in me? When Earth in her gyrations confronts me with the cruelty of life and I find myself ruing it, I must admit that I have, in a way, killed a man I loved. This humbling is one of the desirable spin-offs of this tragedy. There are others. I value what I have become since that moment. I am increasingly conscious of my behavior and relate to people in distress with more compassion. Not always. The die-hard, hold-fast ego that makes itself the center of all life persists, and my Kali/shrew continues to surface, albeit rarely, even in my fights with Payson.

Where was I before this mind storm began? My widowed self is out because P is going to New York. I call out to him again. Soon he is with me on the mat, my head in the crook of his arm, awkwardly, because my neck has been hurting, and I know I will suffer for doing it, but it is the only way I can drape my body over his and hold him close. I frighten myself with my sweet codependence on him, at his power to lull me in my agitation with his hands of light. The past and future have cast their shadow on my now. I tell him, "I'm missing you already."

"I'm right here," he says. "And we will talk frequently. It will be over before you know it."

23
Hanging Out with Kamla

This time before Payson's trip to NY, I prepared for aloneness. Cognitive intervention worked—to some extent. I said to myself repeatedly before P left, *It is a time to catch up with yourself. You are going to settle into your solitude and love it.*

I drove back from the airport thrilling at the indigo luminance of morning. Romance was in the air. I was driving home to be alone with myself.

The first thing I did on arriving back home from the airport was take off my hearing aids. I must wear them all the time now because GERD (gastroesophageal reflux disease) is wearing away P's larynx, as well as mine. He talks softly and his voice sounds like a mumble unless I wear my ears. I terrified myself by the thought: *He will lose his voice! I don't want to lose his voice!* And resolved to wear them often, even though they aren't comfortable in the canals of my ears, already narrowed by tight TMJ (temporomandibular joint).

I amazed myself by tidying up the kitchen and the house, all in small bites, doing necessary housework, not distinguishing, as Payson so admirably does, between good and bad chores. To him it is all Zen, as he himself says and demonstrates, chopping wood, carrying water.

Whenever I am alone I talk to myself aloud in a sort of running commentary and conversation: *Let's go downstairs to the study now; let's eat. You'd better lie down and relax.* It is not cultivated but a natural tendency. It is the first manifestation of making myself my companion. I had a marvelous day with Cookie as companion, working in the garden for hours. Doing yoga in the sun, grazing on broccoli heads, Swiss chard, kale, cilantro, and basil, I felt fifty years old. Once I caught my reflection in a mirror, my hat like a cone, uncombed gray hair going every which way, and was surprised to see I looked old. I smiled broadly and said *Hi!* as to a long-lost friend.

I adore my old self that is wise to prefer the given, to enjoy my solitude, even the extreme tiredness that comes from attempting too much order, doing too much in the absence of another's presence in the house, without frequent stopping for interaction throughout the day. With no necessity to eat together at a particular time or watch TV in the evening together, I worked all day long. The next day I gave myself permission to recover from the tiredness that accrues from living with another, no matter how much you love the person. I wrote and edited for long, uninterrupted hours. Over the days I began to take liberties with the house, leaving the footrest of the rocker recliner up, my blanket sprawled on it instead of folded and put away into its drawer, dirty dishes in the sink, clothes strewn everywhere, the bed unmade. I inhabited the whole house, turning on several wall heaters and all the lamps in the house without anyone reminding me of global warming and energy bills.

When I got lonely I turned to my birds for companionship. The doves come to the table outside my window where I put out bowls of feed. They are skittish and I must almost hold my breath not to scare them away. Certainly I must stop tapping on the keys and watch. They look back at me with their beady black eyes and slick, tan feathers. Every time I go outside they scatter from the fig tree with a trill accompanied by the flap of wings, as if their voices were in their feathers. I say to them, "Stupid birds. As if I will harm you."

But a WhatsApp message from a friend from India put a ding in my solitude. She is zipping around Rajasthan with her husband on a motorcycle, traveling and going to and hosting reunion parties. My old envying whiner felt, *Everyone else is having fun but me! I am all alone and isolated! I am a drudge!*

"This is your *life,"* my better angels whispered to me. "Envy is ignorance," Emerson scolded. But I was inconsolable, not open to wisdom. In my loneliness I envied my siblings and friends who are embedded in community and family while knowing full well that I have shunned such a life. When my whiner began to pout that I was being a drudge while the sun outside was calling me to another sunny Southern California day, I gave in and decided to go for a walk. Despite the pain in both feet, one from extensor tendonitis and the other from neuropathy, I limped down to the open waters of the Pacific and sat on the concrete wall to watch the green, translucent waters rolling before crashing on the cliffs, the rising waves catching liquid light, licking, leaping on the sandstone wall of the shore, pelicans diving for fish with their folded, angled wings. Sitting by the sibilance of the sea soothed and quelled some of my shadows.

I looked at the beach below me, couples walking hand in hand, friends together, families boogie boarding, children shouting as they made sandcastles, dogs wagging their tails. I fell into my widowed self again, the self that Donald abandoned by his suicide. A few years after mourning and grieving for him, I was gripped by fierce loneliness. A wedding next door of a neighbor's son, the truck with streamers and shoes, sent me into a frenzy of longing. I felt like Katherine at her sister's wedding in *The Taming of the Shrew*: "She must be wed, and I must dance barefoot on her wedding day." Everywhere I went, in nature or the city, at work or at home, I cried to God: *Send me my mate! Send me my mate!* A year later he sent me Payson—friend, husband, counselor, partner, and, to avert the evil eye perfection invites, troll.

I called up my friend, SD, who had just returned from a weeklong trip by herself up the coast through Santa Barbara, Hearst Castle, and Big Sur, and was tidying her studio to begin work. She is an artist who has been single for decades. All three of my artist girlfriends, all my age, are single. I envied SD her energy, independence, and ability to do well in her singleness. I forgot the many, many times she had called me distraught that she was growing old without a partner.

Envy, like all my other shadows, comes with a message: If you envy people who are having fun, you need to have more fun. Whatever your version of fun is. My idea of fun is not everyone else's. Just the sight of the pearlescent midnight blue of predawn, the moment so brief it is hard to catch, passing before I can have my fill of it, thrills me with a feeling beyond fun. Not having to be anywhere at any time is my luxury, and not having to talk and interact more than my soul allows is my freedom. My fun is easy; it is going out—into our garden. I returned home, took my bowl of daal, rice, and a spoonful of ghee—God, how I love fat!—downstairs to my zenana, and opened the door to the garden. The birds scattered in a twitter and whirl of wings. I sat on the one piece of furniture I brought back from my home with Donald: a wooden garden bench, that both P and I use often. I savored my food to a chorus of birdsong.

Envy is also a failure to embrace my life as it is, as it has been, and will no doubt continue to be till death ends it all. *Accept your life as it is,* I told myself as I lay down on my manji and drifted off to sleep, content and happy in my own little cocoon, my own little life.

Psychobiological changes make every morning new and different. The wisdom accrued the night before dissolved, and I awoke unhappy. Without the sound of P's early morning steps coming up the stairs—he always gets up before I do—the house felt too silent. I turned on music, upstairs and downstairs, went shopping, organized a little, played some backgammon, watched a bit of TV, any channel, just to have some noise. I became, like the woman at dinner, "utterly lost."

I called Payson. He didn't answer the phone. I knew he was busy.

He has much to do in New York to sort out Larry's life. Larry is in total denial of his condition. He refuses to sign any papers that would give P the power to deal with his affairs should he become incompetent, mistrusts the man who has kept him afloat financially and emotionally these many years. Larry hasn't paid any of his bills and the electricity and gas is about to be shut off. P needs Larry's bank information to set up auto pay, but Larry won't give it to him. He forgets things from moment to moment within a conversation and has lost quite a bit of his long-term memory as well. He doesn't remember the names of any of P's ex-wives, and his rationale is, "Why should I remember them? They were not my wives." He fell in the bathtub and refused to admit he'd fallen: "I didn't fall, the mat slipped out from under me."

Larry was damaged as soon as he came into the world, then had to spend months in an iron lung before he was able to come home. When he finally did come home it was to a mother who took out her frustrations on her children by beating them. Larry holed himself up in his room, populating it with lizards, frogs, insects, and rarely emerging from it. He has been so scarred by his early life in a violent household that he has never married, has had no long-term relationships, trusts nobody, knows no one, lives like a recluse in his one-bedroom apartment, his "cave" in the heart of Manhattan. He lives a rigid life, eats the same thing over and over. He speaks in whispers in his apartment for fear someone will hear. Risk and change averse, he won't throw anything away. His apartment is stacked from floor to ceiling with magazines and books he has never read but won't throw away to make space in his tiny 800-square-foot apartment because he "might read them some day." Every inch of floor is taken by plants he rescues from the street. He navigates with difficulty his tiny studio apartment because his hip joint is so out of whack it has twisted the rest of his body along with it. P arranged for him to have his hip replaced, but he refused: "I don't want anybody cutting me open! They will cut off my leg." He is, in his own words, "a broken man."

But he is also delightful. He has a heavenly singing voice, has been playing the piano since the age of four, having picked it up by ear as his mother, sister, and brother played. He plays for hours every day, connects with all sorts of people on the streets of New York, stops and picks up varicolored leaves in the fall, admires flowers in Central Park, and reacts to the natural world and animals like a child.

I climbed up to the deck, the evening breeze soft on my skin; the ocean, seemingly still with wide swathes of river-like slicks, merged with the sky with just a hint of color and plenty of streaking, streaming white clouds. I recited God's name with each deep breath and felt steadied.

Payson called several times later and when I told him I couldn't stand the silence, he said, "But by the time I return you will be loving your solitude so much you won't want me to return." I laughed. He knows me well. He also advised me to, "Go hang out with Kamla. She is a very interesting person to know." I was grateful for the reminder and began by learning to love myself, my conflicts, my unpredictable and uncontrollable swings, to be compassionate with who I am, and trust and reaffirm that I am, indeed, a very interesting person.

24

Reading, Solitude, Love

The next day I realized that resting is the way to live well in old age.

You've been doing a lot. Let's rest. Start with meditating even if just for five minutes, my inner companion said. I surprised myself and did it for forty minutes till I reached that space and place above conflict, beyond thought, bliss beyond description. Then I lay on the mat, resting guiltlessly, reading the news on my phone without telling myself it was a waste of time. *I'm catching up with the gossip of my world*, I reframed. In the vacuum of resting I created room for life to happen. Resting turned me to reading. I reached for the book I had abandoned months ago, Pierre Teilhard de Chardin's *The Phenomenon of Man*, voted the "best spiritual book of the twentieth century" by the *Best Spiritual Writing Series Poll*. I bypassed the polemics of the title. For me "man" includes "woman" (or rather, literally, "woman" includes "man"). De Chardin made me feel comfortable and joyous about my innerness. Though I have been conflicted about this natural tendency in myself, vitiating it with thoughts like *Be more active, do more, don't be a nerd, get out, mingle, move*, I now returned to my center, my throne, my hermetic cell that includes the entire universe.

I don't read books, I chew them. I used to be reverential, not desecrate them with underlining or writing in the margins, but now I make them my own. I underline sentences and ideas that strike a chord in me, read only the underlined sentences on a second reading. De Chardin's words and sentences sprang alive like spraying fountains: "Deep within ourselves, an 'interior' appears at the heart of things, as if seen through a rent."

I followed my reading bliss all day. Reading Emily Dickinson, I found another kindred spirit.

The Soul selects her own Society (303)

The Soul selects her own Society—
Then—shuts the Door—
To her divine Majority—
Present no more—

Unmoved—she notes the Chariots—pausing—
At her low Gate—
Unmoved—an Emperor be kneeling
Upon her Mat—

I've known her—from an ample nation—
Choose One—
Then—close the Valves of her attention—
Like Stone—

A mind guided, a psyche articulated, a confusion clarified, our truths reflected in another life, a hand held across centuries, a heart vibrating to another heart, love and camaraderie across nations, across space and time. What more company does one need than a book?

But on days when I am incapable of reading anything that requires the mind, I zone out with a murder mystery not too complicated to follow. I don't even try to solve the mystery because I know the writers have tricks up their sleeves that my mind can't wrap itself around. I just stay with the plot and the suspense keeps me riveted to the story. Or I watch TV shows about serial killers. They provide a prurient focus and fascination with the deviant, deluded mind on the edge of the civilized world, a mind and behavior so different from my own, yet consanguine with whom I could have been in another incarnation. I marvel at the suffering that produces violence and harm; feel compassion for those trapped inside their weaker, thoughtless, unaware selves; rejoice at the triumph of justice. My interest in extreme behavior is a bloodless way to experience violence that the old limbic brain enjoys. In life I eschew it, do not rubberneck at accidents but deliberately avoid my gaze. I prefer fiction over reality when it comes to crime.

When my eyes grew tired of reading, I sat at the synthesizer, piddled with it for more than an hour and a half, mostly deploring how I had forgotten so much and how after all these years of singing I am still an amateur. That thought felt like self-recrimination, so I let it go. I propped up my ego by remembering I have composed no fewer than seventy shabads, and even sung to an audience of five hundred once at a book launch. I have constantly to remember my successes to fend off a sense of failure. I entertained myself by doing some *alaap* (arrhythmic musical vocalization), singing (just a tiny bit), then playing the synthesizer rather loudly and practicing notes.

I have finally slipped into my solitude again. It is the place of alrightness, the body, mind, and soul in synergy. I cooked and cleaned, ran errands, did a little gardening. At night I felt my life energy ebbing, but the next day, though I woke up tired after a bad night of drugged sleep, a bit of yoga got me going and I was energized again. I hope my solitude stays.

Yes, Payson knows me well. I got to wanting more of it. Without guilt. I got to thinking thoughts about living a life by myself somewhere, being the solitary artist in one of the many parallel lives I live.

When P and I got married two and a half years after we met,

my friend and soul sister, consummate artist Marsha Skinner, hermit extraordinaire, who has lived alone for many decades in a small village in New Mexico with a poverty rate of 12.27 percent and a declining population of 1,753, without a TV, computer, or cell phone, asked me, "Why on earth do you want to marry again?"

I know myself. I am solitary by profession, needy in my isolation for affection, contact, caring. I want company in my home, like I want a fridge and larder stocked with food. Companionship is bread. We all seek it—with others, with pets, books, nature, for there is no companion more constant than nature, always right there wherever we may be, waiting for us outside the windows of our shelters.

P knows me sometimes more than I know myself. He said to me once, "You like your solitude as long as I am upstairs." I laughed at the truth.

Freedom, like my friend SD has, to paint her bathroom and bedroom walls the color she wants them, to furnish her house according to her taste, means nothing to me without love. I moved in with Payson with just a carload of stuff after selling the rest of the furniture in my home with Donald at an estate sale. What I have with P is worth far more than a house furnished to my desire. Another single friend of mine, whose house is her work of art, furnished exactly as she likes it, has no room in it for another, even though she frequently bemoans her singleness and runs herself ragged with crammed schedules to compensate for her loneliness, then gets tired and depressed. I would be the same in that situation, crying, "Send me my mate!"

My guiltless enjoyment of my solitude while P was in New York did not threaten our marriage. In my best moments I know that if I don't get greedy about it, if I stay content with what I have now, this arrangement of being solitary in the context of physical, human connection is best. I know the shifting nature of my needs and desires: one day I want solitude, one day I want P. I can't wait for him to come back; I wish he would stay away longer. I can't fix this duality. Everything is a process rather than a state; it's all up and down, and any equilibrium I may attain is fleeting. The polarities, unfixable, are maintained with extreme vigilance by the gods because they are necessary for the dynamic balancing act of life. Solitariness and connection are kept in their place by a force that is at once centripetal and centrifugal.

Perhaps it is best that we cannot fix it. If we could, we would become gods. Or monsters. The latter, more likely, for then we would live with our puny wills instead of revolving on the lathe of contraries that shape us. Though in my youth the conflict was intense, in old age my soul has put its fingers on the scale of solitude in the context of connection with Payson.

Relationships have the added advantage, if we cease to be defensive, of showing ourselves to ourselves in the mirrors of others' eyes, revealing some truths about ourselves. I like having my ego and my self-centeredness pruned by P, even when it hurts. I learn most from analyzing the causes of our fights and noticing my own reactive behaviors. Our fights have also taught me the important lesson of not hugging my hurts but letting them go sooner rather than later. Our make-up, turnaround time is much reduced. I have learned to compromise, live with his preferences, and enjoy them. Our music is half his taste and half mine; his white wool rug with off-white leather furniture and mine with my paisleys and colorful throw pillows accommodate both of us in our nest.

25
Entropic Imperative

I dreamed of speeding on winding roads in a red convertible sports car, my long, wild gray hair flying. On waking I lay about some more, forcing myself to get more rest, doing some breathing to justify lying in bed when I neither needed nor wanted to, but from a desire to be lazier than I felt because it was Sunday, getting more and more depressed by the deafening mental chatter in my head. I popped half a chocolate-covered cannabis blueberry and unhappily lay about some more, getting more and more disgusted with myself. *Sit up, get moving*, commanded my angels. I did. Outside our large window, past our deck, the sky was full of fluffy cumulonimbus clouds with silver edges and dark hearts flowing swiftly east; the moon, in its deciduous phase, its pearly sheen edged with rainbow haloes and veiled with white gauzy strips of cloud curtains, was sailing with some speed as if hurrying somewhere to the percussive roars of the ocean.

Sometimes all you need to get over a depression is movement. Sitting up, standing, folding, straightening up, and the world rights itself. And sometimes, all you need is withdrawal and retreat from the battlefield of life. Rest. Holy activity, holy rest.

I reached for my water bottle to take a swig. Cool. Delicious. Thought about all those TV shots of people in Africa and other developing countries in long lines to get a jarful of water; remembered the video of old women in India descending the walls of a well to scoop up half a bucketful of muddy water, and was shot through with compassion and gratitude. Funny how gratitude springs from others' misfortune. Or just plain scarcity. Ground zeroes—tales and experiences of extreme hardship, thirst, hunger, cold—are good breeding grounds for gratitude. I think often of refugees, of people in war zones, and that keeps me anchored to thankfulness for simple things like hot showers, food whenever I need it, and all the simple blessings of life, peace above all.

Stripping out of everything I have worn for four days with a daily change of underwear, showering, wearing different clothes, combing my hair, brushing my teeth—disciplines that threaten to slip—give me a huge sense of accomplishment and satisfaction. To cheer myself up from something dark and heavy about the heart, I put on lipstick and eyeliner. Perhaps Payson, back from New York, would notice.

Our reunions never turn out the way I hope they will because of our conflicting needs. He returns tired, and I want more from him than he can give—hugs, cuddles, kisses. I forget that our reunions, caught up in counter currents, are rough; that our marriage is not based on romance—though there was plenty of passionate fire in the beginning—but on firmer ground. But an occasional flare up of a need for romance reasserts itself in his absence.

There's a reacquaintance phase, a standoffishness before our relationship becomes smooth and falls into the polished groove of its patterns. This time our reunion has been rougher. He has been absent, preoccupied, tired, grumpy since his return from New York. I wear something more youthful, leggings, better fitting, sexier than the comfortable, shapeless *gatkas* I live in most of the time. I put a brace on my aching knee, wear the carnelian necklaces I made when I was still making jewelry (another casualty, alas, of loss of energy), my favorite earrings, a long, elegant, fine-grained black wool coat I bought at Macy's twenty odd years ago and never wore, and Mom's rich madder-colored shahtoosh. My neck began to hurt; I must wear a brace. The necklaces came off and shortly thereafter, the lightweight shawl and coat, which had begun to feel heavy. Though the earrings get caught in the brace, I wore them out of sheer defiance, to appease the god of appearance. I love to look at these Indian *jhumpkas* cascading in chandelier fashion in tiers of oxidized silver studded with sparkling diamond chips, ending in a circle of the palest of amethyst, green, yellow, and pink tourmaline beads dangling from my ears, framing my thin face whenever I encounter it in a mirror. I do so love myself. *You are lovely still*, I say. And become so. It is a different sort of beauty, not the sort that is affirmed by mirrors or desirability by others. This beauty is self-affirmed.

My body—blessed banks that give the river that I am a form, a home from which to flow everywhere in time and the universe— honored, taken care of, adorned, revered, I sit on the swivel chair in the music room on the second level of our home, looking down at the garden, at P wearing his hat, planting saplings of vegetables he grows for us seasonally. The gardener is coming on his weekly visit today, and I don't understand why P won't let him do it instead, considering how tired he is. The more tired he is, the more he works, and it scares me that he will have a heart attack, as his biological father did at his age. Yesterday, too, he stripped the bed and cleaned up for the maid who is coming to clean. When I told him to leave some chores for the gardener, he exploded: "This is who I *am*. Why can't you accept that and leave me alone?"

Why, indeed, can't I? There's skewed thinking at work here, too complex for me to comprehend. Who I am gets tangled with who and how I think he should be. I am much more laid back, and expect him to become that way, too. I fear losing him, want him to rest and heal from all things Larry, and when he doesn't conform to my requests, I feel there is something wrong with him. He is very different from me, as different as New York and Hoshiarpur, Panjab, where I was born. He is an energy being and lives his life at a New York clip. One word describes him: "energy." Even his paintings, which he calls "energy land-scapes," are dynamic and vigorous. I am the turtle to his hare. When I am going ten miles an hour, he is going sixty. Payson helps the help—carrying the massage therapist's table and accessories into and out of the house to his car after a relaxing massage, for example—because he has the energy, and an innate chivalry and kindness to reduce others' loads. My attitude is, Hey, I want to enjoy my massage, not be lifting things. We pay them well to get our old bods nurtured, touched, caressed, and to supplement our waning energies in the house and in the garden. Having grown up with a staff of helpers for the first two decades of my life in India, I love nothing more than service. It is one of the reasons we have been returning to India for half the year for sixteen years. I have no trouble letting others work for me. I live like a queen in my castle in Behta Pani for six months out of the year. For at least part of the year, I live like an upper middle-class Indian, with a cook, driver, groundskeeper, maid, gardener, and breakfast in bed. I never entertain in Del Mar; it is altogether more work than I can handle, but in Behta Pani we can entertain large gatherings of friends and family.

I like nothing more, now that I am aging, than an extra pair of hands, more muscle, an extra brain, tech help, editors. We have both been frugal with money, having saved it most of our lives. It's time to spend on help to take over functions we are unwilling and incapable of performing. I grow steadily wearier of my many tasks and responsibili-ties. It is time to take care of and nurture my gradually enfeebling self.

Of course I fear aging. I have had many intimations of it in tired, sick moments when I project my helplessness onto the future. I think then that the persistent sharp pain in my temple is an aneurism about to burst; that I will have a stroke, like Mom, or grow blind with glaucoma, like Dad. The muscles of my eyes will lose their tone, their humors and gels will dry up, their crystalline lenses, my windows to the world, will dim. Plaque will build up in my brain and I will gradually lose my mind, the command center of my being.

It is a foolish thing to terrify myself with fear-generated images in the many-angled mirrors of my mind, and still, I do it. However, my angels have been coming to my aid when I am in the icy grip of fears. I roll with the punches, ward off their onslaught with slow, steady breathing, and restore my peace.

Payson is still planting saplings. Our garden, geometry and nature, patterns, colors, music to the eyes, is always a work in progress, always somewhat cluttered by watering cans, implements, pots where they shouldn't be. Even the closets, drawers, pantry in the house are never the way I would like them to be, the way Mother's were, a place for everything and everything in its place. If something is not needed, "throw it over the wall," she would say. Literally. People found the nearest place to dump their waste. If there was anything valuable in it, rags, wastepaper, they were collected by the rag and paper pickers. The cows and crows got to the kitchen waste. This was before the days of plastic, of heavy, hazardous, wasteful packaging, before the days when Indians, like humanity, and I among them, became addicted to consuming. I am a clutter bug. Devama, our *ayah* (nanny) from when I was three to twenty-two, when I left for America, took care of me, folding my clothes, putting away books and toys in my wake. Clothes are a big problem. When I was young I was careless, and now being short, getting shorter to almost five feet from almost five two-and-a half, is making me pay almost too much attention to clothing. When I was younger, youth carried my clothing, but as I grow older I begin, like my parents, to care. Earlier I dressed for others, trying on clothes in the mirrors of dressing rooms at malls, imagining myself in social situations, trying to see myself as others might see me. And I dressed for myself, for that part of my ego that cares how I am seen. I am more conscious of how I dress now to compensate for my age. I want to like myself in the altogether too many mirrors in the house I inherited when I moved into P's house, in which he had been living for twenty-six years with three other mates. The house has moved with time to another place in the universe, other configurations. There are no ghosts here.

We women are altogether too bound and tied to our own appearance, which only adds stress in the aging process. Though never overweight, but bordering on it occasionally, my body, compared to images of bodies I am bombarded with in the media, the white, sculpted body of youth and the lovely ones of our society, looks lumpy in the nude. Increasingly my efforts have been to camouflage it with clothing, and that takes a lot of putting together, trying on, discarding, all of which adds to the clutter. Not to mention hot and cold flashes. I am still getting intense ones: strip off the layers wherever I am, leave them in a heap, and if I am in a different part of the house when the cold flash comes, I must grab something from the nearest closet to keep my body from bone-penetrating chill. Having closets on two floors does not help.

Bathroom mirrors don't bother me because then I need only ensure, should I glance up, not often, that my white hair is not peeking too messily from under my hat riding up on my head in a very comical way, way too high on my scalp, or that there is no food or toothpaste around my mouth. I like my face. That has never been a problem.

And I want to appear good in the mirror of P's eyes, Payson who always notices when I go out of my way, but with whom my schlump is totally comfortable, too.

It says a lot about P, who likes clean, uncluttered spaces like Japanese homes, that despite occasional outbursts he puts up with me. Making me feel more comfortable still, he has begun in small ways to add to the clutter. It is a healthy sign. But recently there is an urgency, incommensurable with my energy, to organize for the coming entropy, age-proof the house, know where my many glasses and keys are when I need them, remind myself over and over where I place something for easy retrieval. Ironic that when I need to do this the most, there is little energy for it.

The tight leggings are chafing my crotch. My vagina is no longer moist and elastic, but dry and brittle now. I understand now why all the older people I knew when I was young wore pants with deep crotches, hanging, rather than flush against the butt. I should go downstairs and change back into my gatkas, but the whole dressing ritual has worn me out and I am only capable of sitting in the swivel chair, my feet up on the ottoman, chewing the cud of my thoughts and feelings as I watch P working in the garden.

A question tickles my brain: What do I do when I don't want to do anything but am not comfortable doing nothing? Do I take that extra step, that push against entropy, or give in? Pushing feels like work; surrendering feels delicious, languid, lazy, easy, in the flow, like a senescent river at its delta, directionless, winding, wandering aimlessly, idly, before merging with the sea. And scary.

Action dispels fear. I get up, straighten a few cushions, tidy up the coffee table, change the tack of my thoughts. I must, while I can, push through. The day I give up effort, I will die. There is always effort, the struggle we inherit from the moment we begin our journey through the birth canal after our peaceful slumber in buoyant amniotic waters, the hardwired push to move, thrash about, not die. Only dead people make no effort. I must keep moving especially on days I feel like a sloth. The battle against what P calls "the entropic imperative" must be ongoing. Nature must be propped up with the human will. The quality of our present and future depends on it. Move. Exert. But effortless effort, as the Taoists say, the kind that comes from moving with the flow, with the rhythms of the body-mind, riding the currents of energy, resting when tired, taking time out—prescribed, if necessary—to do nothing but breathe, exercise whenever possible, eat and think right, do the quotidian, move into simplicity of thought and action, turn away from bitter ambitions and unfulfilled desires. Oh, these recurring demons can be lethal, I know! This, this is my passion now: to live some other way, more attuned to the invisible Spirit that has brought me to this point in the map of spacetime, closer to the mystery toward which I proceed apace.

Who says passion and desire diminish as we age? Through their many manifestations in the body and heart they are what move us, undiminished, till the end. Who knows what happens to them when we go? I rather think they go to make our planet green.

Life is surprising me these days. As I stepped into my study a few days ago, the boombox playing pulsing, rhythmic, Bhangra music, I burst into dance—old granny dancing lithely, swaying, every limb moving freeform to an old joy made present, ecstatic in the undulating wave of muscular sound. For those moments, the body, sound, sense, sensations, feelings, thoughts, all synced. I was the dancer and the dance. The conjunction of the moment, the right song playing, the right rhythm, the body receptive and eager to move was sent; it was a gift, a reminder: Dance! Dance even as you deliquesce. It will give life to your life.

I could barely sustain it for ten minutes. But I did not collapse afterward. Dancing lifted my sinking spirits, energized me to do long-delayed clean up, putting away. But today my arthritis is acting up in my left knee, right toe, hip, neck. Am I too old to dance? There is some despair at this thought. I resolve to push through, dance whenever I can.

It is a beautiful day, and working in the garden, if I weren't aching all over, would take care of all my ills. Such deep solace in the earth, the ground of our being. There's something of eternity in gardening, a deep-root connection with the All, hands and clothes soiled with earth, the mind present, as when I am writing, the words and images falling into place, or when I am singing: fingers, rhythm, heart, and mind aligned, harmonious. Home. How rarely I inhabit it. I have not written for a while; nor sung.

26
Home

Old questions about home, country, tradition, family, came agitatedly alive this morning. On a WhatsApp video call Mishi looked thin, shrunken after being overweight most of her life. My fear of losing her was compounded by my own future fears. Her family was by her side, four grandchildren sitting on her bed, her husband, children, and their spouses catering to her every need, holding her hand as she suffers the ravages of chemotherapy.

Who will take care of me when I am enfeebled, even more than now, when aching wrists render the simplest of tasks like opening bottles difficult if not impossible? Who will be by my side when I am sick and near my end? Payson is a wonderful husband, but will he know when I am incapacitated to feed me the food I would need and like? I have done it for P. Will he be capable of doing it for me? Who will fetch me things that need fetching when I am bed-bound? My mother never stopped complaining that a woman can never retire. Help was the answer, but she had to manage them like a captain running a tight ship, and even management grew more and more difficult and frustrating for her as she aged. Her duties ended on the day she had her stroke: fed through a tube; urinating and defecating in her diapers.

India is knocking at my heart today. I miss my sister's family, my clan, my brethren, children, Panjabi, Panjab, food, help; I miss blessed, mindless, relaxed family reunions, good feeling, laughter. I wish someone, something, would breach the impermeable membrane of my aloneness and set me free from this shriveled life, this unutterable isolation called "loneliness," this suffocation of myself inside my skin, this severance from God alone knows what. I wonder how others deal with isolation as they age. What do they do to lessen it? Believing they have more choices than I do—children, grandchildren, community, family—I feel even more exiled.

First-generation blues? The ice bridge over which the first nomads crossed into America flooded in the receding of ice, cutting them off from their places of origin. There is no way to return home. Other first generations procreate, breed, form clans of their own. I am childless, though not for lack of trying. I recall attempts in an earlier marriage, long ago, taking my temperature in the mornings, intercourse on cue, invariably a little forced; pillows under the butt after orgasms to facilitate the sperm's journey to my egg; carrying ejaculate in a vial between my breasts to keep it warm and alive for artificial insemination. And then the hope, the despair at the sight of blood; envy at others' pregnancies and babies; two miscarriages, one on Mother's Day—the universe thumbing its nose at my attempts. Not meant to be. Destiny.

Where is home? What is home? Mortar, bricks, walls, and roof won't do. A country, a place, a name, geography, locale won't do. I have never had a home though I own several houses in two continents. I have fallen between the cracks. The feeling of homelessness is certainly a prominent strand in my life, even here in our beautiful home in Del Mar.

There is some place I am searching for in the iterating narrative of my dreams, on the wrong road, on foot, on a long, long journey, all alone, the sky darkening, raining, snowing; broken cell phone, forgotten numbers, fingers shaky on the keypad. How do I get home to my parents? Where is home? India? United States? Some other place not here? Eternity? God?

When my heart in the grip of nameless fears weeps and mourns the life not lived, I must let it. There is no getting around the human condition. I must bathe naked in the sea of sorrow. The only way out is through. Feel the feeling; weep, if I can, for my eyes are emptied of tears by a lifetime of loss. Move through it with the help of prayer, with the aid of my diaphragm and lungs that must ceaselessly learn to breathe; carry on, not tarry at loss too long. Regret is a dangerous strait. Many have perished in the bog of self-pity, or lived a life of unhappy bitterness, which is another way of perishing while alive. My task is to keep moving forward, always forward, teach myself, again, for the hundred thousandth time, to make myself my home. When grace returns me to the home of my solitude, my life as it is, as it was meant to be, the roar of my anxiety quiets and I am back in the blessed folds of silence and peace.

Grace and self-examining, I think, pouring rice into the cooker, adding water, oil, salt, and turning it on. Wonderful contraption, the rice cooker, turning itself off when it is cooked and ready.

Truth is, I never wanted an arranged marriage like my siblings and friends who have traditional families, sometimes joint, and live not far from where they were born, in the same town as their parents, children, grandchildren, friends. I fled parents, clan, country in my terror of the arranged life, came to another country to be free to live my life my way, and did. I suffered the suffering every freedom-seeker must endure. I don't mind. Doesn't *every* way demand a price?

If I have a home, it is childhood. But where in all our galaxy is that, in what loop or gyre of space outside space, time outside time, where location ceases to exist, where nothing is separate from anything else? Is there a place where everything exists simultaneously, unclassified into tense—was, is, will be, and all the words we use, so inadequately, to represent deep time's many layers, dimensions, and mysteries?

In childhood I saw none of the fights my parents had after Dad retired from the army, the construct that had kept their life regimented, and they discovered how different they were from each other. I grew up happy and free, safe in the knowledge of my father's unconditional love and my mother's deep-rooted attachment to me, which was obscured and complicated by her jealousy of my close relationship with my father. I especially loved holidays in the village we went to during my father's annual month-long leave from the army. Life in the village where my mother was born was so different from the life I lived in the suburbs of cities, in sprawling army cantonment houses. The village was poor, without electricity, walls made of plaster and cow dung, no sanitation except the fields and public latrines for emergencies. Most people went to the fields carrying their *lotas* of water to wash themselves after defecating. But my holidays in the village felt like home. Here, in the first decade of my life, I felt entirely free and irresponsible running around with my friends from the village, Tokho, Premo, and Paro. My days were spent playing marbles, their swirling colors astonishing my youthful eyes; going to the fields past the *gurdwara*, the house of worship at the edge of the village; past the open air *shamshaan ghat* with its heaps of ashes, white bundles of bones hanging from the palm trees nearby—"flowers in the bags," I was told. When families go the day after cremation to sift through the ashes for bones, the ritual is called "picking flowers." The place always frightened me. I hurried past it. Death lurked in my paradise even as I, forgetful of it, raided guava and mango trees and broke stalks of sugarcane from the field, peeling them with my teeth, starting at the broken end, stripping down one section of the shaft at a time, biting off succulent chunks, sucking sweetness, the juice inundating my mouth, singing on the tongue and all the way down. We ate the fruit of someone else's labor. We knew nothing of labor, only play, in which thieving was not thieving but adventure. We stole mangoes in summer, guavas and sugarcane in winter without a qualm, for how could such deliciousness not be communal, not meant to be eaten by young girls on the prowl? We owned it all and owned nothing, for we hadn't yet thought about accumulating, succeeding, making something of ourselves. There was no future; today was all there was of fun and, sometimes, tears. No place is free of tears. Our very sea is salty.

Let me not gloss over those photos in the family album of a very grumpy me at about six: in school uniform, a white shirt under a navy-blue pinafore with straps, my hair in two tight braids folded up and tied near the scalp with white ribbon bows, my face swollen and lumpy with anger, eyes droopy, sullen. What had made her unhappy? No doubt the same thing that makes me unhappy now. What was she not getting? Isn't wanting and not getting at the bottom of all our gripes against life? Or was I grumpy because my obsessive-compulsive mother controlled how my sister and I dressed, always neat, the first twist of our pigtails tight and pulling against our scalps to the degree of discomfort? Later, the harness called a bra was an ordeal, too. I had learned to free myself from it discretely even in public, a trick I had learned from my mother when she took hers off at night: pretend to scratch your back, surreptitiously unhook the fastening at the back, slip one strap down the arm through the sleeve, then the other, and with one deft move, pull it out from the edge of the sleeve, or grab the contraption from under the shirt and stuff it in the satchel. I have never worn it since. Or was I grumpy because I simply did not want to go to school that day? I never did like going to school. Not since the time my mother made me stand before the class and apologize to the kids for stealing their slates and chalk. I did not know it was a crime. I knew only that I loved slates and chalk so much I had to have more and more of them, an endless supply. I simply took them, one at a time, from the khaki satchels of other students when they were out for lunch, stacked them under my bed at home where my mother discovered them one day.

It is the immorality and insouciance of childhood I miss. I recall clambering on the dining table where my mother invariably displayed a large bowl of seasonal fruits, taking a bite of each to see which was sweetest and best, turning the bitten fruit I had rejected bite-side down to disguise my trickery. It was the best I wanted. And had.

Lying on the dining table on my stomach at three, naked. They were going to put ash in my crack, which was itching. Dev Amma said that was the remedy for an itching and scratching butt. My mother, sister, and Dev Amma were separating my cheeks, peering down and placing a handful of it on my anus when I let out a big fart that blew smelly ash into their faces.

With life on the cusp of ending, the gaze turns backward. I see the arc from where I began, a zygote in my mother's womb to now, sitting in Del Mar in this chair looking outside at tiny birds in bursts of flight, wings lit in the morning sun, the kiss of light on the Torrey Pine trees. I'm gazing at the garden I love so well, and the sight of the man I love so well except when we fight, mature adults reverted to children. And we have been fighting lately. And when we fight, I neither like nor want to be around him. His troll elicits my essentially free self that wants to bolt from the relationship.

Patterns persist. Bolting began in early childhood. I was told of, and remember, premature flights of freedom. Each time I felt scolded by my father, I stripped off my clothes, including my underwear, and said, "Because you give me these clothes and feed me you can tell me what to do?" And then I ran out of the house naked. Dad would run after me, pick me up—kicking, screaming, beating his chest with my fists—and bring me home from however far I had gotten in the compound or street. This must have been at an age when nudity didn't bother me. Then something changed at about the age of four or five when I kept my underwear on while fleeing. And Dad would joke, "Those are mine, too. Leave those behind, too!"

P is also an escape artist. Like me, he always knew he wanted to be independent and free. He tried it once at the age of four, ran away from home in Manhattan, but when he got to a large intersection he began to cry. When a cop approached to ask him what the matter was, he said, "I ran away from home but my mother doesn't want me to cross streets." Propelled subconsciously by the urge to be free and independent, he began to work at the age of seven, much to his well-off, world-renowned dental surgeon mother's embarrassment—walking Mr. and Mrs. Moore's dogs, delivering newspapers, mowing lawns in summer, raking leaves in autumn, shoveling snow in winter, delivering fruit and prescriptions. He had always meant to leave home, get away from the physical fights of his mother and stepfather and the demands of his self-willed mother. Once she dropped a sculpture on his head as he stood on the landing of the stairs below and cracked his skull during an argument. With blood streaming down his face, his nine-year-old brother, Larry, clinging to his leg, screaming "Don't go! Don't leave me here!" Payson walked out of the house. He was sixteen, on his own in New York City. It was the '60s, everyone was welcome at everyone's parties, and there were parties everywhere, and that is where he ate and crashed. Till he met Steven M—still a good friend—a few years older than he. They became good friends, and he put up P in his apartment, which his wealthy parents financed.

Our fiercely independent natures, our will to freedom, is one of the fault lines in our marriage. Every fight contains the possibility of one of us bolting. But love, financial security, comfort, compatibility on many levels—intellectual, artistic, emotional, spiritual—interests in common, old age, an increasing need for companionship, fear we may be too old to attract others, loneliness, and a certain undefinable glue hold us together. We make each other our homes.

P is pruning the nectarine. How sweet and juicy its fruit! What a paradise our garden is, our own little bit of fruiting, flowering earth. I could put some roots down into this home if there weren't some fear and wisdom. This is all a passing show, not only through death, but the moment-to-moment vagaries of life.

Our haven sits close to the San Andreas "continental transform" fault. Who knows what quakes life has in store? I have never allowed myself to get attached to this house, in which I have lived for more than twenty-one years, for various reasons. I still think of it as "P's house." I have never had a home I felt I belonged to or that belonged to me. I learned early as an army brat not to get too attached to any of the many homes we lived in, though I had my preferences. My ongoing search for home has perforce become metaphoric and internal. My philosophic leaning has always been to be more and more detached from people, homes, desires. I haven't always succeeded, which is just as well.

A few months ago, standing in our music room looking at the view revealed by tree trimming, the Pacific Ocean to the south, blue on a chilly day in Southern California, I felt the stirring of an intense love for this house and my life within it. Shifting positions, looking at the back garden, I fell in love with the view of the lap pool and jacuzzi surrounded by sunlit bamboo. What enhanced the picture of my life within our life together in this home was P's slight figure, his curly hair still black in several places, tying the bamboo with a rope.

My many losses, through death or separation, have made me, perhaps overly realistically, expect more of it in the future. Loving the home and partner that I know I will have to bid goodbye to aroused fear. Is it why we don't let ourselves truly love? To truly love is to know that love and loss are one.

How inextricably intertwined love and fear are! I wondered then if this fear wasn't at the root of most of our relationship quarrels. Psychology names this pull-push tendency in human nature "approach-avoidance." P and I have both, over the years, become aware of this phenomenon in our own relationships, the tendency to get close and then have a fight because we were frightened of that closeness. My mother, when she was alive, invariably pushed me away before each of my departures for the States; someone I hoped would be a close friend still withdraws for years out of fear of closeness. It is well known that people cannot die in the presence of loved ones. It binds them too much and keeps them from that eternity to which they must go.

I had asked myself, *Is it the fear of having a home I am certain to lose sooner or later that keeps me homeless? Can I learn to accept this intense love bordering on fear in gratitude, without letting my holdfast attach to it? Let go when letting go is in season, trusting that no matter how brief or otherwise, these blessed moments will return and return for as long as I am alive?*

When I told P about my experience of scary-in-love-ness, he said, "Love for the moment; love for now." Much wisdom in that.

Where was I in this rambling narrative I am compelled to write? The jumbled spool of unraveling memories is not always coherent. Damn coherence! Damn audience, that I so crave. The greater need is to give my mind the freedom to bound where it will in the meadows of time, getting lost without care, without the harness, the bit, the whip. The mind is weary of reason, chronology, linearity, of any structure imposed upon its natural flow. There is a different structure here, beyond geometry, as of a river, as of a tree. Movement is the only imperative. As I age, I become pregnant with that swell of abstraction that is my matrix, the vast astronomical, interstellar spaces to which my boundaries extend. So tempting, so scary, this unraveling of the brain.

Abstraction, the comfort of the old, is not, after all, mandatory just yet, I tell myself. It can wait. Matter must cohere till the very instant we step through the door to the invisible. Not yet. Thank heavens, not yet. Let me stay in my material, time- and space-bound home. I ballast my movement toward the soup of consciousness, the invisible radio waves and electromagnetic spectrums from which I came and into which I will return, with the myriad material things that spawned me: with shopping. I order onyx lamps and hobbit-like, hand-smoothed silver maple wood stump tables on eBay. I bring out

Mom's exquisite shawls from the cedar chest, and her jewelry. Matter most beautiful.

There is some comfort in knowing that the material world will outlast me.

> *Beauty is momentary in the mind—*
> *The fitful tracing of a portal;*
> *But in the flesh it is immortal.*
>
> *The body dies; the body's beauty lives.*
> *So evenings die, in their green going,*
> *A wave, interminably flowing.*

WALLACE STEVENS,
"PETER QUINCE AT THE CLAVIER"

27

What Endearing
Fools We Are

*H*aving put up the rice I return to the chair in the music room. Even the simplest of tasks exhaust me some days. I marvel at P, who does so much more than I, though I am three-plus years younger.

One way Payson and I assert our independence in our marriage is to each do our own thing, P in his studio, me in my zenana, my "cave." My space is a large basement with two sides underground; one side has a wide window facing the fig tree and garden, the other is shared by our separate spaces. My cave is a study cum bed cum music area cum beading table, closets, and bathroom. If I am not here in my cave I am in the music room, reading, lying about, napping, chatting on the phone. We are separate and connected, free to do what we want, follow our own rhythms and inclinations. Each is aware of where the other is, and at the best of times we are the best of friends in our spare time. There is plenty of time and space for me to be with my favorite person in the whole world: myself. We are two coexisting solitudes.

In the best of times this arrangement works. But we run into trouble when I am wrenched from my solitude by an emotional upheaval, like now, triggered by the sight of Mishi and her family, the darksome abyss of failure as a writer, and P's distance and unavailability. Weaned from my usual activities by lack of energy, I revert to my carefully camouflaged little girl-child, desperate for the kind of loving she received in her childhood. I begin to expect more from P. The arrangement between P and me breaks down. We haven't connected at all since his return from New York a few days ago. He is exhausted physically from being in the frigid city, and emotionally from the prospect of losing his brother the way he lost his mother, to Alzheimer's.

Payson, seven years older than Larry, loves him dearly and has taken on his responsibility, supplements his meager social security benefit, and has helped him buy his apartment. But their relationship is also contentious. Larry resents his successful big brother, doesn't like being dependent on him, won't let P take care of the things that need to be fixed in his apartment, or help him toss useless possessions to create more space so he can move about easily in it.

P's reality and my reality diverged in every way on his return. Though I had resolved when he left for New York to slip into my solitude, subconsciously the groundswell of loneliness, oozing out of subterranean aquifers despite my intentions and resolutions, gathered force. I was looking forward to his return, to interacting, to touching. In the absence of children, extended family, close local friends, and an inherent tendency to introversion, I depend too entirely on P to fulfill my emotional needs in times of distress. His proximity means everything to me in my exile. There is dependence here.

I wish he would be more obedient, come when I call. I know he is tired, locked inside a garment bag in a closet, his fingers in his ears. Why can't I understand that and hold my own needs in abeyance? I complain he isn't emotional enough, doesn't cuddle and hold me enough, is too busy. My inner nag, who comes out when I need more loving and attention than I am getting, complains it has been ages since we had a sweet, loving moment. He doesn't notice I am absent from the house when I go for a walk; usually he comments on a new outfit or jewelry but now he doesn't notice what I am wearing; doesn't know how to relax; hasn't bought me a sports car (he bought one for his ex-wife!); and hasn't thought about going on vacation in such a long time.

I recall how Mom frequently fell into this pit with Dad, comparing him with other men she knew: "So-and-so is so jolly at parties; so-and-so demonstrates affection for his wife in public; so-and-so is jovial and has a great sense of humor!" It was another way of making herself miserable about the life and partnership she had. But after Dad died, she couldn't stop singing his praises.

What fools we are, appreciating things only after they are gone. Mom suffered and bemoaned her blindness, caused by a self-serving ego that wanted always to be right, that made itself the measure of all things (a thimble thinking it is the ocean), to the richness that Dad was. Why do we have to lose people to see their worth and value? Isn't there a lesson here? Learn gratitude, fool. Isn't it wonderful that P channels his gravest vice—workaholism—in creative ways? Isn't it absolutely marvelous that work gets done around the house: lettuce is planted, bamboo trimmed, dishes washed, taxes done, the house maintained.

But the hungry heart won't hear reason. I wish he would stop, come hold me, touch me. Or we could sit, he with his coffee, me with my ginger chai, which I continue to drink despite my better judgment. Simple pleasures like coffee and tea in the morning have become dangerous. We both suffer from GERD and caffeine is murder on the worn lining and narrowing sphincter of the esophagus. Freud, despite his throat cancer, had his cigar; I have my chai. I do enough out of necessity and must push back a little at death with my pleasure principle, even though what I do to feel alive could kill me.

What a ritual of togetherness my parents' morning tea was. In summer and winter, one of them would make the early a.m. tea before the cook came to work. Even the making of it was a rite, the careful proportion of boiling water and milk, a bit of ginger powder, so many teaspoons of sugar, a tablespoon of Lipton Green Label tea leaves in a teapot, strained, reheated, poured back into the heated teapot on the tray on which the cook had set two glass tumblers. It was their version of modern. Their ancestors drank their chai in brass tumblers with floral engravings polished to a shine, sitting on their manjis in their courtyards, wrapped in their *loees* (large woolen shawls) in winter, in thin, muslin clothes in summer. Just sitting, the men were frequently stoned on opium, conversing with God, sipping, slurping with pleasure the tea sweetened with homemade lumps of brown sugar called *gud*. Chai in the small village we visited annually during the holidays, sometimes for months in my childhood, was always a communal thing, the morning ritual of social togetherness before the business of the day began.

My parents never took to mugs with handles. Sitting in bed in winter by the glowing warmth of radiant electric heaters, they would wrap napkins around their glasses, warm their hands as they sipped their chai, telling each other their dreams, discussing relatives and neighbors, recalling their memories. In winter Mom would be wrapped in one or other of her favorite pashmina shawls, Dad in his favorite maroon sweater, a little shrunken with use, but beloved by him because Mom had knitted it in her younger days. In summer they would sit under fans whirling overhead in their cool cottons and muslins, facing the back garden/orchard, sipping and slurping warm, energizing chai.

The empty space in my heart where children and grandchildren should be is taken up by my parents. They grow huge in proportion to the emptiness of the space. Someone I knew removed all the pictures of her children and grandchildren a few years before her death and replaced them with photos of her dead parents and family. "This is where I am going now," she had said.

Is this why I am missing them so much? Am I going to die? I'm not ready. I haven't loved or been loved enough. I want to learn to love more, finish some more writing projects; I want to become an old lady in a funky hat, my skin thin and bright with the luminescence I so admire in some old faces that reflect, as the outer light dims, some inner glow. I want. I want. I want.

When I am not angry and resentful at P for being unavailable, I am worried. A few days ago he kept saying, "Everything is so hard." I hear Donald's refrain before his suicide: "I'm tired." I fall into catastrophic thinking, into scenarios of abandonment, disease, helplessness, loneliness triggered by the dark memories of others' disasters: someone who slipped and fell in her tub and lay there for three days and nights, her skin burned by the acid in her feces and urine; a friend who woke up one morning to find her husband dead in bed with her. P is all the family I have. He is my anchor, ballast, emotional and physical support, my house, my home. How will tomorrow be? Will P get Alzheimer's? Will he die first, or I? If I survive, I shall return to India where I have my sister's loving, welcoming family. And if I go first, well, then, all my troubles will be over.

I don't know if my concern that he is working too hard is for him or for myself—that he will die on me. Such is the entwinedness of partnership. Two become one. Yet distinguished. What happens to one happens to the other.

Going to bed last night alone—he was in his study—hugging my cuddle pillow, I felt the old darkness gather in my heart. It was time to turn to my guides, face my fears, snip off the invasive weed of dejection. If being widowed again is an inevitability, I must get used to it. I have survived my worst fear. Who would have thought before it happened that I could survive a husband's suicide? I reaffirmed the purpose of fear. It guides us toward life and light. It saves us in many ways, physical and literal. Our existential fear turns us toward God. It makes us cautious where caution is needed. My fear of poverty propelled me to find a job. My fear of being old, alone, poor, eating cat food, made me seek a partner and save money for old age. As my mother used to say in Panjabi, *"Paisa dua khasam hai,"* or, money is a second husband.

I have no control over P's destiny, though I try, often too hard, to push him into rest. He doesn't take kindly to being told what to do. "Don't nudge me" is his standard response.

The crux of the problem is this cursed desire to see the world and the people in our lives in our own image. This ego expects those we love to act and react the way we do, be our clones, in fact, love us the way we want to be loved, be as we want them to be in the light of our innermost desires. This is the Everest standing in the way of love. This ego is the same that more damagingly demands from our days and the circumstances of our lives that they be what and how we want them to be. We plaster ourselves all over the world we see, and see what we have plastered instead of what's beneath it, the person, the thing itself, independent of us, forever independent of our own desires and demands.

This is the cause, I must admit, of much of my misery. My task now is to relinquish control, put my raised hands together in prayer pose, and dive under the waves where there is calm, where I won't be tossed about in the rip tide, where my hand is held, though I sometimes doubt it is. It is time to trust now. To let it go, to let it be. Whatever is happening is good. *Will you ever know it once and for all, for good, you silly human fool? Observe him, be compassionate, give him all the space he needs and love him, troll and all.*

The future has a way of taking care of itself. I need to trust, not fear the future, trust even death, one of life's greatest boons.

P is still working, digging up dirt for the compost bin, turning it over. Both of us need a vacation. Being responsible people we are too bogged down with doing practical things that people like us undertake and fulfill. The practical comes first for us; I border on a type B+, hoping to graduate to a C, and P continues to be an A+. I am procrastinating more and more these days. For a whole week I have procrastinated on mailing an important letter to India. What an astonishing accomplishment! I have always put myself in the tourniquet of time. Now I parse the necessity of each task, see if it can bear delay, and act accordingly. The proactive sphincter is relaxing, and I am glad. It's the perfect time to put off, be lazy. I deserve it after a lifetime of getting things done.

It is life I want now, the simple things, chai together in the mornings, work in the context of life, not life in the context of work. Though I strive for balance between work and rest, if I must wobble and err, let me err on the side of rest. "It is better to do too little than too much," says my wise ancient ally Lao Tzu. I will take as many breaks and naps as needed. No more self-bashing with guilt, regrets, recriminations, small mistrustful thoughts. This cannot happen without rest. I must take full and total responsibility for my own happiness.

28

Living Like a River

*P*ayson has moved to watering and feeding the plants. His workaholism is beginning to get on my nerves. But it dawns on me as I go downstairs to do the laundry that his unavailability and distance is not the sole cause of my current unhappiness. At the best of times I like the distance. It gives me space, solitude.

Sorting the laundry and putting it in the drum, I acknowledge why I am unhappy, with myself, my life, my husband. I had spent months writing a proposal for a book and felt certain I would land the ideal agent I longed for—an editor, a friend, a champion of my work. I sent it off to fifteen agents. It's been months and none of them have responded. I have been seeing my worth as a writer in objective, universal terms and coming up pathetically short. I have been confronting the utter, indissoluble limits of my success as a writer. A lifetime of endeavor, dreams, ambition feels all over. Fin. *Khalaas.* Enough! I have been thinking I am a fool, deluded in my sense of my own self-worth. Shorn of my illusions I am naked, vulnerable, helpless.

This periodic sense of failure drags me by my hair over burning coals and hot sands for days on end, disempowering me, sapping me of self-confidence, locking me in the dungeon of my own ego, afraid, naked of illusions and hope, drowning in the well of my insecurities, chewing my own limbs from envy of others who have "made it." Blighted dreams, I hear from a chaplain in the news, is a common regret in old age. Ambition and desire vitiate our peace, whisk away the feast before us, substitute ashes in its stead.

Adding detergent to the laundry, I am reminded of Guru Nanak's image from the *Japji*, the *Song of the Soul*: "When your clothes are soiled with urine and dirt, you wash them with soap; when your mind is polluted with sin and toxic thoughts, wash it with the color of *naam*."* I take a deep breath. I call out to my Beloved, "Help me! Take away this ambition or give me a bone for my hungers!"

Having screamed out my pain, I am calmer. The truth is I am sick of my greedy ambition for more and more success and my lack of spiritual evolution, the same lessons over and over. *Everything, including my failures, is hukum* (established order), I remind myself. *Accept. Accept. Accept. Hug the thorns to the heart and bleed, impaled upon the cross of ambition, for it is Divine Will that you do so.* I cry to God again, "Please make me happy or let me be content with my unhappiness."

I would drop out of the harlequin hot air balloon of success. It is a chimera, a fata morgana that can lead to ill-health and death. Donald committed suicide from his sense of failure in getting a job and getting his writing published. I cannot let my hungers get out of control. Frustrated ambition that has made me unhappy for much too long must be managed, muzzled, pounced upon at first appearance, dialogued with, embraced.

I accept and embrace my failures as something desired by God. I forgive God, forgive myself, consent to my destiny, whatever it may be, angle the mirror of my consciousness inward, make that infinitesimal fraction of a degree turn that remakes my world. I return to my solitary center, to safe, still harbors. This is how it is; this is who I

Naam, "name," is very central to Sikhism. The only thing solid, and hardly that in the sensory sense, that we have of God is his or her name.

am; this is how I write, these are the limits of my luck, protest it as I may. Adaptation is the highest creative activity, call it what we may in spiritual terms: submission, humble acceptance of the given. There is a point at which science and religion converge. Adaptation has created the world we live in and the world that we are. Adapt or die, is the rule. Who can make a home in the churning? I have lived too frequently in this uncongenial place, in the boiling and frigid hydrothermal vents of poison gas in the abyss where no light ever reaches. The work of leaving this uninhabitable cauldron of suffering and arriving at the house of peace, my dearest, fondest desire, must begin now. I refuse, after a lifetime of suffering, to let ambition hijack my life. I will surrender a dream to get a life.

I look clear-eyed at my greatest fear, go all the way to the end of the thought I dared not think before: My writing may not be "good enough," I may be mediocre. This book in which I am communicating the intimate details of my life, this book I am compelled to write with a thrust to go deeper, put my skin in the game, reveal as much of myself as possible—although always some secrecy, some privacy to which I am entitled must remain—may be of no use to anyone else. I reaffirm why I am writing this book: because I must, and because I am infinitely curious about how others navigate their days, what their inner drama is. That is why I reveal my process, write the book I would like to read. If it's useless, so be it.

What a load off to let the boulder I have been pushing uphill throughout my life finally roll down the hill and smash into bits. Not being good enough is fine. I may never get any more recognition than I have already gotten, and that is good enough; it is plenty. How many people have five books published by a reputed publishing house?

To prop up and affirm my ego—a necessity—I also remind myself of my heroes who thought they had failed. Charlie Chaplin in his autobiography expressed toward the end of his life his fear of being mediocre: "What have I accomplished? I have made people laugh and cry." Or

Walt Whitman, who said in his deathbed edition of *Leaves of Grass*, "I have not gain'd the acceptance of my time but have fallen back on fond dreams of the future—anticipations." William Blake's poetry and painting were thought too strange, too exacting in their private myths, "the conceits of a drunken fellow or a madman," portrait artist John Hoppner called them. Blake was ignored and unrecognized while all around him his friends were winning accolades and acclaim. Despite finding himself in "pits of melancholy, sapped of confidence," he kept writing, engraving, painting, and wrote, "As to myself, I live by miracle... but as I know that he who works and has his health cannot starve, I laugh at fortune and go on and on." In 1999 *The First Book of Urizen*, published 1794, sold to an anonymous bidder at Sotheby's auction house for $2.5 million, the highest price ever paid for a piece of English literature.

I dive under the waves where all is calm, where I am not tossed about in the rip tide, mangled by self-doubt, where my hand is held. I want to live in a home not shaken by every gale that blows. I must change in a crucial way if I am to go into the rest of my life with a certain degree of health, sanity, and yes, joy in the life I have been so kindly gifted, experience it in some other, less conflicted and unhappy, way. I will now follow my will to happiness instead of the will to power, haul myself out of the fallacy that my life and work matter. I don't want to become one of those bitter-till-the-end people. The grain of sand in my fleshy interior may not become a pearl but the agony will have to be circumscribed, contained. Like Shiva holding the world poison in his brilliant peacock-blue throat, not letting it course through his body, I will attempt to circumscribe my failures, write despite doubt, do the work that is the solace of my days. Refocusing the lenses of youth to this new, happier goal is the gift of aging.

I saw an interview on YouTube of a 103-year-old man who loves to bake cakes. He had forgotten his recipes but continued to bake anyway. "I have no failures," he said, proudly, impishly. "If I bake a cake and it fails, it becomes pudding."

It made me laugh so hard I knew it was a message. I will make pudding out of my failures. To do this I must let go my idea of the perfect cake. What I don't let go will drag me to the depths, stones tied to my ankles.

There is a reason we use the present progressive tense in "letting go." It's because the process never ends. Just when I think I am mastering the art, something crops up to show me how deluded I am. The practice must go on till the final letting go. "Let go, let go, let go" will be my mantra going forward into this adventure. More and more letting go till the final and absolute letting go of everything I have, everything I think I have been and am. I must let my sister go, too. She will die when she dies. My hope is later rather than sooner. I will grieve and mourn if I don't get what I want, whenever it happens, then must consent to the ever-passing, impermanent gestalt, the whole that some call God.

It is time to find a way back to my humanity from the writing machine I have become, put a space between my identities as a writer and as a mere human, destined to die and be forgotten. Nameless and naked I came, a pulp of palpitating protoplasm on its way to becoming what it came here to be. There is yet another identity beyond my identity as a human strung together with words. When I was a child I scared myself once by looking at my eyes in a mirror and asking myself, *Who are you?* I must have enjoyed the scare, for I repeated the activity many more times till I became older and jaded and the sight of my eyeball looking at my eyeball without knowing who was doing the looking failed to amaze me. It is time to look into my eyes and scare myself once again with the question: *Who are you?*

I will never know because the "I" who wants to know is too bounded by ego to know anything beyond itself.

My resolutions notwithstanding, I expect to fall, fail, be devastated by other rejections. I expect many more, for I am persistent and will keep casting my net in the marketplace. Holy ambition cannot be extirpated. It was woven into my cells when they multiplied, grew, formed the fabric that is me. It is something I must live with, like an affliction of the soul, like an ailing, cranky child. My ego is a stomach with a mouth crying out for recognition, acknowledgment, love. I want these mouths to be fed. I must let my hunger and ambition be and take the hard knocks that are their consequences. There is an abiding purpose to them. I have no hope of controlling my ambition till the universe takes it away from me—not yet! Not, oh God, yet! Let me stay with my urge to reach even an audience of one, like Coleridge's ancient mariner who was haunted by his story and had to tell it to someone.

When the monster of failure pounces again, I will be prepared, go limp, refuse the tussle, announce calmly that I am not going to play the game. I have played it altogether too long, sacrificing parts of myself, depriving myself of a life, like a good workaholic hardwired to suicidally achieve more and more. No, Payson is not the only one in the family. I, too, have been losing out on life, losing God, love, the ordinary life, sitting doing nothing, talking, being together, small joys that we have been sent hither to experience. My perception of P as always busy is nothing but a projection. I too have had obsessive work instead of a life. I have been thinking in a worn-out groove that unless I am writing, my life is meaningless.

I met an older man in the dining room of the bed-and-breakfast we stayed in after sailing with friends to Catalina Island last year. He looked crestfallen as he warned me, "The coffee in the carafe is luke-warm, it has been sitting there from the night before. Things at this place are not what they used to be."

His face lit up when I suggested, "Put it in the microwave." He could get his hot coffee after all! When his wife arrived on the scene, he told her what had happened and how this lady had told him to put it in the microwave. That is the success I seek, to have the presence of mind, flexibility, resilience to dance through my life, swivel from one way of thinking to another more helpful one, adapt to circumstance life throws my way, think solution instead of problem, transition from unhappiness to happiness, be grateful for even lukewarm coffee when there is no microwave. How easily we forget essential truths, how easily we get fixated and resistant to change. God the Gardener prunes us, sends us in directions not of our choosing but in the direction, always, of light, of simplicity.

Chuang Tzu calls the house of peace the magic storehouse that "makes a springtime it shares with everything. The man who at every encounter generates the season in his own heart, his stuff is whole."

My magic storehouse is so huge the whole universe fits into it. My home, in a little corner of it, is a cottage nestled in a clearing in an orchard bearing all sorts of magical fruit, fruit that has no names but satisfies all sorts of hungers till no hunger remains. There are treasures in it: the riches of my senses, eyes that make meaning of electrical pulses and turn them into pictures for my understanding, ears to listen to the name of the Beloved that calms my storms, mirrors that cast light in darkness, mirrors that remind me of Chuang Tzu's guidance to use "the heart like a mirror; do not escort things as they go or welcome them as they come." In this storehouse I evolve eyes to see the ever flowing and changing waves that are mountains, trees, homes, bodies, me. The magic storehouse's greatest wealth is that it is empty, and I am empty within it, a ghost through which the wind blows: blessed vacancy, *shunya*, the void from which we come, of which we are made, and to which we return.

My greatest fear when I was drinking the dregs of failure was, *Will it take away my work from me? Will I die without it?* Writing is how I cohere, where I breathe. The fear is baseless. I return to my desk, write because in the process of writing I discover more of that gold that transmutes my suffering and desperation into purpose and direction. It would be self-destructive to succumb, to give anyone in the world the power to make me give up what I love and adore. Success and failure are ultimately quite beside the point. I do what I do because I must; because so much of who I am and want to be depends on it. If no one likes what I love and live for—I am an unabashed admirer of my own work; why else would I do it?—or wants my wares, so be it. No amount of success and failure can keep me from doing what I was born to do. It is my supreme adventure. I am a woman made of words, a word warrior. Nobody can tell me what to write and how to do it. I glory in the unique expression that I am; I re-create my beloved life in these pages, live it all over again by telling it. The wind is in my sails. Who cares who's watching? I do, but hopefully less and less. I don't know where I'm going but I know that wherever I end up—shipwrecked or golden dawn—I will be safe.

It is failing, falling, forgetting, fighting that unveils God. Without them we would be incapable of learning about ourselves, incapable of learning to love.

I will milk my failure, take even more freedom in my writing, spread out my wings in these pages, write how and what I please, flow as I am flowing, with only self-imposed checks and censoring, letting my heart meander where it pleases at its own tempo, no external pressures, no deadlines but my own flexible ones. What a wide, wide space-time this failure has bequeathed me! It takes me in directions I need to go, directions I have forgotten, the journey to the heart that I am here to make. If I can turn even a few steps closer to God, failing would be a good bargain.

I intend to live my life with trust, moment by savoring moment, make going the goal, at ease with structureless structure, living as my body-mind-soul lives me. It is the only way to live, not getting stuck anywhere, like a river going acceptingly where I am taken, hopeful about my destiny of death and indestructability. If there is anything eternal on earth, it is water. Though it disappears, it never dies. It may change its shape again and again, fluid to solid to vapor, but it is never wasted, never vanishes.

29

Learning Love and Softness

*P*ayson is in the garden, hauling, feeding, digging. He is getting on my nerves. I'm beginning to bubble and boil inwardly. I open the window and shout:

"Stop working so hard!"

"Don't tell me what to do!"

The harshness of his words sends me tail-spinning downward. I know with my head why he is prickly and short-tempered, but I am hurt that he has cut himself off from his life with me. A few days ago I warned him when he began to butt heads with me in the kitchen: "You are tired. I am tired, back off." But he didn't drop whatever he was upset about. I lost it and called him an asshole, twice, even though the first time he went ballistic when I used the word. He hates it when I call him that, but hell, I must when he is being one. I must speak my truth, even when it is harsh and shrewish. His troll and my shrew are well matched. As I turned away from him in the kitchen, I caught a glimpse of my shrew in the mirror: gray hair coming out in unruly waves from under her hat, face contorted in rage, lips set hard. It is how I felt, undoubtedly.

I get off the chair, open the window, and yell, "You are not a husband to me; I am just your housekeeper who makes sure there is food in the fridge and on the table," then shut the window with a bang. I heard my mother say to my father, "I'm just your servant! I am just your housekeeper!" I sympathized with her. Husbands don't think, when they are being busy with "important stuff" or in their own, cut-off worlds, that they need to be emotionally engaged with the woman with whom they are living.

After our fight we are withdrawn from each other. Silences between us are loud noises. I feel the knot in my stomach no cognition or wisdom can unravel. We are locked in temporary marital disharmony.

I dislike my inner nag, a complainer whose counting skills are all skewed. She counts what she doesn't have, wants her husband to be someone other than who he is, and occasionally becomes ludicrously unhappy. I begin to hate my unhappiness, hate myself for failing myself and others, and recognize at once the urgency for intervention. *If a thought hurts, get rid of it. Replace it with one that soothes. God made you in all your contradictory fullness. The nag you can't banish has a purpose. She is the expression of your dark, feeling, needy self. Embrace her.*

I do. She and I calm down.

My practice of living an aware life, though I often fail at it, has its reward: after much dunking in boiling dye, fading, returning to the cauldron over and over, my color is changing from fugitive to semi-fast. My guides return when my desperate need summons them. I remember to move, get up from my chair, lie down in the *shava asana*, the corpse position, breathe deeply; relinquish. *Let go, let go, let go.*

I lie prone on the floor, arms at my sides, palms facing up, hands open, eyes shut as in death, and breathe deeply. It restores my rhythm, rests my brain. Life becomes luminous in the light of death; I have an insight into my own behavior.

"Stop working so hard" was harsh; it sounded like a command, perhaps the kind he got from his mother when he was little. I need to hear my nag, explore my own rampant expectations and demands. In wanting my own needs met, I'm self-centered instead of compassionate; I have failed to provide him space he needs to just be after his frustrating and tiring trip to New York. I rise momentarily to my goal, become what the *I Ching* describes as "the superior man who is able to bear with people and things." To bear with. And strategize. The best way for me to live in this relationship is as a single person who has many perks of companionship. Shorn of expectations the relationship, and life itself, will become smooth sailing. Letting go of my expectations will become a part of my practice. The sacred shift in perspective of a fraction of a degree works its miracle. I begin to see the good, acknowledge it, be grateful. I remember that my troll is also a prince with whom I can be myself, crone, bag lady, farts, and all. He may not be a cuddler, but he holds and strokes me when I ask for it; he is supportive, loyal, steady in his love, committed; we stand on the same plane intellectually; he has and continues to illuminate me with his far-spreading knowledge of things scientific, political, historic; and we still have a spark. We occasionally hold hands while we walk together and when we sleep, tell each other our dreams. He offers me his hand to haul me up on hikes. I lean on him in my feebleness and he is present most of the time, regales me with the piano when he is in the mood, heats water in the kettle and fills my hot water bottles, which I am addicted to because they are so warm and soft on my perpetually cold feet. I am so accustomed to P's presence in my life. I am a one-person person, even though I do have friends with whom I stay in touch. I prefer P's presence to anyone else's. We are, for the most part, harmonious companions, giving each other as much space as we need; we don't generally vitiate our relationships with too many expectations. The lesson: I fall into discontent when I am not content with myself. It is projection, pure and simple. He is my best friend. I can tell him my all, or most of it; not that when he is distant I dream of other men. I also love the way he steps out on the deck, looks up at the stars and says, "Magic, magic." How can I complain about a guy who keeps wonder and beauty in my life? And yet I do.

We will spar again, maybe even draw blood. But I'm not going any-where. I am, as he has said to me countless times, here till the end.

I will build with the nerve fibers of my corpus callosum that spans my yin-yang cerebral hemispheres a rainbow bridge that unites the polarities of troll-king, crone-queen. In the thick of darkness, remem-ber light. Just when our relationship is bitter I will remember the sweet things. I reach for the phone and call him. I see him stop, pruners in hand, take out the phone from his back pocket and say, "Yes?" in his "I'm busy" tone. I don't let it put me off.

"Don't you absolutely want to come in, hug and kiss me and tell me you love me, and tell me how important I am to you, and hear how important you are to me?"

"I'll be right there," he says in his youthful, loving, enthusiastic voice that I haven't heard in a long time.

"Here I am," he says, standing near me. His words bring tears to my eyes. They remind me how steadfast he is in his love, even when I doubt it, even when we fight and almost break up.

He lies with me on the manji and begins to stroke me. His hands don't lie. He loves me even though he says it infrequently. My nag and unhappy child are instantly dispelled.

"I understand you are feeling neglected," he says, quite simply. "Thank you for saying that," I reply. "I am." How simple the fix, now, after all that complexity. When the ego abates I become supple and soft and love flows in both directions. He has returned from wherever he was that excluded me and us. No wonder I was feeling so isolated.

And I learned, as in the Yiddish phrase, that honey works better than shit, love and softness better than expectations and commands.

30

Leave the Crusty Chrysalis Behind

"*I* feel young enough to burn some rubber," I tell him as I recount my dream about driving a red convertible sports car on winding roads, wild gray hair flying.

"Let's go to Idyllwild. I need nature."

Idyllwild, in the San Bernardino Forest, a place of pine trees, boulders, high mountains, snow covered peaks in winter, is one of our favorite places to vacation. And it's only two hours away by car.

"Yes! Let's go for your birthday!" I love the spontaneity of it. We have lost quite a bit of it lately, perhaps as a symptom of aging. Payson is turning seventy-five and I have had trouble thinking of what to get him. He dislikes parties, thinks they are too much work. I agree. He dislikes getting gifts. I bought him a pair of expensive slippers because he had complained the cheap pair he bought were not comfortable. "I don't need any more things," he said, when I gave them to him. Then he went into a diatribe about consumerism, stuff, plastic, packaging, carbon footprint. The next day when I put the new slippers where he keeps the old ones, he slipped into them, smiled, and said he liked them. A few days later he complained they had no arch, so I ordered him another pair of black leather slip-ons. When they arrived, he went ballistic. "You don't understand, I want less, not more!" I swore to him I would never buy him anything again. I told him I would return them, but he wore them to the New Year's Eve party, and later complained they were a little big. His reaction to my gifts used to annoy me because I love giving gifts to those I love, till he explained that his mother gave gifts to her children instead of love, and the gifts were tied to conditions.

"Ten days in Idyllwild will be my birthday gift to you," I say. He accepts graciously. There is nothing dearer to him than nature.

In the evening we watch TV, my head in his lap, our squawks and squabbles, the gold together with the black, braided into one. At night he strokes my head and I drift off to a long, dreamless sleep, waking and staying in bed, just touching, for more than nine hours.

The whole sexual thing has been over a long time. It doesn't matter now. The heart hungers for the comfort and solace of physical closeness, kindness, care, concern.

P booked a place in Idyllwild—he takes care of practical stuff like that—and looked at the weather. It was going to rain our whole vacation. We couldn't get a refund and were both a bit bummed at yet another busted vacation, like our two-day visit to a high-end spa in Desert Hot Springs a few months ago. We got lost five times on our way there; it was cold and rained the whole time; the food was expensive and over-rated. My idea of a vacation is feeling at home in a comfortable, clean room; being lazy, writing, reading, preferably outdoors doing whatever. The room was dingy with bad lighting, and not furnished with a desk and chair. But the acreage was well landscaped, with thermal baths and steaming lakes with ducks and palm trees. And we got some marvelous soaks in blue tiled pools of steaming mineral waters.

While I was packing for Idyllwild, P said he wanted to have his close friend of sixty years and his wife visit us in Idyllwild; he had booked a furnished house with two bedrooms. I went into an emotional spasm. I was so looking forward to my solitude in the mountains, just the two of us, and my laptop. I worried about having to interact with his friend's wife, whom I hardly know and with whom I don't have much in common. Though in times of isolation I bemoan the community I do not have, guests in the house always remind me that my essential nature is solitary, becoming more so as social energy diminishes with age. Guests in my house warp my days. I am at someone else's disposal, instead of my own. I like to putter through my days at my own tempo. I am defensive of my space and time.

My expectations of myself, based upon what I think his expectations of me are, kept me from saying, "Please don't invite them." I wanted to, but it was his seventy-fifth, how could I? Every arrangement—and every relationship is an arrangement—has its obligations. After a day of tying myself in knots over this new development, I let go. Whatever. Too much resistance to the flow sucks energy better diverted to living in fullness. "Invite whom you like, darling," I said, and meant it. "But," added my nag, who has my welfare at heart, "they have to take care of their own food. I don't have the energy to shop, pack, and cook for four."

P was solicitous. He called them to tell them to bring their own food. I was proud of myself for not taking it on, as I may have in the past. Let it be a group effort. My angels helped, too: *You can do it. What you can't, let others take on. You can stay in your room for as long as you like, and their company, when you are ready for it, will be fun. Learn to sit comfortably at your center; don't push, pull, force, twist, tort, and exhaust yourself.*

I have noticed that whenever I am reluctant about a social event, the universe obliges. His friends backed out. I was thrilled. This left me guiltlessly free. I have suffered too long the Indian "wife" syndrome I inherited from my mother, my culture, my gender.

I have never wanted to be in the traditional role into which my mother very unwillingly had fallen. I would see her sweet, social face when interacting with house guests—there were so many of them when I was growing up, it is an Indian thing—and see an entirely different, grumpy one when she turned away. She did it so perfectly that toward the end the mask cracked entirely and she let herself become the harridan she had repressed all her life. Because she did not allow herself to express her shrew in small ways, she burst out in full force in what Freud calls "the return of the repressed." Dad couldn't understand why she would happily host tea parties for her card buddies but did not want to cater to his friends; why she never wanted house guests from either side of the family. After Dad died she became a hermit, having given up a long-standing compulsion to gamble with horse races and cards, unwilling to have even family visit.

An Indian wife is very obligated. That is why I never wanted to be one. I remember a conversation I had with a friend who had an arranged marriage. She hosted a lot of dinner parties and houseguests, her husband's relatives and her own. She has the requisite space and domestic help.

"I had a nightmare last night," she said.

"About?"

"Four people were coming for dinner." Long pause.

"And?"

"That was the nightmare!"

Women the world over have internalized patriarchal, cultural imperatives. We inherit much from our mothers. Formed in their wombs, flesh of their flesh, their blood whooshing though our veins, their thoughts echoing in our earbuds, dreaming their dreams together with our own through the umbilicus, our brains within their brains within the world and universe they inhabited and experienced, we perpetuate their history and roles. We, daughters, are fashioned by our tropism away from and toward our mothers. Their bio-physio-psychic gravity is inescapable.

Payson, who had a single working mother who was a feminist and a founding member of NOW (National Organization for Women), has never expected me to be anything but myself. I wouldn't be with him if he had. My relationship problems have always come from my own expectations of myself in my many roles. What I think are his expectations of me are mostly imaginary. I recall a day when we were both eating a meal we had prepared together—a soup into which each of us threw ingredients: broth, vegetables, quinoa, persimmons, apples, nuts. The kitchen was a mess and while we were eating, I said, "I'll put all this away in a while." And he replied, "Nobody's asking you to do anything."

He has since taken over the clean-up whenever I cook, and I appreciate his attention to, and participation in, domestic detail.

I create my own problem. I *think* this is what he wants me to do/be in a particular moment, but my notion of what I think he wants me to do/be in a particular moment puts me in a hall of mirrors trying to guess which reflection is the true me. It is my own guilt around housework that is the culprit here.

Disentangling myself from what I am expected to be and who I am is my ongoing work. For me, individuating* means distinguishing between values that my Indian culture imposes on me and my true needs. The former come from historic, collective standards. Sometimes the two coincide, but where they chafe and constrict, I endeavor as gently as I can to molt out of them and leave the tight and crusty chrysalis behind. Not as easy as it sounds, but hell, at seventy-one I have the time, the leisure, the space to sift through myself and consign the chaff to the winds.

---

*Carl Gustav Jung's term. It describes the process of emerging from an undifferentiated unconscious into a person distinguished from group attachments and thinking. It implies movement from an immature existence to wholeness.

31
Promises to Myself

The sky is thick with dark nimbus and gray and white cumulus clouds against patches of sapphire blue, illumined by the early morning sun pouring its gold over green trees as we head from the ocean we adore to the mountains we worship. Even the thought of rain that would confine us indoors did not dampen our excitement. I was determined to love and live every minute of it. I drove, my eyes feasting on the green and lavender fuzz on the earth's hide, my brain empty like a large room, silent as muslin curtains blowing in the breeze, taking my turns at ease through the meandering, canopied roads through Rancho Santa Fe, neither slow nor hurried, feeling youthful, bold, ready for yet another way of being, living, experiencing. Life, with its ever-moving thrust toward death, feels like adventure once again. Payson echoes my thoughts: "I feel there is another adventure left in me." His idea of adventure revolves around nature, as does mine. We discuss buying or renting a house in Idyllwild after our India and Behta Pani lives wind up, a discussion we have each time we drive up, and do nothing about.

Everything is possible as I hit the highway, get into our lane and cruise, my eyes delighting in new sights, thick avocado groves, hills thickly strewn with boulders. The sounds of "Evening Reflections" by

Karunesh are drumming through my bones, beating in my heart as I fall in with the traffic, synchronize with it and flow in the very artery of existence. I am speeding and it feels great, but I listen to P when he tells me to slow down. Caution above thrills: that is our mantra since we took a hot air balloon ride. It was thrilling at first, rising above the earth, drinking champagne and eating gourmet food, but it ended in a very bumpy landing that threw out my neck and knees for weeks afterward.

The sunroof of our car, Rani, is down. The wind blows my long hair wild as I drive the gradual incline up the San Bernardino mountains. Rani is named after a car we had in my childhood, an old Vauxhall with a sunroof. Once we were driving through a crowded bazaar in Jallandhar in Panjabi, barely moving on the street, jostling with rickshaws, pedestrians, dogs, and vendors. When two bulls sat in all their bulk on the road impeding our progress, I boldly stood up on the seat, thrust my head out of the sunroof, and shouted at them in Panjabi: *"Teri maan dee, teno ug lag jaai, chal maadar chod."* My mother frantically pulled me down; my father, red with embarrassment, shut the sunroof. What had I done wrong? I was only speaking the language of the bulls. I had learned it from listening to the guy who worked the Persian wheel around the wide-mouthed well in the mango grove in the large compound of our home. Two bulls yoked to the large wheel went around and around the well, bringing up buckets of sloshing water to irrigate our garden and vegetables. I watched for hours on end their muscular bulk, their large, liquid black eyes in tan hides, massive in their humps and horns, their dewlaps rippling down their necks in folds of skin. My South Indian *ayah*, Dev Amma, who had an altar with idols of Hindu gods, Jesus, and calendars of the Sikh gurus, told me a bull, Nandi, is the mount of Lord Shiva. If we say our wish in Nandi's ear, she told me, it will reach Lord Shiva. I *had* to learn this language. How was I to know the phrases I yelled— your mother's cunt; you sister fuckers; move, motherfuckers—were obscenities? This was the language in which the man spoke to the bulls to make them move.

Back on our present journey, winding up the lower hills covered with evergreen California live oaks, gnarly giant bonsais with dark bark and scraggly canopies thrilling the eye with their twisted, proportioned beauty, I decide I won't let old age hijack my life.

I make promises to myself that I bake into memory. Primary among them: discovering and creating new avenues of being. The old me whose lopsided definition of being has always been working will have to die and reincarnate as someone for whom being alive is enough, and more than enough, abundance. I had to be utterly lost in time, reach the nadir of meaninglessness to feel the necessity for reformatting myself, returning to school, beginning all over again with the alphabet of right thinking and action, keeping myself from falling into my default modes, learning to make my days vast, purposeful, new, and joyous. I want to plunge my proboscis into the nectar of life again: dance gently, vitally, for ten minutes many days a week to Bhangra music, get my old body and muscles reacquainted to rhythm; take singing lessons, bring out my flute, listen to a wide variety of music; write, hike, become material again, refurnish portions of the house, a few more of those onyx lamps I love so well, a rug or two. My mother upholstered her furniture and bought new curtains for her bedroom when she turned ninety. She wore her silks and fine pashmina shawls around the house because it was easy; her maid laid out her clothing and later folded it and put it away. Because it was easy, for this vacation of ours I packed just sufficient, comfortable clothing—I had to bring earrings, of course—but I want to start dressing up again for that person I meet daily in the mirror. I want to embark again, after a long hiatus of flagging brain and interest, on reading, if only a paragraph or two of the dense books I like to read; commit to reading *The New Yorker*, which stacks up each month on the coffee table. I want to push forward with muscle to make myself a cozy, comfortable, peace-and-soul-filled perch of a higher, more imaginative perspective; build a rainbow bridge, stretching across and reuniting the polarities I swing between to navigate my interminable ups and downs. Can I do it given that reality, the world, the universe is dual? I will try, keep a graph of my daily highs and lows, draw a straight line in the middle of the graph and see the two from that perspective. I want to live in *sehej* (calm, easy, natural, spontaneous), let my small boat sail without oars or paddles, freed of volition, to the breath of the breeze, wind, storm; go where I am taken. I want to trust, even when the creature in me is in the throes of suffering, that I am always in a safe place, that I *am* taken care of, even when I don't know, or believe, or trust it. There is health in this surrender and a life that never truly ends. My hope flows outward to the horizon and beyond; even death will be the greatest adventure of all, painful, depressing, dark till the ultimate release from the confined womb of existence through the birth canal to death, the letting go, sliding into ease, stillness, silence, and God alone knows what else. I trust Thoreau's cryptic words to his sister a few days before he died, "Now comes good sailing." I want, once more, to live with hope that transcends circumstance and endures beyond death. Not hope for this or that—like that this book will get published—but hope in the miracle and possibility of transformation, especially in old age, and faith in this incomprehensible existence of which we are intrinsic parts. I want, above all, to become the slave of that Power in whose servitude alone I am the lady of the universe.

Rani was moving smoothly, effortlessly up the mountain range even though loaded down with a week's worth of cooked and raw food. We prefer our own food to eating in restaurants. Every time we eat out, we invariably eat too much of the wrong thing and suffer afterward from GERD. Payson has developed it and I inherited mine from both my parents. My mother was as loud and obnoxiously vocal with her digestive sounds as I am.

Preparing a week's worth of food is work, but it would give me a week off from cooking and allow me to meander in and out of my days in nature, grazing on beauty, hiking, just being, writing. No day, no vacation is complete and fulfilling without it. My laptop is my most important gear. Even on vacation I plow my illusion. I am compelled by a power that has me in thrall; I must write the story of this mote in infinity, this diminutive, ever-shrinking body, this little life as it unfolds from day to day, hour to hour, constantly in flux though seemingly defined and fixed. I am the happy victim of my writing muse. He has hooked me through my tongue and the tendons of my heart. I am his doormat; he rubs his grubby feet on me, and I am happy. I am his footstool. There is a degree of sweet violence mixed in with our tender lovemaking. My muse, demon lover, is a benign, cruel, demanding master. When he calls I go willingly, no matter the time of day or night. I will be his slave even as my skin falls away from my bones and I, wordless, meld and merge with him.

Somewhere along the marital path I slid into the role of kitchen-keeper. I don't mind it most of the time, even enjoy it some days when it isn't a "have to do." I don't perform well on demand, only when the moment and mood bring me to it. I follow, happily, the whims of my psyche. None of my mates have been demanding, and that's probably why I picked them. P has been very easy this way, not demanding anything of me, taking care of himself most of the time, cleaning up after I cook. I have never slaved over housework but am responsible enough to do it. It is satisfying to know the fridge is stocked with good, cooked food: brown rice, vegetables, and proteins.

I grew up with help and though I have gotten by well on my own, when I turned seventy I knew with certainty where I wanted to put my money: into getting whatever help I need. Tech help, a second brain where mine flags; two or four more hands as ours become arthritic. In this part of my journey toward abstraction I want comfort, ease. This is what I worked and saved to have.

My urge to be closer to my parents, to move to India, was equally matched by the desire for a more comfortable life. I longed to live, for at least part of the year, as my parents and all Indian families with some means live, with a staff of household help. Our houses are cleaned, gardens tended, food cooked by a genie in the kitchen, meals served, and dishes cleaned and put away.

Much as I enjoy service, however, the accepted situation in India has always appalled me. Household help, servants really, are at the beck and call of their employers for pay that makes even subsistence impossible. The perks for domestic help are food and lodging. They save their salary, send it home to poor relatives in Nepal or Bihar. They do not get Sundays off from work. Life and living must go on, and they must be there to facilitate it. Sundays are when socializing takes place. They are the first to arrive at work and the last to leave.

This was not the sort of employer either of us wanted to be. Payson, who had had a staff of tens of people when he owned his business, wanted to treat our staff as employees with benefits of health insurance, sick leave, Sundays or any four days off a month, and annual leave. My model for help was Deva Amma, who had been more than a mother to me, bathing and clothing me, washing my hair even when I turned twenty and had long tresses that needed managing. As a child I slept with her, close, whenever I was afraid or simply needed some cuddling. I took care of her after she retired till she died, but not as much as I would have wanted to because I didn't have much at that time.

In America I took care of my home on my own, including cleaning the house, toilets and all, till a year after Donald's death when I was forty-five and hired someone, as much for companionship as for help with chores around the house.

After she was widowed my mother relied heavily on her help for company. They kept her isolation at bay. She was fortunate enough to have a maid who took care of her well. Mother had always had long-term staff. She was very short-tempered and intolerant of people who did not do as good a job as a servant as she had done when she was her mother and sister-in-law's A++ servant, as Indian culture requires, those many years her husband had been stationed in non-family army bases. Being highly efficient and subordinate herself, she did not tolerate inefficiency and "talking back." Her tongue and volume were not kind or soft when she encountered it, but they stayed because she made sure they ate well and got bonuses, gifts, and advances.

I have followed in her footsteps, minus the short temper and feudal intolerance. After seventeen years we still have the original staff we hired at Behta Pani. When we were building our home in the high Himalayas, our staff came to us serendipitously. Our groundskeeper, Himat Ram, was brought to Payson by his good friend Sanjeeva Pandey, the director of the Himalayan National Park. "Hire him," he said. "He will become indispensable to you." He persuaded P despite his remonstrations that he did not need anyone to wash his clothes or polish his boots. Sanjeeva's prediction came true. Our house would not be complete without Himat's management. He is our right-hand man, taking care of so many things inside and outside our home. With him came Meera, his wife, whom I loved instantly. She keeps our home clean, manages laundry, linen, cooks for Bhalli, our shared dog, bathes, brushes, and feeds her. She gives me gentle massages, kneads my body when I am strung out, and puts me at rest.

When I moved in with Payson in Del Mar he had women coming to clean the house twice a month. They continue to come. A few years ago I hired Tiffany, who was sent to me when I asked. The first person I told I was looking for help—the very same day I first thought of getting help with the kitchen—was our neighbor when we met her in her driveway as we were going for our walk. She knew someone who would be happy to get the job, and I got Tiffany. She gives the best hugs and is my angel in the kitchen.

For our trip to the mountains, Tiffany had baked banana walnut muffins, sweet potatoes, parsnips, brussels sprouts, kale chips, meatloaf, and salmon and egg salads with celery, onion, olive oil, and mustard.

P packed up the ice chest with more food from the freezer. I bought some treats we don't allow ourselves normally: chips, a fruit tart, slices of cheesecake.

There was a sudden, loud clap of thunder as we entered the house P had rented in Idyllwild.

32
How We Stay Together

What turned into an ideal vacation started off with a fight. We were bringing boxes into the house, one of them containing a canister of antiseptic wipes. I heard him say. "I'm going to wipe down the counters with antiseptic wipes." I had no energy for it and I was glad he was doing what he thought necessary. I am far lazier than he is. I began the urgent task of putting the food from the icebox into the refrigerator. He came into the kitchen after carrying the last bag into the house (he did most of the moving, though I helped).

"Have you wiped down the counters with the wipes?" he asked. It was the twelfth of March 2020. Coronavirus was lurking on the periphery of my consciousness as something happening in China, but not to us. Even the initial news that it was spreading in Seattle and had killed several elderly people in nursing homes rang no alarm bells. I was not old, and I was not in Seattle. But Payson, a scientist who has studied and written books about biology, did not take these 3.5-billion-year-old infectious submicroscopic viruses lightly.

I said no and he, harshly, "Why not?" That got my goat. "Don't treat me like your employee!" I shouted. It wasn't a good start to the vacation. I felt that knot in my stomach when harmony turns to cacophony and our rhythms clash.

Payson was affected by my words. He became loving almost immediately, and though I took my time sulking till lunch, eating it alone and grumbling inwardly that the food wasn't warm enough, I came around. What I am loving more and more about P, whom I sometimes call Your Ass Holiness to his face, is that he realizes his mistake, even if he doesn't always apologize. He becomes gentler. This is cause enough, among many others, for me to stay with him, put up with his troll, iron out the kinks in our relationship, learn the art of letting go of my piques and hurts, and proceed on the path to love. But I'm glad we got the fight over with, first thing.

After the initial upset I looked around at where we had landed.

What a beautiful place P had picked for us! It was a clean, spacious, well-furnished, open A-frame house surrounded by redwoods, sugar pines, oaks, firs, large scurrying squirrels, and blue jays. Many large windows brought the outdoors in, views of Lily Rock, the San Jacinto ranges, and towering boulders. A bedroom and study on one level descended a few steps to the living room that had a wood stove, plenty of firewood, comfortable sofas, couches, and chairs, a dining area, and a modern kitchen. Payson had gone to a lot of trouble to book the perfect place. He always does. Everything I needed was here in someone else's well-furnished house that felt like home.

I was cold and P spent a lot of time and energy figuring out the heating. Then he tended the fire in the wood stove that needed some getting to know, and turned the car around, "in case we have to get out in the snow."

After he had made me comfortable, he said, "I'm going for a walk while there is still light." He didn't ask me to accompany him. Our last trip here two years ago—ah, I was younger then! and loved to hike—we got into trouble because he couldn't understand why I wouldn't accompany him on his hikes, and would try to persuade me gently, and sometimes manipulating me to come with him. Now, over the years, with my increasing lack of energy, after an initial "Want to come?" he has ceased to push.

"Want some?" I asked, popping a cannabis sativa gummy. Cookie is just the thing to kickstart the holiday. It intensifies and deepens my experience of a new place.

"No thanks."

"It will relax you and you will have a magical walk." I don't know why I asked. Cannabis has never been his drug of choice.

"It doesn't do that for me."

"Come on, be adventurous. Take some. You are always so resistant."

"One day I'll surprise you, take that whole thing and you will come back to a puddle."

"I'll suck you up with a syringe."

"And only take out as much of me as you can handle. Or keep me in the bottle."

We had a good laugh.

"You have to admit I am your genie in a bottle," he said.

"Sometimes a troll."

"Or a gnome."

We were laughing about serious things that gather more gravity from secrecy. Laughter is the antidote to anxiety. I was a bit fearful, too. I had already tripped on a rug. P hit his head against a pane of glass, thinking the outside ledge was inside. "This is new terrain," I said. "Let's be cautious."

P's behavior before leaving the house also showed his anxiety. He put a handwritten note in his jacket with our address in Idyllwild; he didn't want to take the only key we had because he was concerned I may not be able to get out should there be a fire. He asked me to lock the door after him.

I lay on the long white leather couch under piled blankets, my lungs catching up with the altitude, watching the flames, looking outside the large picture window, realizing how tired I was. Preparing for a trip like this exhausted me. I wondered how long we would be able to continue coming to Idyllwild. It was getting too much for us to pack and unpack.

Vacations are so much work. It has taken decades for me to admit, "I am tired." I used to turn my tiredness into a lot of mental and emotional chatter. I drifted into a sweet nap till P returned, hungry, and we got into the kitchen. I put out some snacks, a bowl of nuts, raisins, sesame sticks, bean chips, and hummus. We sipped red wine as we made salad and reheated Tiffany's pasta with chicken balls in tomato sauce. We even had some cheesecake for dessert. When we settled down before the fire, my feet on his lap as he sat on the other end of the couch, I felt that melted feeling called love for this man, this stranger I have lived with for so many years. *Let him be who is he in his entirety without forcing him into the molds of your needs*, my angels instructed. What a huge relief to let people be who they are, not what you expect or want or fear them to be. No need to change, prod, pull, push him or the world to fit some conception of what it should or ought to be. How liberating to take my selfhood out of the equation. I owe this to old age, to the atrophying of energy and the muscles of the brain that thought they held up the world.

I looked at Payson's profile, curly graying hair, his Jewish nose above his moustache and beard, the folds on his neck, and wondered how many vectors crisscrossing from so many directions, the many synapses and intersections, conjunctions and dispersings, death, trauma, suffering came together to make the meeting of a Jew from New York City and a Sikh born in Hoshiarpur, in the heart of Panjab.

I turned to P's arms two and a half years after Donald's suicide. I was hungry for touching, holding. My heart had begun to wither. I wanted love present and pulsing in my life. Donald's ghost that kept me company for those years, and for long after P and I married, wasn't enough. I was forty-five when he died, and still had life and loving left in me.

Payson and I were cosmically prepared for loving each other before we met. After Donald's death my friends Susan and Sara came to live with me in the house Donald and I had bought together barely two years before his suicide. My friends helped pay the mortgage on the house, which I would have lost otherwise, and gave me much needed companionship. Sensing my loneliness—both Susan and Sara were in relationships—they began matchmaking for me. I allowed Susan to persuade me to put an ad on a matrimonial site. I met one man, a wealthy Indian widower who tried to put his arms around me and kiss me the first time I met him. That was that. Nobody touches me until I am good and ready.

One day, sitting on the back lawn of the house, Susan and Sara recited a list of known men they thought might be eligible for me. They mentioned Larry, John, Tom, Rick, and when they came to Payson I said, entirely unexpectedly and spontaneously, "I want him!"

Susan had dated P some time before her current boyfriend and they were still friends. I had been attracted to P through the things she had told me about him: how kind he was, how creative—an artist and a scientist, a meditator and activist, pianist, author, photographer. He sounded like an attractive bundle of contraries. *And* he owned a house and ran a business. I had never, in my previous marriages, married for money; quite the opposite. My parents' injunction that a husband had to be economically stable seemed too bourgeois to me. However, Donald's suicide, partly due to economic insecurity, left no doubt in my mind that economics play a large part in the stability of a marriage.

Susan and Sara moved out of the house and rented their own apartments after two and a half years. Susan invited me for her fortieth birthday party. I had a feeling I would meet P there. Susan gave me tips on how to appeal to him: "He likes sweet and loving women who wear long, flowy clothes. If someone offers you a joint at the party, don't smoke it; Payson doesn't like marijuana."

I ignored her sartorial advice and wore tight black jeans, boots, and a leather jacket to Susan's party. *He must like me for who I am, not what I wear,* was my reasoning.

When I saw a short man with dark curly hair in a black cotton shirt and drab olive camel hair jacket, I knew he was the guy. There was something sparky and quick about him, a grounded, engaged presence.

Nobody introduced us. We gravitated toward each other. We found ourselves sitting at the small table by the refrigerator in the tiny kitchen, talking. When someone offered me a joint, I held on to it and inhaled deeply.

Payson didn't waste any time with pleasantries. He got right to Donald's suicide. P knew what had happened because Susan was dating him at the time it happened. They were comforting each other after breakups with others: P from his wife, Susan from a boyfriend. Susan was one of the first people I called after Donald's death. She was with P when I called. Later he told me that when he heard what had happened, he felt as if someone had punched him in the chest. He didn't know me, though he had visited our house once when Donald and I had gone to India and Susan was pet-sitting our cats, Chua and Purry. P had seen a picture of Donald and me together. He later told me he was very attracted to me.

Sitting in the tiny kitchen at Susan's party, I found myself responding easily and openly to Payson's probing questions. He elicited my confidence. He was a good listener, quick, vital, and engaged. It got deep, fast. Later, when we moved to sitting around on the floor, Susan and a friend of hers whom P had also messed around with, and who had written a beautiful poem dedicated to him called *The Green Man*, which I had read and admired, rubbed P's shoulders as he sat on the carpet leaning against the sofa. He was like Krishna. He had many admirers and an active and far-ranging romantic life before he met me.

I left the party earlier than the others. I did not want to be another hanger-on or send him the message that I was angling for him. I am deficient in the art of flirting. As I got into the red pick-up truck I inherited from Donald, I did wonder whether I would see him again.

When Susan called the next day to say P had asked if he may call me, I said yes, of course.

When we talked on the phone, he said he had "a window of time" at three the next afternoon and invited me for a hike at Torrey Pines. I wore blue jeans, gray and blue hiking boots, a purple parka, and of course, earrings. We met by the "No Stopping Anytime" sign, an augur of things to come. P was wearing a blue parka, already showing some wear when we met on our first date by the ocean, the one he still owns and uses after all these years.

We walked up into the reserve, dense with brown and withered chaparral and many Torrey Pines, and down the sandstone cliffs through sweet coastal sages and Yerba Buena, plants whose names P told me. He rubbed his hands gently on their leaves so as not to crush them and I inhaled the strong perfume on his palms. We talked the whole time and I discovered some of his family history: His mother kicked out his biological father when he was two years old, told P and his sister that he had died, and married several times after the divorce; Larry is his half-brother. P had a conflicted relationship with his mother and left home at sixteen. A man of many passions, nature and art foremost among them, P also had a background in biology and oceanography at the Scripps Institution of Oceanography. He had worked with NASA, and his design firm had won a Presidential Award from President Clinton.

His questions as we walked were very probing. I found myself telling him how I came to America after cashing in my dowry money, about my parents, my family, my passion for writing, and my previous marriages, even though I heard my mother's words in my ears after Donald died and they were matchmaking for me with a high executive in Apple: "Don't tell him about your previous relationships! He will think you are a loose woman." I told P about my job as a tenured faculty at Grossmont College, teaching classes in composition, grammar, literature, creative writing, Shakespeare, theatre, and mythology. He shared my passion for these subjects. We descended to the sea and walked back at dusk along the beach in a rising tide, getting soaked but oblivious to it.

At the parking lot he invited me to his home. I followed him in my car. He unlocked the front door, stood inside his house with the door wide open, and said, "Welcome to my home." It was such a wonderfully old-fashioned thing to say.

He made me soup and toast and we ate sitting before the fire. We dated for two more years. On our wedding day on the cliffs of Torrey Pines, the woman who was supposed to officiate our marriage fell and hurt her ankle and didn't show up. We married ourselves with the sky, sea, dolphins, pelicans, sea gulls, wind, ocean, clouds, all of nature as witnesses. A red-tailed hawk flew overhead—a message from the universe—as P and I broke the champagne glass. Hawks have always come to P at critical times in his life. My own dad named his house White Hawk, after Guru Gobind Singh's hawk/falcon perched on his gloved hand in popular images of him.

I looked at P as we relaxed across from each other on the white couch in Idyllwild and marveled at the transformation time had wrought in him since we'd first met at Susan's birthday party. I wondered how I looked to him. I was thinking about our romantic beginnings when a loud fart annunciated itself.

"You had your cannon ball aimed right at me," P said, jumping up, at once annoyed and amused.

"At least it wasn't stinky. If you don't like it, you can divorce me and get yourself a Barbie doll with no asshole."

"I'm checking eBay right now," he retorted.

We lay about some more by the fire, speaking of nothing till we rambled into our careers as artists, and how, though we have had successes here and there, we haven't "made it." For every artist who makes it, like the sperm that enters the ova after a herculean journey, a billion die and are reabsorbed. We reflected on innumerable artists who were never discovered, and artists who were discovered after death, like Vivien Maier, a nanny, who died in obscurity and left behind 100,000 photographs hidden in suitcases in storage lockers that were discovered decades later. *The New York Times* called her "one of America's more insightful street photographers." We write and paint because we must, because it is as natural an instinct as breathing, because not doing so would destroy our lives and even kill us. As poet John Ciardi said, "An ulcer, gentlemen, is an unwritten poem." P and I talked about Joachim Martin, a nineteenth-century carpenter who left a secret diary under the floorboards of the Chateau de Picomtal, excavated in the 2000s. He had to unburden himself of the dark secret he couldn't keep in his heart. He *had* to tell the story about his neighbor who committed infanticide several times and hid the bodies under a stable; he couldn't report him because he was a childhood friend, and because his mother was the neighbor's father's mistress. The stories *must* be told; the paintings painted.

P talked about *The Gift: Creativity and the Artist in the Modern World*, a wonderful book by Lewis Hyde that we both love. In distinguishing labor from work, Hyde puts things in perspective. Work is time-bound, done by the hour for remuneration, will-driven; labor, he says, "sets its own pace, has its own schedules, things get done but we often have the odd sense that we didn't do them." Both P and I feel the most fulfilled when we are laboring at our projects.

The sight of the Milky Way, dense with stars, spread out in a wide path through the sky in the frame of the window put our striving in perspective and we fell asleep in the warmth of the fire.

33
Grass Growing Mood

I am in what author Herman Melville, struggling over *Moby Dick*, called "the grass growing mood," waking from a sticky sleep whose silence and lethargy lasts for hours, sitting in bed talking with P before loafing through my days. I brush my teeth while admiring the old oak whose roots encapsulate granite boulders, its three dark trunks thick and brown, its roots spread wide to anchor itself in the slope. I make chai in the company of junipers, resting, enjoying the stillness, lingering on my tasks. I loiter and lie about in bed or on the couch, just lying quietly, all thought stilled. My eyes absorb the sunshine crawling down the San Jacinto range, trees out of every window, a bird carrying gossamer in her beak for her nest, a crow breathing in the cedar, and once, Oh heaven, a family of deer, the stag with his heavy, far-spreading, branching antlers and two others, a juvenile and its mother with sleek velveteen bodies and large round eyes. In a place like this, nature is the matrix in which we live.

P and I are each doing our own thing, he hiking, I in bed scribbling, or stretching, eating, and drinking warm teas. I am sleeping well, not worrying about the encroaching pandemic, putting together meals supplemented by Tiffany's dishes, or just making a soup of leftovers and broth that we help ourselves to all day.

I indulge in what I call "geriatric yoga," gently, always gently, careful to not overstretch, to not break anything, small movements done slowly, thoughtfully, resting between and breathing through the poses, doing only brief and easy stretches on tired days, doing it as if time exists only as a medium for me to move through, light and invisible, like air. Now that the body is crumbling, the weary structures succumbing to the gravity they have fought all their lives, entropy must be intercepted, maybe even delayed, by stretching out the limbs, keeping them limber, flexible. Where in time past I could function with just twenty minutes of yoga a day, now I function poorly even after an hour of it. The difference in stamina between then and now, even from our visit to Idyllwild a few years ago, is pronounced, but the battle against the entropic imperative must be ongoing.

Payson has laid down a thick piece of cardboard on the counter that divides the kitchen from the living room, his brushes aligned in a row on a bamboo mat, a white sheet of paper, and lumps of Prussian blue, olive-brown, violet, red, sap green, turquoise blue pastels, siennas, and umbers. Though he is painting long hours, he has taken time to connect with me during the day. He goes off for a long hike and I plug into my solitude and my laptop or go on my own hike. I found a little rivulet in my walk the other day and followed it downstream over boulders strewn in the backyards of abandoned homes, under old oak and cypress trees. Wearing a back brace—my lower back was talking to me—I climbed a few hills, slowly, surely, the old muscles holding up, the knee buckling only once when I overextended it by jumping from a boulder.

A few mornings ago, turning my head on the pillow toward this many-windowed house, I gasped in awe at the miracle I was hoping for but did not expect—snow-dusted pines, snow on the limbs and leaves of trees, white slopes and peaks, the textured white of the ridge illumined by the gold of first alpine light. I wanted to be out in it. I hiked for more than an hour, up and down the steep slopes of this neighborhood overflowing with the vegetal world, snow falling on me gently, my eyes drinking in the beauty of this white bowl thick with trees surrounded by tall mountains and bare peaks. We call them *chataans* in Hindi, the onomatopoeia echoing their naked mass and majesty. Slowly my body pumped its way uphill past a stone-strewn creek. I followed it downstream on high banks, negotiated my way on boulders, under trees, on the soft mulch of pine needles and leaves.

Payson has been at peace for the first time in these many long months of worrying about and taking care of Larry. He has been a mountain goat for as long as I have known him. He has hiked two thousand miles in the Great Himalayan National Forest not far from our own home, Behta Pani, in a remote canyon by the Hirab. Now the mountain goat's knees are hurting. He is slowing down, tiring easily. He can't understand why. He has been doing his knee exercises and he had a great score in his recent treadmill stress test. Yesterday as he was walking to the kitchen I saw his old man, as I am sure he sees my old woman from time to time, glimpses of dilapidated appearances to come in the years ahead. But there is a very youthful and vital side to him, too. Our past selves are not rubbed out. We are like palimpsests, the past visible through the new.

Though I was tired, when P suggested we hike the Ernie Maxwell trail in Humber Park the next day, the weather was so tempting, the sun shining on the white shagged trees, some green still visible, the sky a brilliant blue with shades of grays, everything pristine, cleansed by this visitation from the skies, I thought I would be a fool not to take advantage of it. As soon as we entered the trail, my tiredness fell away. We were in and vibrating with the forest. The bright sun, pouring through dark shades, made the perfect combination of light and shadow; it illumined the scales of the thick, textured, patterned, varicolored barks of pine, redwood, and fir, their lace-like canopies, green dusted with white, shimmering. Sunlight bounced off boulders and lit our dappled path winding lyrically before us as we walked on a soft spongy carpet of dead leaves, pine needles, spiraling cones, frilly fronds of cypress trees, tiny twigs, seedpods of unnamed vegetation, and glimmers of copper and gold from decomposing granite, the jeweled detritus of a forest.

Further into the trail another mythic encounter awaited us, the sudden appearance across the bend in the trail of three wolves on leashes held by a group of tall, Amazonian women. My first reaction was fear, and I retreated to a lower slope. When they passed me at the safe distance of a few yards, held in check by the women, and I looked at the leashed animals—a black one with silver hair, a beige with black streaks, and a silver with dark edges—all three large and well-groomed, I broke out in admiration and awe, "They are beautiful!" The fleeting sight of them, too fleeting, alas, will stay with me forever. It was a *darshan*, a glimpse of the divine.

"Are they wolves?" I asked the older woman, probably the mother of the younger three, walking behind them with two hiking poles. "Wolf dogs," she replied. P asked, "How much do they weigh? Seventy pounds?" She told us the black one weighed 150, the beige, 130, the silver 110. Her last words were, "They are very high maintenance."

As we walked ahead, I was in love. I wanted to follow them, I wanted to be with them, know their owners, spend time with them. It was an old, mythic, all-too-fleeting encounter.

I live many alternative lives. In one of them we live in Idyllwild all year long, in that wonderful house we saw in the wilderness with acres of land around it, wild deer and bobcats. I added another: I am younger and have three wolf dogs I walk daily into Humber Park.

I walked lumberingly from being tired by the hike the day before, weighed down by gear, a thick long down coat I was grateful I had brought, a backpack in which I carried half the picnic—I insist on it. P tries to carry it all and then his back begins to hurt. The coat kept me warm but overheated me on climbs. I wore a back brace, and one for the wrist of the hand that held my hiking pole. Though I was slowed by an increasing stiffness in my joints, I was determined to make it to the beautiful meadow we call Dad's meadow, where we picnicked with Daddy when he visited us in 1997. It is a fond memory and an inspiration. He had hiked up here at age seventy-nine. P and I weren't married then. I had been living in the old house ten miles south, and Dad knew P was sleeping over because we would have dinner together and P would still be there the following morning. Dad, a conservative Indian man, had a liberal heart. He even suggested I live with P before marrying him to see how it went.

On all our hikes P and I give each other enough space so we can have our own individual experiences of nature. Often, being far faster than I, he is ahead of me, and sometimes, being a photographer of his god—nature—he lags behind to do his own thing. I used to pause with him when I was younger in the interests of togetherness, but as I age, I want to do my own thing more, harken to the beat of my own drum. I have done my own thing most of my life, with all my other mates, but with Payson I was cautious, tentative, careful, more submissive than ever before, knowing my responsibility in Donald's suicide. Though small, P is a powerful man. I restrained my Kali with him earlier, but she still resurrects and jumps in with both feet when P and I are fighting, becomes a well-matched adversary of P's troll, his sharp tongue and temper. Harkening to my own drum even more and more is becoming an imperative I cannot ignore. I have been meek and fearful in this context too long. Now, in closer proximity to the inevitable—hopefully not imminent—dissolution, I would birth the mother in me who nurtures her infant self, herself.

Payson and I met up near the manzanita trees. P photographed it, then did a manzanita dance, his arms twirling up and away like the manzanita's limbs spiraling in different directions. The old manzanita's beauty consists in incorporating life and death in almost equal parts. The fleshy, silk-smooth red limbs of its live bark intertwine with the rough brown of its dead bark. They coexist and dance as one, the old and new together.

Earlier I could do the whole trail from top to bottom and back again. This time I was grateful for making it halfway one way, to Dad's meadow. We sat in a clearing in the warming sun, surrounded by dead trees deliquescing to mulch, ancient and adolescent junipers, stunted pines, and bonsais growing out of boulders, their aged, serpentine roots coiling around, cracking rock, their crooked trunks and winding branches twisting at aesthetic angles. Behind the vibrant green of trees, the sky an intense and cloudless blue. There was no indication of more snow. We sat in an ocean of atmosphere, 7,000 feet above our home at sea level, the currents of the wind sounding like the ebb and flow of waves. We ate our raw veggies and fruit, banana nut muffin and nuts, drank our hot green tea with honey, a little bit of chocolate, and talked. We have begun in the past year to have conversations about our deaths. He reminded me where the will is, where the key to the lockers is, who to contact for help in figuring out the finances, and reassured me I will have no financial worries. I told him in our last conversation, "Don't be lonely when I am gone. Find a companion." I said it because I don't want to rule out the possibility for myself should he go first. In case I get lonely, if I can, I will find someone. P would be a very hard act to follow. I looked at his profile, his gray beard, his maleness, his stance as he pees, his independence and strong preferences, and realize how deeply I am bonded to him. But should he go first, I may fall finally into the arms of my demon lover, solitude, also attractive as a possibility, become an old widow puttering through her days with the aid of lots of help. It could only be in India. But when I am feeling vulnerable, I am terrified at the thought of losing P, fear I will fall apart, be utterly lost, and think it would be such a relief to go first.

"I wonder if squirrels get Alzheimer's and forget where they buried their acorns," P said. We laughed, but it also pointed out his constant worry about Larry, and possibly himself.

I encouraged him to take off his shirt, lie down on the spread, and sun himself. There was a chill in the air and the sun felt like warm honey on our skins. I did the same. First the tops came off, then the bottoms, then everything, including underwear, and we lay about soaking light and warmth like lizards in the sun. "The bears ran away when they saw us," P described to a friend, later.

Payson went off further into the wilderness to draw and sketch—he always carries his kit with him on hikes. I lay back, watched the moving tapestry of the sky, observed the leaves of the spreading California oak sparkling in the sun, the pine needles shimmering. When I felt like action, I sat up. My gaze was riveted to a huge, multi-trunked oak tree, its blackened body charred in a fire, with many mouths, boles, and burls on its trunks where storms had torn off its branches, concentric arrangement of branches that never developed or developed, had their day, then died. It had taken beatings from fires and storms. I wanted to get away from this scene of death and walked to an oak, the matriarch of the land. It was the sort of tree I would have climbed in earlier days. I tried climbing it several times, but my knee did not cooperate. I turned away, defeated. But before the defeat could do any damage and drag me down to "I'm getting older, I will never climb a tree again," I let the failure go. No pausing at regret as I walk through my days achingly. Who knows, I may climb another tree yet. The progress of time, of aches and pains, is linear in a circuitous way. They come and they go, all the way till the last letting go. I had, just this past fall, a few months ago, climbed our Fuji tree to pluck some apples. I felt strong, healthy, girl-like. I have always loved to climb trees, especially fruit trees, sit on a comfortable limb, and eat.

Returning to camp, instead of avoiding the sight of the dead oak I veered toward it. No turning your face away from it, I told myself. I saw how it had grown smooth, round, heart-shaped skin-like lips around the hollowed mouths of its wounds. And when I got closer still, I saw the tips of its branches edged with tight, budding green blooms. It was still quick, only slumbering, its sap armored by dead-looking live scales. The sight made me very happy. There is always hope.

Sometime later P came back and showed me his drawings, energy vortices in nature, at once turbulent and calm; his abstract manzanitas, colored by red sienna from earth and leaves, whirled in a dance of energy. I was reminded that it was his artwork, and his beautiful book, *Embracing Earth*, and his old-fashioned, almost Indian gesture of standing inside the house with the door open, saying, "Welcome" and making me a delicious soup that impressed me about him that first time I went to the house I would end up living in for two and a half decades. When he took me to his studio and I saw the paintings on the easel, in violets, blues, and white, abstracts of water in thick impasto, I sat down on the stairs, filled with awe.

P strewed the drawings he had done in the meadow on the forest floor, thick with pine needles and swirling cones in a haphazard way, then took photographs of them and titled the series *Forest Litter*.

P is a JewBu, a Buddhist Jew. In one of his trips to Nepal, long before I met him, he had witnessed an entire *Kalachakra*, Wheel of Time ceremony, the grain-by-grain painstaking construction of a mandala with powders of precious and semiprecious stones: lapis, turquoise, coral, pearl, emerald, sapphire, gold, silver, crystals, and rubies. When it was complete, awe-inspiring to behold, beautiful beyond description, the monks swept it away with a broom, the mixed colors carried to the river and immersed. Nature destroys all its creations, turns them to litter, including our lives in *samsara*, the cyclic existence of nature, its diastole/systole pulsing in our own bodies.

34
Corona Cocoon

*P*sychobiological turnings tied to the twirling of the earth through time, my own lack of awareness, and global events plunged me into darkness again. The hikes tired me. And when I am tired, I get depressed. If I could remember this causality, knock myself out with some Indica and/or a low dose of valium, forget all about productivity, get into bed, fall asleep, I would be a wise woman who knows how to circumvent her funks. Instead I try to fulfill the agenda for the day, and once again the old darkness in different permutations and iterations gathers in my brain. All my shadowy regrets, gripes, insecurities, and fears crawl out of the umbra and drag me all the way down the ladder from angel to suffering creature.

Lying on the white couch, in the interest of productivity, of learning something, I picked up an old copy of *The New Yorker* and read an article about Sylvia Plath's letters, and some poetry that made no sense to me. Exposure to *The New Yorker*, which has repeatedly rejected what I submit to it, took a bite out of the ozone of my existence. At night, blanketed under the down quilt, my old, bitter self, which I thought I had transcended, came out of hiding, full of jealousy at others' success, even if they were so unhappy they had to kill themselves and leave behind two beautiful children.

An email from a friend telling me about the many friends helping her through an illness of the lungs plunged me into another old funk about not having a community, not being in my country. My "poor me," torturing herself with cruel "self-objectification," was in the ascendant all night. I felt life had passed me by; I have won no major awards, just a few here and there, so it felt as if a lifetime of writing had paid no dividends. It felt like death. I was worrying about pandemic news, the shelter-in-place orders. California was locked down, panicking, food and supplies were reportedly dwindling. Coronavirus hit us where we are creaturely, human, fearful. P, who studied microbiology, said it was going to last years. I feared I would not be able to return to India, to my sister now kept alive by chemo infusions, to my dearest young grandnephews and grandnieces, to Behta Pani, to our dog Bhalli, whom I have been missing with a passion since I met the wolves, for she, too, is a sleek black wolf with silvering hair.

I mercifully remembered to meditate. I arrived in the presence of God and there, right in front of his majesty, I lay down naked, unzipped myself from my neck down to my pubic bone and exposed all the amorphous, blobby, pathetic malformed creatures, spitting poison on the flower of my gratitude. I surrendered them to God. "Take them, they are yours."

In the morning, lying in bed, I told Payson how I was feeling. He listened. His response was, "You are suffering a crisis of faith." Exactly. Faith in myself, my life, my writing, God. "You are beating up on yourself." Exactly. *I am not good enough, my writing isn't good enough, nothing about me is good enough.* How difficult it is to see one's truth when one is in the cauldron.

P organized my amorphous feelings of inadequacy into neat piles. He told me his ideas about a book he had meant to write, called *Lifelines*, in which he had categorized relationships into primary, secondary, and tertiary. P is primary. Close behind, bordering the primary space, is my family in India, where there are open arms and hearts.

Secondary, five friends and a cousin with whom I am in regular touch, some of our mutual friends with whom there is mutual goodwill and caring. Tertiaries are kind, friendly neighbors and all our other contacts. Next, he addressed my publisher pique. He reminded me I have no fewer than five evergreen books published by reputable publishers.

P counted for me when I was incapable of mathematics and made me see how false my feelings of inadequacy were. "You know, in your life you have gotten most of what you wanted," he reminded me.

I counted my fulfilled desires and saw how overflowing my vessel was and continues to be. Some of my fulfilled desires were dark: the death of my baby sister at the age of one because I didn't want to share my father's love with her, and repeatedly told them to throw her in the well; Donald's suicide after I thought, when he was drunk, *Enough of this!*

Other fulfilled desires were not so dark. I attended the best school for girls in India, Welham Girls' School. I came to the United States on dowry money and got a fellowship on my first day in college as a consequence of stuffing my poems in the mailbox of the English Department chair, Jake Leed. I got a full-time teaching position when I was hurting financially. A mate was given to me after my prayers of *Send me my mate! Send me my mate!* Behta Pani, which we acquired after I said to P as I stood on the banks of the Hirab, "I want it." Losing Behta Pani but returning to it in one and a half years, in time for my seventieth birthday, something I had prayed and hoped for, as it allowed me to spend more time with my parents and family than I would have if I lived in the States year-round. This was something to be grateful for when I was bemoaning that I didn't spend enough time with them. And now, at almost seventy-two, I am in relatively good health and my partner is, too, well enough to still hike and pack for a vacation such as this. The gifts are uncountable, starting from the functioning of my little pinky, my toes, the pulsing of 40 trillion cells and the universes within them pulsing rhythmically to keep me alive, upright, balanced. How many little accidents avoided, little trips in which I did not fall, and was rescued repeatedly?

But as I age, I will have to think of even my falls as gifts. And I have had several that have brought, after the first swear words, the gifts of resting and reflection.

I realized while talking with P that most of my problems stem from wanting more, from a basic greed that is hardwired into our species. How insidious and destructive of our happiness is the default wanting of more, always more. We can't unwire our brains, but we can strive to remember when the very existence that the hardwiring protects and enhances is threatened. Donald killed himself in just such a funk of "not enough." Wanting more and more of everything, including time, energy, health, is corrosive to our peace and happiness.

I was flooded with gratitude for my innumerable blessings, primarily P who can straighten me out when I am tottering. After he so magically turned my world around by tweaking my perspective, I got under the covers, watched the snow falling gently like grace, pulled my cap over my eyes, felt the warmth of two layers of down, retreated into a safe and cozy spot within myself, and fell into the sweetest slumber and healing dreams.

I dreamed of my Holy Marriage with the Beloved. The one I have loved all my life has chosen me as his. I weep because I have found him and he, me. I am orchestrating, because he has asked me to, a symphony in which every grain of sand, everyone, including me, the lost, the confused, the depressed and crazed, and everything, animate and inanimate, are notes.

When I awoke, sunshine was flooding the white mountain peaks in luminescent pink and baby blue glows. I awoke to the paradise that, because of darkness, this earth is. I will stay in this glow of supreme alrightness till the darkness returns and skews my perspective again. It will happen; I must expect it to, not cling to or resist it, know that darkness and funks are necessary for me to re- and relearn the lessons I am here to learn, lessons I so unerringly forget.

Payson and I cuddled in bed the morning of his birthday, then brought our hot drinks, chai, coffee, nuts, and ate and drank in bed the way my parents used to, dipping their biscuits and rusks in the tea. Often we children would wrap ourselves with the lower half of their quilts and drink tea together as a family. P has slowly adapted to my need to re-create a warm, living memory. As we sipped he told me about his dreams from the night before.

"I'm in New York," I said. He smiled. Most of his dreams begin that way.

"I'm in New York in one of them. Another anxiety dream. I have to take a bus. My luggage gets left behind in another bus and I'm getting more and more agitated and then a voice says, 'Don't worry. There'll be another bus.'"

We laughed over the dream and told ourselves to remind each other when we are agitated that there will always be another bus.

His other dream was about being somewhere in the mountains, reminiscent of the actual place he fell off a ledge as he hiked down in a downpour after hiking up to Lambri, a 14,000 foot range in our back yard in Behta Pani. It could have proved fatal if our groundskeeper had not descended the muddy embankment to rescue him. In his dream P is coming down a narrow path when pack horses come from the other direction. He doesn't know what to do and he keeps climbing up the mountain to safety but then keeps coming down again repeatedly. Finally, he climbs up a bit and lets the horses pass.

I knew instantly what his dream meant. I let him do his interpretation first, without paying attention because I was so fixated on my insight. When it was my turn, I said, "The 'pack horses' gave it away to me."

"That's exactly what Mother used to call herself: a pack horse!"

"You work too hard for your own good."

"She was like that, too."

"You must slow down. The Lambri connection is telling you there is danger here. You must slow down, do less, not get into every project that comes your way."

I was amazed he was listening to me calmly. His usual harsh reaction is, "That's who I am, don't try to change me please," or "Enough, enough, don't be a nudge. You are not my mother." I pushed my luck. I had been meaning to tell him all these things and the dream was the opportunity for me to do so. The dream had opened him up to listening.

"That backache you had last month, for the whole month, was exacerbated by your inability to rest. Every day I had to remind you of RICE: rest, ice, compress, elevate. You have a compulsion to keep doing. You have *shpilkes*.* But I refuse to accept you can't change your conditioned doing, doing, doing. What should have taken a few days to heal took a whole month because of the stubbornness of *Randolph, the Bear Who Said No* and brought on his own misery."

I hoped he was paying attention to what I said. I push so hard because I have learned these lessons the hard way. Not paying immediate attention to ailments when they first appear, a backache not tended to for too long, unsteadiness that does not make me turn to the cane has led to prolonged problems and falls. I know how essential it is in old age to slow down, pay attention, be still in bed for long stretches when needed. If you don't adapt to changing circumstances you will suffer and even die. It is a workaholic's nightmare from hell: *In bed all day! What, no do, do, do? Shame on me!* It is also practice and preparation for when we are more and more bedbound.

But somewhere at the back of my mind I knew that my words would make no difference and I would have to put up with his folly together with my own, and ultimately abandon him to his fate.

After breakfast I gave him three poems I had written to him. This is the sort of gift he values, something created by the hands, mind,

---

*Yiddish word for impatience, restlessness, "ants in your pants."

heart. We had a special meal of leftovers, wine, chips, dip, nuts, salad, and some cheesecake we had picked up in our only visit to town. For the rest of the day we allowed ourselves to rest before the fire, doing yoga, reading, hanging out, doing nothing.

"See? I let the pack horses pass by," P said.

A few days before we were to return to Del Mar, I got sleepier than usual, even during the day. I packed up somnambulantly, at an easy, unhurried pace. The magical drive home after celebrating P's seventy-fifth birthday inside Mother Nature was the icing on the cake of the perfect vacation before the pandemic lockdown. All the way down from the mountains, with P driving in the hypnotizing snow amid flakes like feathers, small and large, swirling all around us, I kept yawning. For almost an hour we drove in a snow flurry with large, wet snowflakes lashing our windows. P loved the snow so much he stopped many times to film it. As if one can capture a snowflake. It is a lesson I am only just beginning to learn while knowing full well that I will never learn it fully. Capturing this ever-evolving story, which moves on even as I write, is yet another attempt to capture a snowflake.

P said, "Call Alicia and Tiffany and tell them not to come. We are isolating." My luxurious life of help with these two wonderful workers was the first casualty of the pandemic. I bemoaned it at first, then embraced it. I know the quality of my life will depend on my plunging headlong into my external-internal life, saying yes to it all. Sleepily I resolved to return in these stormy times ahead to practice more and more innerness, float on my tote, drop anchors in Ariel, music, reading, weave a corona cocoon, return to what the fourth guru of the Sikhs, Guru Ram Das, calls *nijh ghar mehal* (the inner home palace). It is the place you reach when, in Guru Nanak's words, you go on *atam tirath*, or the pilgrimage to yourself. I will turn again and again to my guides and gurus whose words light my way, feed me wisdom, and hand me the philosopher's stone that turns lead into golden feathers for flight.

P talked about how pandemics are paradigm shifts; they cull populations. That it is a good thing, he said, even if we are the culled ones.

He looked at me sideways, smiled, and repeated his mantra:

"Happy to be here, ready to go."

Darkness was gathering like a dark fog bank on our psychic and global horizon. I asked God for the gift to endure. We do not know what to expect. But whatever happens, I will take it in the spirit of adventure. The word, concept, image of adventure has served me well as a survival tool. Certainly my perspective will be changed by planetary events and our changed circumstances. What is old age but the opportunity to experience yourself and life from another perspective? If I survive to tell my story, you will hear from me again.

Acknowledgments

*G*ratitude is due foremost to my dear friend and agent, Joe Kulin, who long ago, as publisher of *Parabola*, encouraged my career as a published writer. To Jon Graham, Inner Traditions acquisitions editor, for giving this book a home; to Ehud Sperling, longtime friend and publisher of Inner Traditions for his enthusiasm and support; to Jamaica Burns Griffin, my editor, for her encouragement and kindness; to the wonderful crew at Inner Traditions for their support: Erica Robinson, Courtney B. Jenkins, Jeanie Levitan, Aaron Davis, Priscilla Baker, Ashley Kolesnik, and Manzanita Carpenter Sanz. Thanks are due also to my dear friends who read the manuscript, gave valuable feedback, and supported me when my confidence flagged: Marsha Skinner, Phyllis Kahaney, Diane Stacy, Gloria Sandvik, Libby Jennings, and Jillian Hensley; to Charanjeet Singh for all the help he has rendered me over the years; to my dear cousin Billo Jolly for her loving support; to Dan Burrus, Ken Druck, Lori Fox, Christof Bove, and Jessie Simmons for being there. Last, but never least, my partner and husband, Payson, who suggested the title and kindly allowed me to make him a character in this book, and with whom I share the privilege of aging.

Books of Related Interest

The Inner Work of Age
Shifting from Role to Soul
by Connie Zweig, Ph.D.
Foreword by Harry R. Moody, Ph.D.

Meeting the Shadow on the Spiritual Path
The Dance of Darkness and Light in Our Search for Awakening
by Connie Zweig, Ph.D.

The Spirituality of Age
A Seeker's Guide to Growing Older
by Robert L. Weber, Ph.D., and Carol Orsborn, Ph.D.

Change Your Story, Change Your Life
Using Shamanic and Jungian Tools to Achieve Personal Transformation
by Carl Greer, Ph.D., Psy.D.

Herbs for Healthy Aging
Natural Prescriptions for Vibrant Health
by David Hoffmann, FNIMH, AHG

Witch Wisdom for Magical Aging
Finding Your Power through the Changing Seasons
by Cait Johnson
Foreword by Caitlín Matthews

Walking Your Blues Away
How to Heal the Mind and Create Emotional Well-Being
by Thom Hartmann

An Energy Healer's Book of Dying
For Caregivers and Those in Transition
by Suzanne Worthley

INNER TRADITIONS • BEAR & COMPANY
P.O. Box 388
Rochester, VT 05767
1-800-246-8648
www.InnerTraditions.com

Or contact your local bookseller